FOR DUMMIES
BESTSELLING BOOK SERIES

Coaching Junior Foo[tball] Teams For Dummi[es]

G000255127

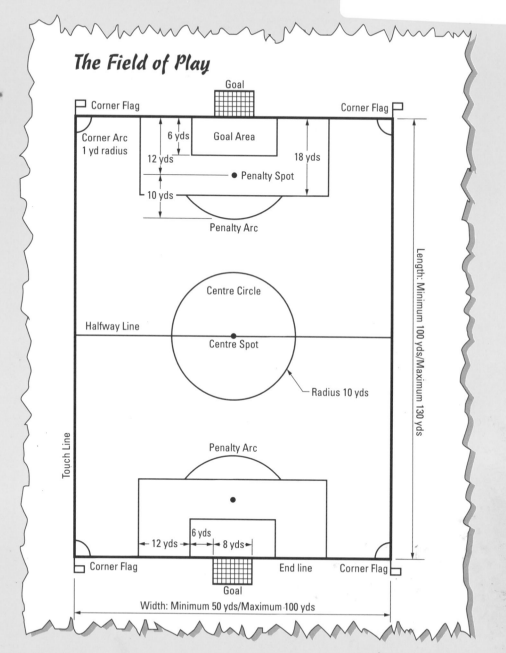

The Field of Play

Goal

Corner Flag

Corner Flag

Corner Arc 1 yd radius

6 yds — Goal Area

12 yds

18 yds

● Penalty Spot

10 yds

Penalty Arc

Centre Circle

Halfway Line

Centre Spot

Radius 10 yds

Length: Minimum 100 yds/Maximum 130 yds

Touch Line

Penalty Arc

●

12 yds — 6 yds — 8 yds

Corner Flag

End line

Corner Flag

Goal

Width: Minimum 50 yds/Maximum 100 yds

For Dummies: Bestselling Book Series for Beginners

Coaching Junior Football Teams For Dummies®

Cheat Sheet

Supporting Your Players

Your players are counting on you for guidance and support all season long. The following are some helpful ways to meet their needs.

- Be specific with your praise.
- Stop training sessions to point out when a player does something well rather than when they make a mistake.
- While providing feedback, use the 'sandwich' method by placing a critical remark between two encouraging comments.
- Pile on the praise for kids giving their best and displaying good sportsmanship.
- Provide constant positive reinforcement – it's the key to improvement.
- Focus on fun and safety instead of wins and losses.
- Be passionate and enthusiastic – it carries over to your players.
- Have reasonable expectations and set attainable goals for the kids.
- Remember that kids making mistakes is all part of the learning process.

Following a Pre-game Routine

A good pre-game routine helps set the tone for a safe and fun-filled day of football. Keep these tips in mind before the game begins.

- Inspect the pitch for loose rocks, broken glass, raised sprinkler heads, or anything else that could injure a child.
- Verify that all the kids brought the proper equipment.
- Have the kids warm up. Keep the drills light, cover all the muscle groups that will be used in the game, and involve a large number of football skills to properly prepare kids for the game.
- Give the kids a water break before the game begins.
- Provide encouraging words and a pat on the back to boost kids' confidence and enhance self-esteem.

Delivering the Pre-game Talk

What you say to the kids before the game, and how you say it, makes a big difference in how they approach taking the field. Here are some helpful pointers to prepare them for competition.

- Speak in a calm and relaxed manner.
- Be brief.
- Conduct the talk away from any distractions.
- Stress the importance of having fun and displaying good sportsmanship at all times during the game.
- Stay away from overused clichés; speak from the heart to get your point across.
- Avoid pressure phrases like 'Let's score five goals today.' Kids can give you their best effort, but they can't control the outcome of games.
- Be enthusiastic with your tone of voice and body language. The kids will be more responsive.

For Dummies: Bestselling Book Series for Beginners

Coaching Junior Football Teams

FOR

DUMMIES®

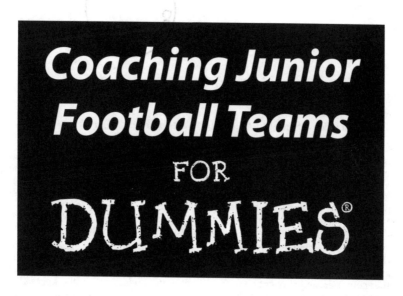

Coaching Junior Football Teams FOR DUMMIES®

by the National Alliance For Youth Sports with
Greg Bach and James Heller

BICENTENNIAL
1807
WILEY
2007
BICENTENNIAL

John Wiley & Sons, Ltd

Coaching Junior Football Teams For Dummies®

Published by
John Wiley & Sons, Ltd
The Atrium
Southern Gate
Chichester
West Sussex
PO19 8SQ
England

E-mail (for orders and customer service enquires): cs-books@wiley.co.uk

Visit our Home Page on www.wiley.com

Copyright © 2007 John Wiley & Sons, Ltd, Chichester, West Sussex, England

Published by John Wiley & Sons, Ltd, Chichester, West Sussex

For general information on our other products and services, please contact our Customer Care Department within the U.S. at 800-762-2974, outside the U.S. at 317-572-3993, or fax 317-572-4002.

For technical support, please visit www.wiley.com/techsupport.

Wiley also publishes its books in a variety of electronic formats. Some content that appears in print may not be available in electronic books.

British Library Cataloguing in Publication Data: A catalogue record for this book is available from the British Library

ISBN: 978-0-470-03474-3

Printed and bound in Great Britain by Bell & Bain Ltd, Glasgow

10 9 8 7 6 5 4 3 2 1

WILEY

About the Authors

The **National Alliance For Youth Sports** has been America's leading advocate for positive and safe sports for children for the past 25 years. It serves volunteer coaches, parents with children involved in organized sports, game officials, youth sports administrators, league directors, and the youngsters who participate in organised sport. The Alliance's programmes are used in more than 3,000 communities across the USA by parks and recreation departments, Boys & Girls Clubs, Police Athletic Leagues, YMCAs/YWCAs, and various independent youth service groups, as well as on military installations worldwide. For more information on the Alliance's programmes visit www.nays.org.

Greg Bach is the communications director for the National Alliance For Youth Sports, a position he has held since 1993. Before joining NAYS, he worked as the sports editor of the *Huron Daily Tribune* in Bad Axe, Michigan, where he captured numerous writing awards from the Associated Press, Michigan Press Association, and the Hearst Corporation. He has a journalism degree from Michigan State University, which he earned in 1989. He's an avid sport fan and has coached a variety of youth sports.

James Heller has been involved in football on and off for over 35 years. As a player, he played from youth-team level through into senior football. He has also helped to coach and manage football teams at several different age levels. In his time associated with 'the beautiful game' he has seen junior football coaching in the UK improve from a situation where 20 children ran around a muddy park aimlessly chasing the ball, watched by two cold goalkeepers, to one where the focus is on mini-soccer, skills improvement, and 'one child, one ball' training sessions.

Dedication

National Alliance For Youth Sports: This book is dedicated to all the volunteer football coaches who give up countless hours of their free time to work with children and ensure that they have positive, safe, and rewarding experiences. We applaud their efforts and commend them for making a difference in the lives of youngsters everywhere.

Greg Bach: This book is dedicated to my mom and dad, the best parents anyone could ever wish for. I am truly lucky and forever grateful for their never-ending love and support.

Authors' Acknowledgements

From the National Alliance For Youth Sports: A successful youth football programme doesn't just happen. It takes a real commitment from not only dedicated volunteer coaches, but also parents who understand their roles and responsibilities and league directors and administrators who know what it takes to ensure that every child who steps on the football field in their community has a safe, fun, and rewarding experience. Football plays an important role in the lives of millions of children and provides them with the opportunity to learn the skills of the game and the chance to develop both emotionally and physically as individuals. The National Alliance For Youth Sports extends a heartfelt 'Thank you' to every person who makes a positive difference, through football, in the life of a child.

From James: My thanks to Jason Dunne and Simon Bell at the Dummies team, and John Moseley at Capstone, for their help and support. Also to the numerous coaches of children's mini-soccer teams and footballing brains who offered valuable pointers along the way.

Publisher's Acknowledgements

We're proud of this book; please send us your comments through our Dummies online registration form located at www.dummies.com/register/.

Some of the people who helped bring this book to market include the following:

Acquisitions, Editorial, and Media Development

Project Editor: Simon Bell

Content Editor: Steve Edwards

Commissioning Editor: Jason Dunne

Copy Editor: Kim Vernon

Technical Editor: Graham Reed

Executive Editor: Jason Dunne

Executive Project Editor: Martin Tribe

Cover Photo: JupiterImages

Cartoons: Ed McLachlan

Composition Services

Project Coordinator: Jennifer Theriot

Layout and Graphics: Carl Byers, Heather Ryan

Proofreaders: John Greenough

Indexer: Stephen Ingle

Publishing and Editorial for Consumer Dummies

    Diane Graves Steele, Vice President and Publisher, Consumer Dummies

    Joyce Pepple, Acquisitions Director, Consumer Dummies

    Kristin A. Cocks, Product Development Director, Consumer Dummies

    Michael Spring, Vice President and Publisher, Travel

    Kelly Regan, Editorial Director, Travel

Publishing for Technology Dummies

    Andy Cummings, Vice President and Publisher, Dummies Technology/General User

Composition Services

    Gerry Fahey, Vice President of Production Services

    Debbie Stailey, Director of Composition Services

Contents at a Glance

Table of Contents

Introduction

· ·

*W*elcome to *Coaching Junior Football Teams For Dummies,* a book dedicated to volunteer coaches everywhere who work with kids in the wonderful sport of football. We hope you find it informative, entertaining, and – most important of all – useful in helping ensure that every child in your team has a fun, safe, and rewarding experience. After all, that's what it's really all about.

About This Book

We wrote this book for first-time volunteer football coaches looking for some guidance before they step onto the field, as well as for coaches who've been on the sidelines for a season or two and are interested in gaining more insight into specific areas of the game to benefit their young squads. If you're new to the sport, you may be somewhat nervous or a bit apprehensive about what you're getting yourself into. You can take comfort in knowing that this book will kick those concerns into touch and fully prepare you to enjoy a rewarding season with your team. Each chapter is filled with useful and straightforward information. The more chapters you knock off, the more knowledgeable you're going to be about this great game and how to teach it.

We also have plenty of information for the veterans who've spent countless evenings at the local football pitches. We wrote plenty of chapters specifically for you, covering everything from drills you can employ to upgrade individual skills to examining in detail the various systems of play that are available and how to choose the one that best fits your team's talent level.

One of the neat things about this book is that you can jump in anywhere. If you're a rookie coach, you probably have several questions swirling around in your head on everything from how to plan an effective training session to what to say to the team after a loss. Just check out the table of contents or the index for the topic you want to read about and then flip right there to get the scoop. Each chapter is divided into sections, and each section contains information on a specific topic concerning coaching youth football teams.

Conventions Used in This Book

To help you navigate this book, we use the following conventions:

- ✔ *Italic* text is used for emphasis and to highlight new words and terms that we define in the text.

- ✔ **Boldfaced** text is used to indicate keywords in bulleted lists or the action parts of numbered steps.

- ✔ `Monofont` is used for Web addresses. If you find that a specific address in this book has been changed, try scaling it back by going to the main site – the part of the address that ends in `.com`, `.org`, or `.edu`.

- ✔ Sidebars are shaded grey boxes that contain text that's interesting to know but not necessarily critical to your understanding of the chapter or topic.

In football-speak, many people still use yards to measure distances, so we have used yards as our unit of measurement in this book.

We've also packed this book full of diagrams of training drills and plays that you can work on with your team. The following chart is the key to understanding all the squiggles and lines:

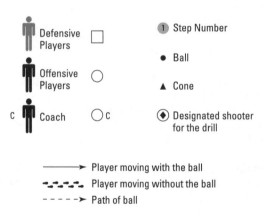

Defensive Players   ▢

Offensive Players   ◯

C Coach   ◯ C

① Step Number

● Ball

▲ Cone

◉ Designated shooter for the drill

———▶ Player moving with the ball

-◄-◄-◄- Player moving without the ball

- - - -▶ Path of ball

What You're Not to Read

Personally, we would read every word of this book if we were you. That's how good we think it is. But we may be biased, and you may be short on time. So, for your convenience, we're telling you that you don't have to read everything. In fact, when you see text marked with the TechnicalStuff icon, feel free to skip it. It isn't integral to your understanding of coaching or football. We also include grey-shaded boxes called *sidebars* that we fill with interesting (but totally skippable) information. Read at your own pace, and if you have time, let us know what you think of the book.

Foolish Assumptions

Here are some things that we assume about you:

- ✔ You know that football is played primarily with the feet and involves lots of running.

- ✔ You have a son or daughter who's interested in playing football this year, but you're unsure how to go about teaching him or her the game.

- ✔ You're a novice youth football coach, and you need to get your coaching skills up to speed.

- ✔ You don't have any aspirations of climbing the coaching ladder and overseeing a high school or college football team in the near future.

- ✔ You want the basics on things like what to do during the first practice of the season, how to determine who plays where, and whether teaching youngsters how to head a ball is safe.

If any of these descriptions hits the mark, you've come to the right place.

How This Book Is Organised

This book is divided into parts, each one pertaining to a specific aspect of coaching a youth football team. Here's a quick rundown.

Part 1: Getting Started Coaching Football

Coaching youth football can be a real challenge, but what you do before you and your team ever step on the field can make the difference between a smooth-running season and one that dissolves into total chaos and confusion. In this part, you get the inside track on how to develop a coaching philosophy that you're comfortable with and one that your players and their parents will embrace rather than reject. You also discover what all those markings on the pitch really mean and get an overview of the rules of the game.

Part II: Building Your Coaching Skills

Fresh air. Green grass. Colourful kits. This is where the real fun – and actual coaching – begins. Before you step on the field, though, this part provides valuable information on how to conduct a preseason parents' meeting, an often-overlooked aspect of coaching youth sport that's crucial for opening the communication lines, reducing the chances of misunderstandings and hurt feelings, and keeping your sanity. It also answers questions such as:

✔ How do I create training plans that aren't the same boring thing week after week?

✔ How do I work with the uncoordinated kids or the shy youngsters who won't stop staring at the ground?

✔ What about the kid who doesn't even want to be here?

Plus, we show you the game-day ropes – from pre-game routines to your post-game speech – and help you assess your team and your performance at midseason.

Part III: Beginning and Intermediate Football

Teaching kids the basics of the game – from passing and defending to dribbling and shooting – is crucial for their long-term enjoyment of the sport. This part shares how you can go about teaching by providing a variety of fun-filled training drills that are highly effective in communicating skills. Also, when your team has a pretty good handle on some of the basics, check out the chapter devoted to taking those skills up a notch.

Part IV: Advanced Football Strategies

When your players have a pretty good grasp of the basics of the game, they're eager to learn more advanced skills and continue their development. Part IV serves you well in this aspect. You discover more in-depth attacking and defensive techniques – such as overlaps and counterattacking – while being presented with an assortment of drills that you can use to help your players maximize their development. From indirect free kicks to defending a 2-on-1, this part examines it all.

Part V: The Finer Details

Part V is a smorgasbord of information on several topics that we hope you won't be dealing with much this season, such as recognising injuries, confronting problem parents, and dealing with discipline problems on your team. You also find valuable information on pre- and post-game nutrition that you can share with your team to help maximise performance. And for those coaches looking to coach a team in a league, you find all the information you need to help make your transition to a more competitive level of football a smooth one.

Part VI: The Part of Tens

It just wouldn't be a *For Dummies* book without the Part of Tens. Here, you find all sorts of precious information that you can put to use to boost the fun and enjoyment your team has playing for you this season. We include information on ways to make the season memorable and fun ways to end on a high note and keep 'em coming back next year.

Icons Used in This Book

This icon signals valuable tips that can really enhance your coaching skills. If you're scanning a chapter, take a moment to read these tips when you come across them and then put them to work.

When you're coaching youth football, you have a lot to comprehend. This icon alerts you to key information that's worth revisiting.

Watch out! This icon alerts you to situations that can be dangerous or derail your instruction.

Football can be a pretty complex game, particularly at the more competitive levels, so at times throughout this book, we present some rather technical information. You may want to skip some of this information if your young squad isn't ready to get too in-depth in the game.

Where to Go from Here

If this season is your first on the touchline as a volunteer youth football coach, you may be most comfortable digging in with Chapter 1 and moving forward from there. Please note, though, that the book is structured so that you can easily move around from chapter to chapter at your convenience. So if you need answers to some of your most pressing early-season questions, you can scan the table of contents or index for those topics and jump right to those chapters.

Part I
Getting Started Coaching Football

'He's very proud of his son.'

In this part . . .

*B*efore you take the field with your young troops for the first time, do yourself, and your team, a big favour by diving into some behind the scenes homework to lay the foundations of a smooth-running season. The homework includes outlining your coaching philosophy, understanding how your league operates, and learning the basic rules of the sport. You find all the information to get your season headed in the right direction in this part.

Chapter 1

Coaching Children in Football

- -

In This Chapter

▶ Coaching your own child

▶ Getting up to speed on the rules of football

▶ Planning training sessions

- -

Congratulations on your decision to coach a youth football team this season. You are embarking on a wonderful journey that will be filled with many special moments that both you and your players – regardless of their age or skill level – will remember for the rest of their lives.

Before you step on the pitch, please be aware that you have taken on a very important role. How you manage the youngsters on your team and the way you interact with them during training sessions and games impacts on how they feel about the sport and even themselves for years to come. How you handle the lengthy list of responsibilities that come attached with the job helps them develop an unquenchable passion for the game or drain their interest in ever participating again.

All you need – besides a whistle and clipboard – is some good information to guide you through the season. In this chapter, you find useful, straightforward insight and tips to help you and your team members have a safe, fun, and rewarding season, and one that they – and you – will look back on fondly for years to come.

Striking a Balance between Parenting and Coaching

I certainly don't have to tell you that being a parent is an enormously difficult job, but here's what I can share with you: Coaching your son or daughter's football team is equally as tricky. After you step inside the white lines and your child straps on the shinguards, you're likely to encounter an assortment of issues. I hope most of them are minor, but some may be problems that you never even dreamed of dealing with. Don't panic! Although the job of coaching your own child can be complex and confusing, if handled properly it can also be an extremely rewarding experience for both of you. Yes, expect to experience occasional bumps along the way, but if the two of you work together, you can enjoy some very special memories to savour for a lifetime.

And take comfort in the fact that you're not alone. Approximately 85 per cent of all volunteer football coaches have their own sons or daughters on the team, so you have ventured into common parenting territory.

Kicking around the decision with your kid

Before you decide to grab the whistle and assume the role of football coach, sit down with your child and gauge how she feels about you overseeing the team this season. If you don't ask her how she feels, you won't know. Many youngsters are thrilled to have their dad or mum as coach, and if you see that sparkle in your child's eyes when you bring the subject up, that makes all the time and effort you put into the season well worth it.

On the other hand, some children – for whatever reasons – aren't going to feel comfortable with the idea and would prefer that their parent didn't coach the team. Take their wishes into account before making the decision to step forward.

Here are a few tips to help you reach the right decision on whether you and your child are ready for you to pick up the coaching whistle:

- ✓ **With your child's help, put together a list of all the positives and negatives about being the coach.** On the positive side, you may list that the two of you can spend more time together, and that, as the coach, you can ensure that your child and the rest of the team have fun as they acquire new skills. Resolve the negatives by working with your child to develop solutions. For instance, your child may expect to play in a certain position simply because you're her parent. Explain that you must be fair to everyone and can't show favouritism, and that your child and her teammates will have an equal chance to play different positions.

- ✓ **Examine your own motivations.** Don't take on the task of coaching your son or daughter if your goal is to make your child a star. You must be willing to do whatever is best for your child's overall development, and harbouring thoughts of professional football and international caps is simply a blueprint for trouble.

- ✓ **Explain to your child that being the coach is a great honour.** The fact that she will be 'sharing' you with the other kids during games and training sessions doesn't mean you love her any less. Explain to her that your responsibility is to help all the players on the team. Taking the time to explain your role to your child helps promote better understanding and reduces the chance of problems arising after the season gets under way.

After the two of you have talked things through, take your child's thoughts seriously. If she still isn't comfortable with the idea, push your coaching aspirations to the side for the time being. You can revisit the subject with her the following season to measure his feelings. Just because she isn't ready this season doesn't mean she won't want you guiding her team next season or at some point in the future. The last thing you want to do is turn your child off the sport and make her uncomfortable.

Focusing on family-friendly football rules

If you and your child agree that having you take up the coaching reins is a good move, keep these tips in mind as you navigate through the season:

- ✔ **Remember that you're still the parent.** Whether the team wins or loses, you've got to step out of the coaching mode and remember that first and foremost you're a parent – and that means asking your child whether she had fun and praising her for doing her best and displaying good sportsmanship. Take your child out for that post-game ice cream or pizza whether she scored three goals or tripped over the ball in front of an open goal.

- ✔ **Keep talking.** To effectively monitor how the season is going, you want your child to understand that she can come to you with a concern or problem at any time. Just because you're the coach doesn't mean that certain topics are now off limits.

- ✔ **Don't push training at home.** If your child has a bad training session, you may be tempted to work with her on specific skills as soon as you get home. Never push your child in this direction. In casual conversation, ask her whether she wants to spend a few extra minutes practicing a certain skill that may be giving her a bit of trouble. If she does, that's great, but if not, let it go. Pushing your child to perform extra drills at home or in the park can drain her interest in the sport.

- ✔ **Never compare siblings.** Let your child develop at her own rate. She should never feel burdened by your expectations to control or kick a football as well as her brother or sister did at her age. If you compare a child like this, you can crush her self-esteem and smother her confidence.

- ✔ **Praise, praise, praise!** Be sure to praise your child's willingness, understanding, and co-operation in this special venture. Coaching your child can be one of the most rewarding experiences you can ever have, but it won't always be easy.

Coaching your own kid can be a great experience for both of you, but the job can feel a bit like walking a tightrope at times as you try to avoid two common traps that many coaches (especially those coaches who are unfamiliar with their roles) tend to fall into. Ideally, your behaviour should fit somewhere in-between these two extremes.

- **Providing preferential treatment:** Parents naturally lean toward showing preferential treatment for their own children, whether they realise it or not. Typically, they provide their children with extra playing time, shower them with more attention during training sessions and games, or assign them special duties, such as team captain. Showing favouritism throws your child into a difficult spot with her teammates and weakens team camaraderie.

- **Overcompensating to avoid the preferential-treatment label:** Coaches can also go too far out of their way to ensure that no one thinks they're giving preferential treatment to their own child. Quite often, they reduce their child's playing time or give their child less one-on-one instruction during training sessions. But, taking away playing time from your child in order to steer clear of the favouritism issue will, in effect, create a negative atmosphere for your own child. She will question why you're unfairly punishing her.

- **Refraining from pushing too hard:** All parents naturally want their kids to excel, no matter what the activity. In a sport like football, parents sometimes go overboard and take their newfound coaching positions to the extreme by viewing it as the chance to control their child's destiny. When this happens the youngster's experience is unfairly compromised because the parent will typically push her harder than the other kids, demand more from her and pile on criticism when she's unable to fulfil the unfair expectations. When parents lose sight of the big picture of what youth football is all about, problems begin materialising that impact on the child's emotional well-being, as well as her interest in discovering and playing football.

Doing Your Homework

Whether you volunteered to coach youth football this season because you wanted to spend more time with your child, or the club had a shortage of coaches and you were willing to step forward, you've accepted a responsibility that should not be taken lightly. You have plenty of work to do behind the scenes before you roll out the balls at your first training session to ensure that the season gets off to a smooth start. See Chapter 4 for more on preparing to run training sessions.

Working with – and not against – parents

The overwhelming majority of parents with children involved in organised youth football programmes are supportive and caring and only want the best for their children. Of course, there are those parents in the minority who can turn out to be a source of season-long aggravation that you may be forced to deal with. You can head off a lot of potential problems by gathering the parents together before you begin working with their kids and laying down the ground rules on what you expect in terms of behaviour during games, as well as their roles and responsibilities.

Coaches and parents who find ways to work together – the adult form of teamwork – is a formula that's going to produce tremendous benefits for the youngsters. Coaches and parents who clash over everything from playing time to why junior isn't getting to play centre forward will spoil the experience for not only that child but quite possibly others as well, if the negativity seeps into the team's training sessions and envelops match day. When it comes to working with parents, it makes good sense to keep the following in mind:

- ✔ **Be proactive.** Outlining your expectations and coaching methods before the season paints a clear picture to parents about how the season is going to be handled. When parents hear first-hand that you are committed to skill development over winning, and that you will be adhering to the league's equal playing time rule, this leaves no room for petty squabbles over how much playing time their child receives. If you don't clarify these issues for parents well in advance, you are asking for a heap of trouble – and you'll probably get it too.

- ✔ **Involve them.** Parents invest a lot of time and money into their child's football experience, and being able to include them will make it far more worthwhile to them and their children instead of simply watching training from the car or dropping their youngster off and running errands. Parents can do more than bring treats after the game, too. Find ways to involve them at your training sessions and recruit the right ones to assist on match day, and turn the season into a rewarding one for everyone involved.

- ✔ **Communicate with them.** Besides that pre-season parents meeting, keep those communication lines open all season long. Talk to parents about their child's progress, share your thoughts on areas of the game that the child has really made improvements in and that have impressed you; offer suggestions for things parents can do to help their youngster develop in other areas; and check from time to time to find out whether their child is having fun playing for you. Including parents in all facets of the season is the right and the smart thing to do, to ensure that their child has a positive experience.

Deciphering rules and mastering terminology

You're going to be coaching kids in the world's most popular sport, and as a volunteer coach, you may not have played much football yourself. That means that in order to fulfil your responsibilities you've got to have a good handle on the basics of the game and be able to explain rules, introduce terminology and pass on strategies to your young players. Sound complicated? It's not; just take a little time and effort to understand some of the quirky rules, like offside; and some of the terms, like corner kicks and indirect free kicks, that are at the heart of this great game. Check out Chapter 3 for more on rules and terminology.

 One of the most important steps that you can take is to find out what special rules your league operates under. Quite often the rules that leagues use vary greatly depending on the age and experience level of the players. Everything from the size of the pitch to what types of rules are enforced change from community to community. Knowing these rules – and being able to share them with your players – will make a tremendous difference in their enjoyment of the sport.

On the Pitch

Playing on the pitch is what coaching youth football is all about: The kids, their smiles, and their eagerness start discovering football and developing skills under you. What you say and do from Day One through the course of the season will have a major impact on whether these kids take a great interest in the sport and continue playing it for years to come or whether they choose to turn their backs on it.

Planning training sessions

The exercises you choose in order to pass on skills to kids, and the manner in which you go about designing your training sessions, will influence your team's enjoyment, and progress, during the season. Training sessions that kids look forward to with the same enthusiasm as they have for the first day of summer vacation are going to promote their acquiring and developing skills. But, training sessions that are not well thought out and are put together in your car in the car park five minutes before the players begin arriving are going to stifle all discovery and put a road block on fun. While working with your team, keep the following thoughts in mind to help squeeze the most out of your sessions:

✔ **Control the tone of your voice:** While correcting errors, do so in a way that's non-threatening and that applauds the child's effort in the process. Also, don't just focus on spotting mistakes in technique, but give the youngster some easy-to-understand feedback that they can use to correct the mistake the next time.

✔ **Create a positive atmosphere:** Turn your plans into sessions in which youngsters can make mistakes without the fear of being yelled at in front of their teammates. Letting the kids know from the first training session of the season that making mistakes is part of the process of acquiring new skills will allow them to relax and, in the process, help them to pick up skills quicker and perform better. Flip through to Chapter 6 for the inside track on running great training sessions.

When it comes to choosing exercises for your training sessions, always go for the ones that keep kids moving at all times and are challenging enough to hold their interest. Exercises that force kids to stand in a queue waiting for their turn are not only boring, they dramatically cut down on the number of touches of the ball each child receives, which minimises their development.

Match day

Coaching is about constantly adapting to ever-changing conditions, and that's more evident than ever on match day, when you need to make all sorts of decisions in a short period of time. With younger kids just starting out in the sport, make sure that you rotate them around to try all of the different positions so they can experience the sport from a variety of different perspectives. When it comes to the older kids, you find yourself making half-time adjustments and determining whether a more aggressive approach would serve the team best in the second half or whether a more defensive style of play is warranted.

Match days also provide many great able moments for the kids. Take the chance to reinforce some of the points you've talked about all week during training, such as the importance of working together as a team, displaying good sportsmanship toward the opposing team and the officials, abiding by the rules, doing your best at all times and having fun, regardless of what the scoreboard reads.

Chapter 2

Getting Organised

. . . .

In This Chapter

▶ Developing a coaching philosophy

▶ Understanding your league

. . . .

Coaching a squad of young football players involves more than showing up with a whistle, a team sheet, and a car boot-full of footballs. Being a coach kids admire and look forward to seeing all season requires a lot of preparation on your part prior to the first training session.

First, think about why you got involved this season, what you hope to accomplish and what your approach is going to be to help your team get there. Have you assumed the coaching role because you genuinely want to help kids pick up and develop skills in a fun and safe environment, or because you want to make a bid for the league title? What's your take on playing time, motivating players, and creating a positive atmosphere?

This chapter considers those aspects, and many others, which form the basis of your coaching philosophy. Having a philosophy in place and sticking to it as best you can sets the tone for a good season. A portion of your philosophy should also be dictated by the league you are coaching in. That's why it's always important to find out as much information as you can about the league's policies before you step on the pitch. Being involved in a league that promotes the values that you are aiming to impart to your team is critical for everyone's enjoyment.

Developing a Coaching Philosophy

Creating a *coaching philosophy* is fairly simple. Living up to it all season long is the tricky part. What is a coaching philosophy? Basically, it reflects the standards you have set for yourself and your team, and is the foundation of your coaching values and beliefs.

Entering the season without a coaching philosophy is like driving across the country without a road map. Yes, you'd eventually arrive at your destination, but not without wasting a lot of time and energy with wrong turns and dealing with unnecessary problems and aggravation along the way. A well-thought-out coaching philosophy should reflect a number of considerations, such as:

- ✔ Focusing on the best interests and well-being of every player
- ✔ Promoting the respect of players and coaches on both teams, as well as officials
- ✔ Upholding the virtues of fair play, good sportsmanship, honesty, and integrity
- ✔ Placing safety, skill development, and fun ahead of any personal desires to win.

Even with a carefully planned philosophy firmly in place, you will find it pretty challenging adhering to it at all times. This can be particularly true when Billy's mum confronts you halfway through the season about why the team isn't winning more games; or Jennifer's dad questions why the kids with less ability are receiving as much playing time as the team's best players. (For explaining your coaching philosophy to the parents before the season gets under way, see Chapter 4, which can help you steer clear of many of these potential headaches.)

Your philosophy is going to speak volumes about you as not just a coach, but as a person. So take the time to put real thought into it. You'll be glad you did. Lead your players in the direction you know is right. Strive to instil in them the values that you want your own kids to exhibit throughout their life.

Tailoring your coaching to your age group

Children are continually changing, and one of your responsibilities as a coach is to know what to expect both physically and emotionally from youngsters at various age levels. Being fully aware of these differences enhances your coaching skills and your ability to relate to your team. It also ensures that you don't favour those players on your squad who are more mature and skilled at the expense of those who are less skilled and developed.

No matter what the age or skill level of your players, always be supportive and enthusiastic. Pile on the praise and never stop encouraging them. This approach builds their confidence and self-esteem, regardless of age, and it's a gift that will last for years to come.

Protecting children

When it comes to coaching kids, first and foremost, before skills and drills and games comes the protection and safety of the children. This is why adults working with children in football are required to undergo a Criminal Records Bureau check. A number of other initiatives regarding child safety and protection are run by the various football associations in the UK, an initiative to ensure that only child-safe goals are used in mini-soccer and other youth football, for example. (Details of all such initiatives are available via the FA website, www.thefa.com (see Chapter 23.)

While each child has his or her own unique strengths and weaknesses, all youngsters possess general characteristics that are dictated by their age. Good coaches are aware of these traits. The following are general characteristics that are applicable for certain age ranges.

- **Age 6 and under:** Children in this age bracket may never have played football, and this season may very well be their first experience in an organised team setting. Your job is simply to introduce them to football's most basic elements and whet their appetite for future participation. (See Chapter 5, which covers the fundamentals that you can focus on with this age group.) Children at this age generally aren't concerned about how well they are performing football skills compared to the others on their team. They are primarily interested in being with friends and having fun discovering and playing the sport. Competition is usually the furthest thing from their minds, which is why scorelines and league rankings are often not that important at this level.

- **Age 7–9:** Youngsters at this age tend to start focusing on mastering the basics of the sport. They also crave feedback from coaches and parents on how they are performing certain skills and how they are progressing in a new skill. They begin noticing how their teammates are faring while practising these skills. As coaches praise their peers for properly executing a skill, the child will want to earn that same feedback as well. The desire to compete carries much more prominence for some youngsters in this age range than others, particularly if they have older siblings who they have watched compete in football or other sports and now feel it's finally their turn to display their skills.

- **Age 10–12:** More than likely, these children have had experience playing football in the past and are continuing with it because it has piqued their interest. Keep the positive momentum going by adding to their foundation of skills and fuel their desire to continue playing by conducting training sessions that are both challenging and fun. Quite often, sports take on added importance at this juncture in their life and they really want to do well. (For more on skills and drills with this age group, see Chapters 10 to 12.) As children reach this age range, many become more competitive and seek to perform better than others of their age. When their ability matches up with their peers, or surpasses it, they feel a real sense of achievement.

✔ **Age 13–14:** Welcome to the challenging world of the teenager! Children in this age category have already developed many of the basic skills needed to play the sport, and now they want to improve these skills. Be aware that teenage children are typically searching for their own personal identity as well. So, it's a good idea to get to know them on a personal level by finding out who their favourite football players are or what football team they support. Of course, this is a great tip for building special coach-player bonds with kids of all ages. (Turn to Part IV, where we cover forward play and defending for older kids, and drills that challenge them.)

✔ **Age 15 and above:** Gaining the respect of your players is always important to your coaching success, and this is particularly true for kids aged 15 and older. These are teens that have developed a real passion for the sport. They attend football tournaments, perhaps play in leagues year-round and, in some cases, may even be more knowledgeable in certain areas of the sport than you are. If you volunteer or get recruited to coach this age group – don't be scared! Don't feel threatened. Instead, welcome the chance to enhance your coaching abilities and embrace the opportunity to coach kids with a deep-rooted love for the game. Be sure to let them know that you value their opinions, suggestions and input regarding the team. A youngster's passion for football is wonderful, and actually helps make your job easier.

Emphasising teamwork

While football is a sport that allows individuals plenty of opportunities to be creative and to run with the ball on their own, you and your team are much better off if you can get everyone to work together as a cohesive unit. Of course, this is easier said then done.

Imagine having 10 kids in front of you. You have one really good toy that they are all eyeing. You give the toy to one child and ask that they share it with everyone. Tough to achieve, eh? The same goes for football. There's one ball that they are all going to have to share in order for the team to be successful. So how do you get the team to that point?

Sure-fire routes to fostering the essence of teamwork among your players don't exist, but the following are some pointers to assist you in your efforts and get the players to begin to see the enormous benefits that accompany working as a team rather than a bunch of individuals.

✔ **Give touchline support.** Encourage players not in the game to stay involved by cheering and supporting their teammates. This keeps them involved in the action instead of glancing over to see what their parents are doing or what kind of food their friends are eating.

✔ **Allow individual freedom – at times.** While you should allow players individual freedom to run with the ball, it must be done within the confines of the team setting. There will certainly be points during the game where a player's close control skills and ability to dribble the ball down the pitch may be called for, and that's part of the game. But when that player then ignores teammates and isn't willing to pass the ball, the team chemistry is threatened. Remind players that they have teammates for a reason and must be sure to look out for them. (The problem of dealing with a player who isn't willing to pass the ball is covered in Chapter 19.)

✔ **Avoid the captain syndrome.** Continually relying on two or three players to serve as team captains throughout the season puts them on a platform above the rest of the squad. By giving every player the opportunity to lead warm-ups in training or be first in a drill infuses the team with that sense that everyone is equal.

✔ **Praise team efforts.** During training sessions, make it a point to recognise the efforts of the team whenever possible. For example, if you're conducting a 3-on-1 drill and the attacking players score a goal, you may feel a natural tendency to applaud the end result and acknowledge the youngster who scored at the expense of the others involved in the drill. Be sure to acknowledge the perfectly executed pass that began the move, or the pass that found the unmarked scorer. If your admiration is spread among all the players who played a role in the goal, players begin to understand that setting up a goal is just as important as scoring in the team framework.

✔ **Get the kids praising one another.** Encourage the kids who score goals to acknowledge the pass from their teammate that led to it. If you get kids into the habit of giving one another high-fives, or telling one another 'great pass', this forges a bond and strengthens the idea of everyone working together for the benefit of the team.

✔ **Recognise the non-scoring contributions after the game.** The kids who scored the goals don't need additional praise after the game because their shot generated cheers and applause from the spectators. How about giving out post-game prizes to the player who began the move with a great pass out of defence? After all, there never would have been a goal without the effort of that child, and it's well worth mentioning that whether the team wins, draws or loses, the whole team deserves the credit and not just any one player.

Motivating players

Regardless of the age or experience level of your players, they arrive at the pitch with vastly different motivations for playing the game. While some will be strongly motivated individuals who will be real gems to work with, others may benefit from your inspiring words.

Some players should respond positively to the challenges you issue, such as seeing whether they can deliver 10 accurate passes in a row. With others, that approach may actually detract from their motivation to participate. Each youngster you come into contact with is different. Discover for yourself what works for each child to help get the best out of them.

Here are a few general tips that you can employ to help spur your players on to become the best they can be.

- ✔ **Share your love of the sport.** If you have a sincere passion for football and for passing this on to children, your excitement and enthusiasm should rub off on the team.

- ✔ **Set attainable goals for youngsters.** By having reasonable expectations for the kids you are coaching, and setting goals that are within their reach, you will stimulate and encourage them to keep working because the goals are within sight. If a child senses that your expectations are impossibly far-fetched, they are going to wonder what's the point of trying and their play on the pitch could suffer tremendously.

- ✔ **Recognise the good things happening on the pitch.** Stop training to point out when a player has done something really well, not when he's made a mistake. Praise is simply one of the best motivational tools around. Think about it. If your boss tells you that you have done a great job on a presentation in front of your colleagues, you are going to give even more effort on your next presentation. The same goes for kids performing skills on a football pitch.

- ✔ **Do not motivate through fear or threats.** Making a child run a lap for failing to perform at an expected level has no place in youth football. These types of approaches typically handcuff a youngster's ability to perform because they're now afraid of making a mistake that is going to translate into punishment. Children have to feel free to make mistakes in order to improve. Plus, this motivation-through-fear tactic has a strong probability of putting them off of the sport in the years to come.

Fostering a positive atmosphere

Creating an atmosphere in which youngsters are prized, respected and accepted is imperative for any improvement and skill development to take place during the season. Youngsters who are comfortable in the team environment that you have created and genuinely feel that they are valued and contributing members will give you their best effort all season long – and have fun doing so. Here are a few ways that you can help make that happen.

- ✔ **Listen to the young voices.** Let the kids regularly make choices. Letting them select a favourite drill to run during training or choosing the team snack at the next game are great ways to involve everyone and make them feel a real part of what is going on this season. If the league allows it, let them choose the team name and the colour of the strip. Or, to help promote team unity, let players pick what colour shirt everyone wears to the next training session. Seeing all the kids show up in a blue shirt at training is one of those little things you can do that can make a big difference in forging a bond among all the players.

- ✔ **Play the name game.** Let players choose nicknames for themselves. If you feel daring, even let the team come up with a nickname for you.

- ✔ **Give constant recognition.** Applaud good attitudes and strong work ethics as much as a properly executed pass or a good tackle. These are the attributes that youngsters often carry with them for the rest of their lives, long after they have put their shin pads away.

- ✔ **Cheer when mistakes are made.** Yes, even when a child makes a mistake or fails to perform a skill the way you just demonstrated, that's a part of playing football, and they need to be reminded of that. Praising their efforts rather than criticising the result frees up the child to keep trying until they get it. They're not going to fear making a mistake because they know there won't be negative backlash from you. This opens the door to all sorts of development during the season.

Making every kid count

As the coach, your job is to to work with, and play close attention to, all of the youngsters on your team, regardless of how fast they run or how hard they can kick a football. Sometimes this can be a lot more difficult than it sounds. After all, those kids that are more athletically gifted than the rest of the team are fairly easy to become enamoured with, and you can end up showering these kids with all the attention, accolades and praise. Spreading the encouraging words around equally takes real focus and effort. Making sure that each child – no matter how big or small their actual contributions are during games and training sessions – feels valued and appreciated for their efforts is the cornerstone of good coaching.

Providing immediate feedback is one of the most effective ways to accomplish this. While the kids who score goals during games hear the gratifying applause from the touchlines, make the time to acknowledge the efforts of your other players that led to the goal. For instance, recognising the youngster who delivered the pass to the scorer, or applauding the defender who won the ball and started the move that eventually led to the goal, goes a long way towards making each child truly feel appreciated and a part of the team.

Even less-skilled youngsters struggling to contribute during games can be recognised in a number of ways to inflate their self-esteem and maintain their interest in participating. You can applaud their chasing the ball down, acknowledge their team spirit and enthusiasm, and even point out to the rest of the squad the good sportsmanship that they displayed during the game and how the rest of the team should follow the example they set. Continually recognising players in this way boosts their self-confidence and fuels their interest in giving it their best effort all season long.

Many coaches enjoy handing out awards to their players at the end of the season. If you elect to do so, make sure that you come up with something for every player on the team. Traditional awards, such as Best Player, do nothing more than pile on the praise to a player who has enjoyed recognition all season long. Plus, everyone involved with the team probably already knows who that player is. Presenting awards to everyone ensures that the entire squad feels valued and appreciated for their efforts, and receiving one may be just the nudge that certain youngsters need to continue with the sport next season. Awards such as Best Player in Training Sessions, Most Supportive Teammate, Most Improved Player, and Best Display of Sportsmanship are just some that you can present. See Chapter 22, where these awards, and others, are discussed in greater detail.

Focusing on fun and skill development

As a youth football coach, make sure that you don't let your vision of what is best for your players become blurred by trying to win every game, grab the league title and show off the shiny champions' trophy on your mantelpiece at home. Your team's win-draw-lose record at the end of the season does not define your success as a coach. The true barometer of what type of coach you are is going to be whether the kids acquired skills, had fun doing so, and if they would want to play for you again next season.

Certainly, at the more advanced levels, winning takes on a more prominent role, and the concept shouldn't be swept aside; winning is a part of playing football. After all, doing well in a test in school is a form of winning. Winning is something that we all must strive for in order to achieve a level of success in life.

But when it comes to youth football, coaches must exercise great caution. Children are highly impressionable. If they get a sense that winning is all that really matters to you then having fun and developing skills suddenly become secondary in their minds, and the season begins heading into a downward spiral. Once you start letting this happen it becomes really difficult to alter the season's course and get everything back on track. The younger and less experienced the children on your team are with the sport, the less you should focus on wins and losses and the more you should concentrate on coaching kids in skills and ensuring they are having fun playing and discovering the game.

Children and their short attention spans can make coaching skills difficult to apply at times, but the short attention spans can also work to your advantage. Many youngsters just beginning in the sport are usually going to forget the score of the last game pretty quickly and direct their attention to something else. So even if you happened to lose 9–0, praise them for their effort; congratulate them on how well they passed the ball; provide them with a confidence boost and a sense of accomplishment that they are making strides in their play.

Keep in mind that simply because your team scored more goals than the opposition doesn't necessarily mean that they performed to the best of their ability. A team can turn in a poor or lacklustre effort and still win because the other team played even worse or simply didn't have many talented players. Conversely, your team can play extremely well and still lose the match, but that shouldn't detract from the kids' performance. So, don't turn to the scoreline for feedback on judging how the team played.

Never let scorelines or opposing teams define how much fun you have on the football pitch, or impede your team's progress in picking up the game. The skill development process evolves continuously throughout the season. Use every training session and game as a building block to acquiring new skills, while never forgetting to have fun along the way. With the right approach, your team will surely enjoy the journey with you, every kick of the way.

Modelling good sportsmanship

Explaining good sportsmanship to youngsters can be tricky, especially as they are bombarded with images on television of professional footballers swearing, diving and abusing the referee. Good sportsmanship is one of the healthiest and most important ideals you can instil in your young players, though. Here are a few ways you can help to accomplish this and make your squad liked and respected.

✔ **Continually stress to your team during training sessions and before games the importance of good sportsmanship at all times.** While your players are going through warm-ups before training, discuss a game on television that they saw and ask them whether they saw a player display good sportsmanship. Subtly reinforcing the importance of good sportsmanship every chance you get, goes a long way toward instilling these qualities in your players.

✔ **Set the tone for good sportsmanship before any game begins by shaking the hand of the opposing coach.** The players, the fans, and the opposing coach should notice, and you will have made a difference.

✔ **Be a model of good sportsmanship at all times.** That means no yelling at officials or questioning decisions that you are sure should have gone your team's way. If you aren't a model of good sportsmanship at all times yourself, you can't expect your players to be. Remember, players are going to take their cue from you, so if you rant and rave about a decision to an official, you can't expect your players to show respect for the officials.

✔ **During your post-game talk with the team, make sure to recognise any players who displayed good sportsmanship.** Perhaps one of your players went out of their way after the game to congratulate an opposing player who scored a goal or played well during the course of the game. By recognising these displays, your players gradually begin to realise that how they behave on the pitch is important.

✔ **Deal with problems**. During the season, the chances are that you may encounter a win-at-all-cost coach who prowls the touchlines yelling and berating his team; or an out-of-control parent who spends the entire game shouting instructions at their child or disputes every decision that doesn't go his child's team's way. See Chapter 19, which includes tips to handle these types of inappropriate behaviour, which have no place in youth football.

Understanding the League You're Coaching In

While several different varieties of youth football leagues exist around the country – same-sex leagues and mixed leagues, indoor and outdoor leagues, for example – for children under 11, *mini-soccer* is fast becoming the dominant game. For children over the age of 11, the choice is often between small-sided games and the 11-a-side adult version. (For more information on mini-soccer, see the upcoming section 'Playing for fun or first place'.)

With all the leagues comes the smorgasbord of rules that are a specific to each league. Many adhere strictly to the official rules of the sport and allow for little modification. Some, however, alter the rules to fit the age and experience level of the kids. Mini-soccer has its own set of rules, which you can obtain from the Football Association, the governing body of football in the UK:

✔ `www.scottishfa.co.uk`: Scotland

✔ `www.thefa.com`: England

✔ `www.irishfa.com`: Northern Ireland

✔ `www.faw.org.uk`: Wales

Knowing your league's rules

Reading the league rulebook isn't as exciting as a Stephen King novel or a John Grisham thriller. You're not likely to be eagerly turning page after page. But this book should be bedside reading for you. To be successful at coaching, you have to know the rules of the game, as well as the particular rules your league is enforcing this season, and be able to explain them to your players. If you don't know and understand the rules, there's no way you can expect your team to either.

If youngsters don't know the rules, football can be a pretty frustrating experience. For example, consider a child who has put in a perfect cross to a team-mate rushing in on goal. He feels a sense of pride and accomplishment for delivering such a great pass, only to hear the official blow the whistle for offside. If your players don't understand the offside rule it's going to affect their play. (See Chapter 3 for your initiation into the mysteries of offside).

Don't assume that older kids have a firm grasp on all the rules simply because they've played the sport for years. If no one took the time to explain the rules, they may be confused over some of them. You can make a difference.

Don't plunge into the rulebook and attempt to memorise all the rules in a single sitting. Review a few pages every night prior to the season getting under way until you are pretty comfortable with them.

Even if you have an extensive knowledge of football and perhaps have even played it at a reasonable level, looking at the league's rulebook is useful. Consider it a refresher before you take to the pitch. Plus, there's a good chance that the league is using rules that were never applied that way when you first played.

Rainy days and postponed fixtures

Days arrive when Mother Nature just isn't going to be on your side, and she's going to create havoc with your season. Rainy weather often forces you to reschedule or call off training sessions. Inclement weather on match days may result in your games being shuffled to another day that you normally don't play on, or being cancelled. Certain leagues may even have a week set aside at the end of the season specifically to catch up with fixtures. Being aware of the league policy regarding postponed games alleviates a lot of the confusion felt by parents and team members once bad weather arrives.

Exercise great caution with approaching storms, as well. Waiting for the first sign of lightning before cancelling training or stopping a game is flirting with serious trouble. Get your players off the pitch before lightning threatens the area. Storms should not be taken lightly, and attempting to squeeze in a few extra minutes of training before the storm hits simply isn't worth risking the lives of your players. If conditions become dangerous during a game, don't wait for an official to call the session off. Get your kids off the pitch immediately.

Training, training, training

The age of your team generally dictates how much time you spend conducting training sessions during the season. With most young children, for example, you spend just one training session a week with the kids, so it's important to be aware of the time you have before you put together your training plans.

The time you spend with your team during these sessions is critical for their success. Training isn't a social hour where you roll balls out on the pitch and have the kids knock them around while you stand by on the touch-lines watching. You've got to carefully plan these sessions and be actively involved in them at all times. Often, kids won't even be able to recall a game they played in, but they will fondly recall a training session and what you said to them, or a drill that was so much fun they couldn't wait to tell their parents about it. See Chapter 6 to get in-depth tips on running a great training session.

Playing for fun or first place

The two distinct differences that exist between football fixtures are whether they are classified as recreational or competitive. Each type requires vastly different approaches to coaching. Do you know what type of fixtures you are coaching for this season?

Recreational games

If you are coaching football for the first time, the chances are pretty good that you're involved with younger kids in a recreational league. The FA recommendations are that children of five and six do not play competitive football. Indeed, many older children aren't involved in competitive football as such, depending on how you define competitive football.

If your club's team is in a league, it is probably a *mini-soccer league.* These types of league focus on coaching kids in the basic skills of the game. Generally, they have rules in place regarding equal playing time. Often, with kids aged 10 and under, teams have fewer players, and games are played on scaled down pitches to allow each child plenty of touches of the ball. The league may not record results, keep standings or tables, or award prizes for first place. Different leagues have different policies in this regard so make sure that you check.

Recreational leagues also feature rules that have been altered to meet the needs of the age and experience level of the kids. Offsides don't exist in mini-soccer. There may be no indirect free kicks. The game leader or referee may stop to explain and demonstrate the rules from time to time.

Outside of mini-soccer leagues, teams may also just play other local teams for fun, with cut-down versions of the usual football rules. With the younger age groups, there may not even be goalkeepers, and just cones for goals.

 When meeting with the opposing coach before the game, encourage her to provide positive feedback to your players when the action is at her end of the pitch, and let her know that you will do the same when the play takes place near you. At this level, you just want kids running around and getting a feel for kicking the ball and being with their teammates.

As children become older and stay involved in the sport longer, naturally they are going to become more competitive. Winning takes on a more prominent role with a lot of kids around the age of 12. While football is still a recreation, some of the emphasis shifts to winning, but not at the expense of league policies regarding equal playing time.

Competitive leagues

Children whose thirst for competition can't be quenched in local recreational football can usually get a taste of competitive football in a local league.

Competitive football may just be a question of keeping records of results league tables and giving out prizes and trophies. As the children get older, though, it becomes a question of which youngsters have demonstrated higher skill levels than other kids their age.

At this level, usually not until kids are into their teens, the coach has a broader set of responsibilities including more intensive and detailed training schedules, away games, football tournaments, trials, and team selection. Results become more important and the idea of equal playing time less so.

Coaches are usually only given the reins of a competitive team if they have a strong coaching background and have proven with their experience to be well-versed in all areas of the game. The higher you go, the more likely it is that you will be taking your FA coaching badges to become a qualified FA coach.

Chapter 3

Knowing the Football Basics

· ·

· ·

*F*ootball is a truly amazing, wonderfully complex, and sometimes even mysterious sport. If you never played it as a child, or have little experience coaching it as an adult, the rulebook may seem more difficult to remember than a foreign language, and the markings on the pitch may seem pretty difficult to decipher as well. But you've got nothing to worry about. In this chapter, we take you on a tour of the pitch, explain all those lines, rectangles and arcs, and let you in on a little secret: The rules really aren't as difficult to comprehend as you may think.

We also talk about the various positions, the skills required to play them, and the secrets to matching kids to the right positions when you are filling out your team sheet. We guide you through the maze of hand signals that referees and linesmen use during the course of games that you need to be familiar with in order to provide your team with the best possible coaching at all times.

Inside the Lines

At first glance, all the markings on a football pitch may look intimidating or confusing, but this isn't really the case. Each is easily identified and each serves a specific purpose. Just like the markings on a rugby or hockey pitch, they are part of the foundation of the game.

In tennis, the size of the court never changes. But football is a completely different story. The size and shape of a football pitch can vary in length from 100 to 130 yards and its width can be anywhere from 50 to 100 yards.

In international matches, games are generally contested on pitches that are usually between 110 and 120 yards long and 70 to 80 yards wide. Of course, in youth football the pitch size is scaled down considerably to account for the small bodies. Often, one regulation football pitch can accommodate at least half a dozen youth games at one time. Here's what the markings (see Figure 3-1) on a football pitch mean:

- ✔ **Touchlines:** These are the outside lines that run along either the side of the pitch. Balls that completely cross these lines can be picked up (touched) by players in order to put them back into play.

- ✔ **Goal lines:** These are the lines at both ends of the pitch and the goals are positioned directly on top of the lines.

- ✔ **Corner areas:** In all four corners of the pitch, there are small corner areas marked by a quarter circle with a radius of 1 yard and a corner flag. These areas are marked off to indicate exactly where the ball must be placed for corner kicks.

- ✔ **Halfway markings:** This line runs across the centre of the pitch and is primarily used for the opening kick-off. During kick-offs, the teams are required to stay in their own half of the pitch. The middle of the halfway line is marked by the centre spot, which is where the ball is placed for kick-offs. Surrounding the centre spot is a circle. When a team kicks off from here, opponents must stay outside of the centre circle.

  The other purpose of the halfway line is determining offside violations, because a player can't be given offside if he is on his team's side of the halfway line. (For more on offside, see the section 'Offside'," later in this chapter.)

- ✔ **Goals:** The goals at each end of the pitch are 8 feet high and 24 feet wide.

- ✔ **Goal area:** More commonly known as the six-yard box, these rectangles are directly in front of each goal and measure 6 by 20 yards. They indicate where the ball is placed for goal kicks; the ball can be placed anywhere inside the marked out area. If an indirect free kick is awarded in the six yard box it is taken from the goal area line parallel to the line across the goalmouth.

- ✔ **Penalty areas:** Also known as the penalty box, this large rectangle surrounds each goal area and measures 18 by 44 yards and includes the goal area within it. The keeper can handle the ball when it is inside his penalty area or goal area. The lines marking the sides of the penalty areas closest to the centre circle are 18 yards from the goal lines and are referred to as the 18 yard lines.

✔ **Penalty spot:** The penalty spot is 12 yards from each goal and centred between the goal posts. If a team commits a major foul within its own penalty area, the referee awards a penalty kick that is taken from the penalty spot in that penalty area. The ball is placed on the penalty spot. When a penalty is taking place, only the goalkeeper is allowed to defend against the penalty taker.

✔ **Penalty arcs:** These semi-circular arcs extend from each penalty area. During a penalty kick, all the players except the penalty taker and the goalkeeper must remain outside the penalty arc, as well as the penalty area. Penalty kicks are not awarded for fouls committed within these arcs, and goalies can't touch the ball with their hands within them.

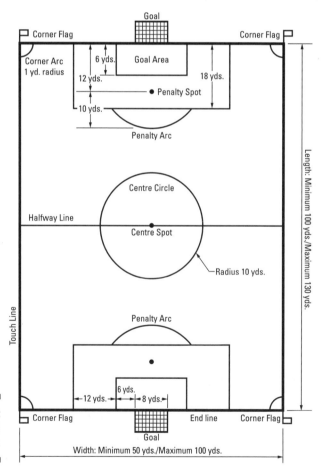

Figure 3-1:
The field
of play.

Taking Up Position

In football, the basic positions that your youngsters play on the pitch are goalkeeper (also known as the goalie or keeper), sweeper, centre-back, full-back, midfielder, and forward (see Figure 3-2). In a typical full-scale football game of 11 versus 11, during the actual playing of the game, you have a goalie, four defenders (two centre-backs, two full-backs), four midfielders, and two forwards. This is the 4-4-2 formation. Of course, as the coach you can tweak and modify your line-up and use all sorts of different formations (see Chapter 14 for more detail on this).

Each position is accompanied by varying responsibilities, and kids are going to be better suited for certain positions than others. Of course, at the beginner levels of football, you want to be sure to introduce all children to each of the different positions and give them actual game experience at each spot so that they have the opportunity to fully enjoy their football experience. As players gain experience and advance to higher and more competitive levels of play, then be more concerned with finding the right position to match each child's talent and figuring out how that child's particular skills can best be used for the benefit of the team.

When it comes to positioning your players, you've got to take into account the positions on the pitch that you need to fill, the skills that are needed to successfully play those positions, the wide range of responsibilities that come with each position, and what types of kids are best suited to handling these positions.

You can pretty much be assured that one of the first questions you are going to face from a parent before the season gets under way will be regarding who is going to be playing what position on the pitch. It may be a father asking where you intend to play his son, or a mother pulling you aside prior to the season's first training session to tell you that her son is probably the most talented player on the team and that you should be playing him in goal because he's really good at making acrobatic saves.

Positions on the pitch

The possible positions on the pitch are as different as the kids under your care who will be playing them this season. Starting from your own goal and working out, you have the following:

✔ **Goalie:** This player positions himself between the goal posts and usually stands a few yards out from the goal line. He is the only player allowed to handle the ball during normal play, other than from throw-ins.

✔ **Sweeper:** This player plays in the space in front of his team's goalie and behind the centre-backs and rarely strays from the goal scoring area.

✔ **Centre-backs:** These players hold down the position in front of their goalie in the centre of defence.

✔ **Full-backs:** These players play either side of the centre-back and provide primarily defensive help.

✔ **Midfielders:** These players play in between the defenders and forwards and provide support in both attack and defence.

✔ **Forwards:** The players in these positions spearhead the attack and focus on making and scoring goals.

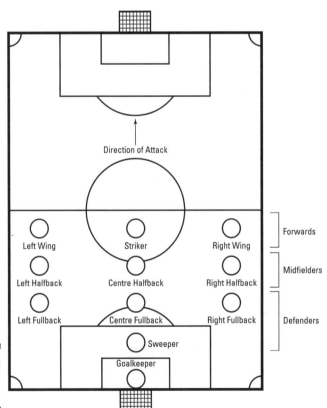

Figure 3-2:
A standard
line-up.

Each position on the football pitch carries with it its own specific set of responsibilities:

Goalie

The goalie's Number One responsibility is to defend your team's goal and prevent the ball from going into the net. While he is allowed to wander all over the pitch, allowing him to do so is not a strategy that is recommended under any circumstance. You always want him stationed in front of your goal and ready to make a save when called upon. Anytime the goalie has the ball in his hands, opposing players are not allowed to kick at it. Anytime the goalie strays outside their own penalty area, which includes the goal area, they are just like any other player on the pitch and cannot touch the ball with their hands or arms. Anytime the ball is within the goalie's own penalty area he is allowed to touch it with any part of his body. So, he can scoop the ball up with his hands, hold it or simply kick it away. Also, when the ball is in his hands he can even take steps before releasing the ball. Anytime a goalie has the ball in his arms opposing players can not interfere with his throw or kick.

When a goalie is positioned inside the goal area, he receives special protection when it comes to contact from opposing players. Only minor and incidental body contact by opposing players is allowed when going for the ball in this area. While the rules in this area of the game are generally left to the discretion of each individual referee, generally speaking most goalies are allowed the privilege of not being interfered with while they are grabbing the ball. Goalies also have limitations that they must adhere to, which are the following:

- **Six seconds:** Once the goalie has possession of the ball, he is only allowed six seconds before sending the ball back into play. Sometimes referees allow an extra second or two, particularly if the goalie has made a lunging save and is trying to regain balance.

- **Back passes:** If the team is under pressure and a defender or another player deliberately passes the ball back to the goalie, the goalie isn't allowed to handle the ball. He must control it with his feet, or other part of the body, and pass it or kick it away. The same thing applies if a teammate throws the ball to the goalie from a throw-in.

- **Doubly possessed:** Anytime a goalie has possession of the ball with his hands and he sends the ball back into play, he can't touch the ball again with his hands until an opposing player makes contact with the ball anywhere on the pitch, or a teammate plays it outside the penalty area. This rule does not enter into play when the goalie is playing the ball with his feet. He can dribble or kick the ball just like any other player on the pitch, regardless of whether he has touched it with his hands. So, he can stop the ball with his hands, put it on the ground and kick it to a teammate. He can even gain possession of the ball with his feet, dribble it, and then scoop it up if he chooses to do so.

Sweepers

The top priority of the sweeper is to make sure that no ball gets behind him. Ashe is the last line of defence before the goalie, the sweeper's responsibility is to 'sweep' the ball out of the goal-scoring area. Sweepers must always be aware of when the opposing players are near the goal and mark them tightly when they are positioned to get a shot on goal. A sweeper rarely leaves the goal area unless there happens to be a teammate available to provide back up while the sweeper steps out to defend another attack. Occasionally, as sweepers are generally unmarked, they can push forward to assist the midfield, but they must always remember their defensive duties.

Centre-backs

The primary responsibility of the centre-backs is to help ensure that players from the opposing team don't get close enough to take quality shots, and to head balls away from the penalty area that are in the air. Youngsters who play these positions are also sometimes referred to as stoppers because they are relied on to 'stop' the opposing team's attack when they are converging on the goal. A football goal is pretty big and it puts an enormous amount of pressure on a goalie to expect him to be able to cover all of that territory all by herself.

Full-backs

The left and right full-backs, as their names suggest, play to the left and right of the centre-back. These players have the task of containing the other team's forwards or midfielders playing opposite them. The opposing team will try to penetrate the defence by attacking down the line towards the corners of the pitch and then crossing the ball to the centre forward or striker. The left and right fullbacks must be focused on stopping that penetration, or at least slowing it down and making sure that they don't get a quality cross in.

Because the full-backs play in the shadow of their own goal, coaches generally don't want them taking any unnecessary risks with the ball. That means they don't spend a lot of time dribbling, but instead their focus is on getting the ball away from their goal and out of danger as quickly as possible. Fullbacks typically kick the ball out for a throw-in to avoid conceding possession to an opponent in a dangerous area of the pitch where an attacking player has a lot of options.

Certain formations and systems of play rely on the full-backs getting down the line into the opposition half and delivering crosses. Others do not expect the full-back to go beyond the halfway line.

Midfielders

When it comes to being successful in football, how effective your team is will often be determined to a large extent by which team controls the middle of the pitch the best. After all, during games the centre of the pitch is where a big chunk of the action usually takes place – and that's where the midfielders enter the picture. These players are stationed in the middle of the team's formation. Their top priority is to gain possession of the ball and get attacks underway by dribbling the ball up the pitch, or getting the ball to the forwards with accurate passes. It's no secret that the team that maintains possession of the ball the longest is the team that is probably going to make more quality scoring chances, and score more goals.

The essential job of the midfielder is to control the ball, distribute it to teammates, and be able to move the ball up the pitch themselves if they are unable to spot an unmarked teammate. Midfielders also handle a lot of the throw-in responsibilities, which can be a valuable attacking weapon at the opponent's end of the pitch. Midfielders must also execute sound throw-ins at their own end of the pitch because an inaccurate throw can quickly turn into a great scoring opportunity for the other team.

The centre midfielder has a number of special roles. When on the attack, the centre midfielder often joins the action as a second striker, and is counted on to deliver shots on goal from a little further out than his teammates on the front line, who usually work much closer around the goal. He also supports attacks and can be effective in taking advantage of any rebounds around the goal. A centre midfielder may often play in front of the defenders, breaking the play up, and protecting the defence. All midfielders have defensive responsibilities as well and must provide support whenever the opposing team has possession of the ball.

If the formation has only one or two forwards, then the left and right midfielders are expected to get down the touchline to cross balls to the forwards.

Forwards

These players are counted on to score goals for the team. Once the team has possession of the ball, these players move forward and look to receive passes from the midfielders that they can then use to deliver quality shots on goal. A forward who plays primarily in the centre of the pitch, rather than on the flanks, is known as a centre-forward, while forwards who operate primarily down the touchline are known as left- and right-wingers, depending on which flank they operate on. The centre-forward's primary focus is scoring goals, while the wingers look to create shots for themselves from the outside, or deliver passes to the striker in the middle of the pitch.

The wingers' primary responsibility is to get the ball down the touchline and work their way as close to the goal line as possible, and then look to cross the ball to the striker for a shot on goal. Because the left- and right-wingers must be excellent sprinters who can outrun defenders to the corners, conditioning plays an important role in how successful they are in this position.

Besides being well-conditioned, which certainly is an important aspect for all players, forwards must possess quality passing skills. A lot of the team's success in the opponent's half of the pitch is dictated by how effective the link-up play is between the forwards as this helps to get the ball to a striker in positions that produce quality scoring chances. Forwards are also more effective in their roles if they develop other skills, particularly one-against-one dribbling skills, which help the forward to deceive an opponent in order to get by him with the ball. If you want to find out more about these important skills, see Chapter 14.

Wingers may also be responsible for taking a large amount of corner kicks, because a lot of their play happens in that area of the pitch when they are attacking with the ball. Make sure that you have players in these positions who are proficient in receiving throw-ins, as well as heading the ball when crosses come in from those corner kicks.

The centre-forward is clearly an important piece in your attacking puzzle. But remember, his skills are suffocated and his ability to score greatly reduced if you don't have midfielders who can get the ball to the wingers, and wingers who can push the ball up the pitch and into the corner areas. The bottom line is that the centre-forward is only going to be as effective as his teammates allow him to be. After all, football is a team game.

Placing kids in the appropriate positions

While any child is certainly capable of playing, enjoying, and excelling at any position on the pitch, certain general characteristics are helpful to keep in mind when determining who should play where:

✔ **Goalies:** Athletic youngsters are naturals for the goalkeeping position, which requires sound footwork, quickness, excellent hand to eye co-ordination, great concentration, the ability to leap into a bunch of players to secure the ball without being afraid of contact, the ability to dive for loose balls and shots, and a strong leg to kick the ball when taking a goal kick, to name just a few important qualities.

A goalie must be a good communicator, because when the team is under attack he's got to be able to shout instructions to his teammates. For example, if the goalie spots an opposing player moving in and none of the defenders have him in their sights, he can call out that number 11 needs to be covered. Because goalies have the best view of play and usually the best angle on what is unfolding, they can't be afraid to share what is going on with their teammates, and the only way that can happen is if they are willing to shout instructions and provide plenty of vocal input to help derail the attack before a shot on goal is delivered.

Put a youngster in goal who is extremely confident in his abilities and doesn't get easily rattled or down on himself when things don't go his way. Keep in mind that for a lot of kids letting in a goal can be a pretty traumatic experience in their young football life, especially if they tend to take all the blame on themselves when in all likelihood it was probably a defensive error, or simply a well-executed shot from the opponent, that produced the goal.

✔ **Sweepers:** These players must be good listeners and be able to quickly react to the goalie's instructions. Because the goalie often has a better perspective on the developing play, he can communicate with the sweeper on where he needs him positioned, and the sweeper must be able to quickly adapt to the opposing team's attack and provide defensive support for the goalie any way he possibly can. An ability to read the game well is an advantage. Players in these positions must be true team players, because they're not going to be experiencing the excitement of scoring goals often, if at all. Rather, they need to derive their enjoyment from stopping other players from putting the ball in the goal, which usually doesn't generate as much attention and applause from spectators.

✔ **Centre-backs and fullbacks:** Kids who are aggressive and possess a lot of determination are usually pretty good fits for the centre-back and left and right fullback positions. These are the kids that you count on to chase down a loose ball in the penalty area with as much enthusiasm as if they were hunting down a £20 note blowing along the pavement. Centre-backs need to be confident headers of the ball, because they need to head away crosses and corners and other aerial threats. Centre-backs and fullbacks must also be unafraid of lots of contact and willing to aggressively go after attackers and use tackles to extricate the ball from the player and regain possession for their team. Full-backs need to be especially fit if the formation uses wing-backs, as they are required to support the attack down the wings as well as defend. Both centre-backs and fullbacks must be content with being defenders, however, because their main job is to stop the other side scoring, rather than to score themselves.

✔ **Midfielders:** In a lot of football teams, the centre midfielder is the team's most talented player. Because he patrols the middle of the pitch, he is going to get a lot of touches of the ball. A skilful player, comfortable dribbling and passing under pressure in an often crowded midfield, is going to be a real asset to the team. A vocal child is ideal, as he's basically the person who creates the attack and directs players and communicates to teammates as different moves unfold during the course of a game.

He also has to have a pretty good grasp of the basics of the game and understand and anticipate when the right opportunities present themselves to join an attack and when to hang back and take a more defensive role. Because the centre midfielders is also in a position to receive a variety of passes from the defenders, as well as intercept passes from the opposing team, they must be adept at receiving passes with their left and right foot, trapping balls with their chest and thigh, and using headers to advance the ball or clear it out of danger. When on the attack, a centre midfielder often joins the action as a second striker and often gets the opportunity to shoot from around the edge of the penalty area, so he needs to have a good shooting technique.

✔ **Forwards:** Kids that love to run are perfect for the forward positions because the position puts a big emphasis on speed, quick feet, and being fast to the ball. Regardless of how many football teams you guide during your volunteer coaching career, you will probably always find that one youngster on each team who just seems to have a knack for getting the ball in prime scoring position and being able to put it in the net with a pretty high rate of success. Of course, all kids love to score goals, because that's the most attractive element of the game for them, especially those just starting out in the sport. But certain kids just seem to have that built-in desire to desperately want to score a goal every single time they get the ball at their feet. These are the kids who make great centre forwards in your team.

Deciphering the Rules of the Game

Football is a complex game, and it involves all sorts of rules. Some are basic and easy to understand, and some may initially leave you scratching your head. Don't worry. If you have never played or coached the sport before, some rules may seem a little baffling at first, but with a little study you'll soon be reciting the offside rule to colleagues at work and rambling on about when indirect free kicks are awarded, to friends at dinner parties.

If you're not familiar with a lot of the rules of football, it can be easy to become overwhelmed by them and all the little nuances attached to many of them. First of all, don't panic, and don't try to mug up every single rule in one sitting. Focus on remembering two or three rules each night and how they are applied, and build from here. You can't possibly expect your young players to remember every single rule during the first week of the season, so don't put that kind of pressure on yourself either. Go through the rules one at a time, build on them, and before you know it you'll be rules savvy – and so will your team. Here are the basic rules:

- ✔ **The start:** A simple toss of a coin is generally used to determine the team that kicks off. The team that wins the coin toss has the option of kicking off or choosing which end of the pitch it prefers to defend. Kick offs are used to begin games, second halves, and extra time, as well as to start play again after a goal has been scored. Both teams must remain on their side of the centre line until the ball is kicked. Players on the opposing team must stay at least 10 yards from the ball until it is kicked, and this distance is conveniently marked by the centre circle.

- ✔ **The stop-watch:** A regulation football game consists of two 45-minute halves, with a halftime of no more than 15 minutes. At youth level, games are much shorter. In mini-soccer, for example, they are either 20 or 30 minutes long, depending on age.

  In regulation football matches, there are no team time-outs but again, at the youth level, leagues may allow coaches to call time-outs to help reorganise their players and provide valuable instruction. The referee keeps the official time of the match on his watch, and time does not stop for minor interruptions in play, such as balls that roll off, fouls or any type of minor injuries.

  Referees can stop the clock for major interruptions in play, which include substitutions and serious injuries. The amount of time that is added in order to make up for these incidents is up to the discretion of the referee. The game ends at the exact moment that time expires. So, if a ball is in mid-air and headed for the net, but doesn't cross the goal line before time runs out, then the goal doesn't count. A half may end while a ball is out of play, such as when players are busy lining up for an indirect free kick and time expires before the ball is put into play. However, time can not run out when a team is lining up to deliver a penalty kick. If a foul is called right before time expires, it entitles the team to a penalty kick, and the referee extends the time in order for the kick to take place.

- ✔ **Off:** The ball is in play as long as any part of it is touching the pitch of play. Because the goal lines and touchlines are considered part of the pitch of play, the entire ball must pass completely beyond the outside edge of these lines for the ball to go off. Also, once a ball is off the pitch it can't roll back and be played. So, if the ball rolls out, hits a rock, and ricochets back into play, you have a dead ball.

Putting the Ball Back into Play

The opponents of the team that last touched the ball before it went out of play get to put the ball back into play. For example, if a player from the blue team kicks the ball and it hits a player from the red team in the knee and bounces over the line, the blue team puts the ball into play because the player in red was the last to touch it.

The three methods that a team can use to put the ball back into play after it has rolled out are the throw-in, the corner kick and the goal kick, which are described in the following sections.

Throw-in

This method puts the ball into play after it has rolled over a touchline. The referee signals that the ball is out by pointing in the attacking direction of the team that gets to put the ball back into play. Players need to put the ball back into play immediately so that they don't delay the game. The following are other points to be aware of regarding throw-ins:

- **The location:** the throw-in is made from within about a yard of the spot where the ball crossed the touchline. Anyone on the team may take the throw-in.

- **Lining up:** The thrower's teammates, as well as the opposing players, may position themselves anywhere they want on the pitch. The only thing the opposing players can't do is attempt to distract or impede the thrower.

- **The throw:** When a player executes a throw-in, he must be facing the pitch and standing with both feet on the ground, and the ball must be thrown from behind and over the player's head using both hands. At least parts of both feet have to be touching the touchline or the grass outside the touchline. The ball must enter the pitch through the air; it can't be rolled in or bounced along the ground.

- **In play:** Once the player delivers the throw-in, which can be of any distance, he can't touch the ball again until another player does so first.

- **Foul throw:** If the player makes an illegal throw, such as not having both feet on the ground, then the opposing team is awarded the ball and delivers the throw-in at the same spot.

Corner kicks

Whenever a ball rolls off over the goal line, either a corner kick or goal kick (see the next section) is used to get the ball back into play. Corner kicks are used when a player knocks the ball off over his own goal line. So, when a player from the blue team knocks the ball over the goal line that his goalie is defending, the red team is awarded a corner kick in whichever of the two corners is closest to where the ball went out of play. If a player on the red team takes a shot on the blue team's goal but misses and the ball sails over the goal line without anyone touching it, then the blue team takes possession of the ball in its own end with a goal kick.

Once the referee indicates which corner the kick is to be taken from, any player can set the ball down so that it is entirely within the corner area. Any player on the team may take the kick. Here are a few other points to keep in mind:

- ✔ **Position of defence:** The opposing players must stay at least 10 yards away from the ball until it is kicked, while teammates of the kicker may position themselves anywhere on the pitch.

- ✔ **Corner flags stay put:** Even though it may be tempting for some of your players to want to move the flags, they must not move flags in order to clear out extra space and make the kick a little easier.

- ✔ **Direct goal:** Players can score a goal directly from a corner kick because it doesn't have to be touched by another player before going into the net.

- ✔ **In play:** Once the player puts the corner kick into play, he can't touch the ball again until contact has been made by another player.

Goal kicks

Goal kicks are used to re-start the game when a player knocks the ball over the opponent's goal line, other than when he scores a goal. Once the referee points to the goal area indicating that a goal kick is to be played, any player from the team is allowed to place the ball at any spot within the six-yard box. Keep the following key points in mind regarding this type of kick.

- ✔ **Position of defence:** Players on the opposing team must stay outside of the goal area until the ball has cleared the penalty area. Meanwhile, the players on the goal-kicking team may stand anywhere on the pitch.

- ✔ **No time like the present:** Once the kick has been awarded, the players don't have to wait for their opponents to get into position before delivering the kick.

- ✔ **Defensive no-no:** If a player from the opposing team steps into the penalty area before the ball leaves the area, the referee has the option of stopping play and allowing the team to retake the kick, or allowing play to continue if it didn't affect the kicking team.

- ✔ **Any direction:** The kick may be delivered in any direction and is in play as soon as it leaves the penalty area.

- ✔ **Goal:** A goal cannot be scored directly from a goal kick unless a player other than the taker touches the ball first.

- ✔ **Don't touch:** After the ball is put into play, the player who kicked it may not touch it again until it has been touched by another player.

A ball that makes contact with a referee or assistant referee on the pitch is still in play, unless of course it bounces off after hitting him.

Adjusting the Game for the Younger Leagues

One of the great things about football is that the game can easily be modified to match the age, experience, and skill level of the players participating. The pitch is scaled down so that their young legs aren't forced to cover large expanses of open pitch; the number of players in the game is trimmed back to allow each player more contact with the ball; certain rules are radically altered, adjusted or simply ignored to keep the game moving and ensure that the fun keeps flowing; and the equipment is tailored to match the age and development of the kids.

Smaller pitch size

The way pitch size typically works in youth football is that, the younger the kids, the smaller the pitch is going to be. If you threw small kids on a large pitch for a game, they would be huffing and puffing and out of breath and too tired to do anything with the ball once they finally got to it.

Depending on how much pitch space a recreation agency has, the size of a youth football pitch is going to vary largely. A four-on-four game with beginner players can easily be played on a pitch measuring just 30 yards long and 15 yards wide. Keeping beginner players confined in a small playing area allows them to get lots of touches of the ball, rather than spending all their time aimlessly running around in a wide-open area.

As players get older, they can expect to play on pitches 60 to 100 yards long and 35 to 50 yards wide. In mini-soccer, the recommended pitch size is 30 by 50 yards maximum for under-8s and 40 by 60 yards for under-10s.

Smaller balls

You don't give a Shakespeare play to a child just discovering how to read, so it makes little sense to give a youngster just starting out in the sport, or even one who has just a year or two under his belt, a regulation-sized football. A child's small foot isn't able to control a football that is intended for an adult, and it doesn't speed up skill acquisition and development by forcing a regulation ball on a child just starting the game. In order to build a child's confidence in the sport, he must continually experience success and notice improvement, and that can only happen if he is playing with the appropriate-sized ball for his age. Here are the different- sized balls available for kids to use these days:

- **Size 3:** These balls are typically used for kids age 7 and under.
- **Size 4:** These balls are generally for kids age 7 to 11.
- **Size 5:** Youngsters age 12 and over are usually ready to handle these size balls.

No-goalie games

At the complete beginner's level of youth football, games often don't involve a goalie. Because the kids don't have many skills at this point and are in the infant stages of acquiring the basics of the game, it really doesn't make a whole lot of sense to put a kid in front of the net where he probably sees more butterflies during the course of the game than shots on goal. And even if a shot on goal happens, the goalie is probably playing with an insect in the grass or waving to his mum on the touchline.

In the beginning, a couple of cones are typically set up a few yards apart to help ingrain in the youngsters the concept of moving the ball down the pitch and putting it into the goal. At these early stages of youth football, you simply want to introduce the kids to the concept of kicking the ball, running after it, and kicking it again. Executing passes, headers, and throw-ins all come later on, as does dealing with a goalkeeper.

Fewer players

While a regulation football game features 11 players on the pitch for each team, the younger the children, the fewer kids are on the pitch at any one time. The idea at the youngest age levels is to introduce them to the game by giving them lots of touches of the ball, which can only happen if only a handful of players on the pitch at one time. Just imagine having a full squad of 6-year-olds on the pitch at once. The players would be lucky to touch the ball a couple of times during the game, which isn't going to be any fun at all.

That's why games of anything between four-on-four and seven-on-seven are quite common nationwide. These scaled-down games are great for promoting an interest in the game because the kids are experiencing the thrill of kicking a ball in a team environment, and being actively involved in the action. These types of approaches stir interest in the sport and open kids' eyes to how much fun it can be playing this great game. Positioning takes a backseat at this level, because you basically just want the kids to start going after the ball and begin building foot–eye co-ordination skills in making contact with the ball and getting it to go in the general direction intended.

Special substitution rules

At the beginner's level of youth football, you coach kids in the basics of the game, not adhering to the rule book that is used in the upper ranks of organised football. In a regulation football game, only three substitutions are allowed, and any player that is substituted may not return to action. In mini-soccer, the substitution rules in place are far more lenient, and with good reason. If you've got a squad of 10 players and your team plays in a five-a-side league, you've got to be able to interchange players more often to keep their excitement and interest levels high.

With the youngest age groups, coaches may have the luxury of swapping players in and out at any point during the game. Players who are substituted can return to the game; and players can be substituted several times and allowed to continually re-enter the game.

As the kids get a little bit older, the rules on substituting become a little more strict. If you are coaching in a mini-soccer league, then substituting players becomes more formal and needs to follow the proper procedures, which include securing the referee's permission before sending a new player out onto the pitch. Substitutions can generally be made during the following times when play is stopped in a mini-soccer game:

- ✔ **Prior to a throw-in:** If your team has possession of the ball, you can usually make a line-up change prior to a throw-in.
- ✔ **Before a goal kick:** Usually both teams can make player switches when the referee has signalled one of these kicks.
- ✔ **Following a goal:** This happens to be one of the most convenient times to substitute players as you have a little cushion of time before everyone is set up and ready to resume play again.

✔ **Injury stoppage:** When a player has suffered a minor injury and the referee halts play so that the injured youngster can be helped to the sideline, both teams can use the break to make a substitution.

✔ **Halftime:** Halftime is another convenient time to make a line-up switch.

✔ **Following a caution:** When the referee stops play to issue a caution to the player, you might want to remove that player. You can use the opportunity to bring the youngster to the sideline to go over what he did wrong and make sure that he clearly understands the ruling so that the same thing doesn't happen again later in the season.

The Men (and Women) in Black: Referees

Perhaps no other sport leaves such a wide margin for individual interpretation of the rules than football. Knowing what a referee has signalled during the game, and understanding why he has made that particular decision, are essential in order for you to fulfil your coaching responsibilities and for your players to acquire skills and grow in the game.

Hand signals

This section takes a look at the most commonly used hand signals a referee is likely to use in your contests this season. You may think thathe is using signals that look like he's involved in an intense game of charades. Check out Figure 3-3 for the range of hand signals a referee can make.

✔ **Indirect free kick:** The referee initially points in the attacking direction of the team taking the kick. Then, he holds one hand up in the air until the ball is kicked and touched by another player, or until it goes off the pitch.

✔ **Drop ball:** A drop ball rarely happens during the course of a game, but every once in a while, the referee may have to stop the game for some reason, such as a small child running onto the pitch of play during a game. To restart the game, he gives a drop ball. The drop ball is used at the spot where the match ball was when play was halted. The referee holds the ball out at waist level and drops it to the ground between two opposing players. He can drop the ball at any time without any warning, though usually he holds the ball until both teams are ready. Players cannot touch the ball until it hits the ground.

✔ **Corner kick:** When a corner kick is to take place, the referee points briefly to the proper area to indicate that a corner kick is to be taken.

✔ **Off:** At the more advanced levels of youth football, there is an assistant referee, as well as a referee. When a ball goes over a touchline, the assistant referee uses his flag to point in the attacking direction of the team that is putting the ball back into play.

✔ **Play on:** Sometimes during the course of play, a foul may be committed, but if the team that that is fouled still maintains an advantage, the referee will allow play to continue. To indicate that he has made the play on call, he extends his hands with palms facing up to indicate that he wants play to continue.

✔ **Direct free kick:** The referee points briefly in the attacking direction of the team taking the kick.

Indirect free kick

Direct free kick

Corner kick and penalty kick

Out of play

Play on

Substitution

Misconduct

Offside

Offside Far, Centre, Near

Figure 3-3:
The most common hand signals a referee and his assistants use.

✔ **Substitutions:** When a team wants to make a substitution, the assistant referee holds both ends of his flag above his head to signal to the referee.

✔ **Misconduct:** The referee displays a yellow card when issuing a caution to a player and a red card when sending the player off.

Major fouls

Nine major fouls can result in the opposing team receiving a direct free kick. These major fouls are especially troublesome when committed within the penalty area because they result in a penalty kick in which the player gets to take a shot on goal with only the goalie defending. The following list takes a look at the major fouls:

✔ **Kicking:** Either kicking an opponent, or attempting to kick him, is a big no-no.

✔ **Tripping:** Tripping is often given by the referee after a player has failed to make a successful tackle and instead of knocking the ball away, he takes out the attacking player's legs.

✔ **Jumping:** This infraction involves jumping or lunging at a player, and most often is given when an opposing player or the goalie is in the air attempting to play the ball.

✔ **Charging:** Referees signal charging when a player charges into an opponent with an intent to harm. If the player has attempted to play the ball and the contact is incidental, then charging does not apply. A player may never knock an opponent to the ground by charging from behind.

✔ **Striking:** Any attempt to strike, or the actual striking of an opponent, is never allowed. Striking includes intentionally throwing the ball at an opposing player.

✔ **Holding:** Players must not grab an opponent's shirt to slow him down, or stick out their arms to obstruct another player's movement in any way.

✔ **Pushing:** Players must not push, shove, or nudge an opponent in an effort to gain any type of advantage.

✔ **Spitting:** Players must not spit at another player.

✔ **Bad tackles:** When attempting to tackle an opponent and gain possession of the ball, players must not touch the player before the ball, or instead of the ball.

✔ **Handball:** Football is played primarily with the head, chest, legs, and feet – not the hands. Handball is one of the most basic rules of football. Besides the goalie being able to use his hands within the confines of the penalty area, no other players are allowed to touch the ball with their hands on the pitch. Any player, not counting the goalkeeper, who intentionally touches the ball with their hand or arm to gain control it is committing handball and the opposing team takes over possession of the ball.

Types of penalties

There are three types of penalties that can result from fouls: Indirect free kicks, direct free kicks, and penalty kicks.

- **Indirect free kicks:** These are awarded to the non-fouling team and result in a free kick from the point of the foul. A player cannot score a goal from an indirect free kick unless the ball first touches another player.

- **Direct free kicks:** These are awarded for fouls that the referee considers careless or reckless. These kicks do not have to touch another player before a goal can be scored. The kick takes place where the foul was committed, unless it occurs within the penalty area. Such cases results in a penalty kick.

- **Penalty kicks:** Players look forward to penalty kicks as much as the first day of the summer holidays. Penalty kicks are the chance to score a goal for their team going one-on-one against the goalie. These kicks are awarded for fouls occurring inside the penalty box. The ball is placed on the penalty spot, which is 12 yards from the front of the goal on a regulation football pitch. On a smaller scale pitch for younger players, the spot is much closer. During the kick, all the other players must remain outside the penalty area. The penalty taker only gets one shot, unless an infringement occurs and the referee calls for the penalty to be retaken. The goalie must stand in the goal with his feet on the goal line. He is allowed to move on the goal line but not towards the ball until the penalty is taken. The kicker, who can be anyone you choose from your team, must wait for the signal from the referee before he can proceed with the kick.

The referee shows players yellow and red cards at the more advanced levels of football to signal minor and major infractions.

- **Yellow card:** The referee issues this card when a minor rules violation has occurred. Common scenarios where yellow cards are issued include when players enter or exit the pitch without prior permission from the referee. Players are allowed to temporarily go off the pitch during corner kicks, lining up for free kicks, handling throw-ins, or playing the ball near the edge of the pitch, for example, but at virtually any other time they need permission from the referee. Yellow cards are also issued if players argue with the referee over a call.

- **Red card:** Referees issue red cards for major violations, such as being overly physical during the course of play. Players committing a particularly violent foul, such as intentionally tripping an opponent who has an obvious scoring opportunity, or using their hands to stop a shot that has a good chance of going in the goal, usually result in the referee issuing a red card. Once a red card is issued, the player is immediately sent off the pitch and out of the game and he cannot be replaced, so his team plays with one person less for the remainder of the game.

Minor fouls

Minor fouls and rules violations are penalised by awarding free kicks to the team that was fouled. Here are the most common minor fouls and violations that you are likely to come across:

- **Obstruction:** The referee whistles an obstruction infraction if the player's primary intent was to block the other player. The player can use his body to block an opponent's route to the ball, but only if the ball happens to be in range where he can gain control of it. If the ball is obviously not within the player's reach, then an infraction has occurred. If a player uses his arms or simply stands in an opponent's way, those are all deemed as obstruction fouls. Obstruction can also be given against a player who is disrupting a goalie's attempt to put the ball back into play after gaining possession of it. Obstruction is punished with an indirect free kick.

- **Dangerous play:** Players who put themselves, or an opponent, in danger are whistled for this infraction. Examples of a dangerous play are swinging a leg near another player's head to kick the ball, or diving low to head a ball that opposing players are attempting to kick at the same time. Even if the foul is completely accidental, it can still be given.

- **Charging the goalie:** Goalies do receive a thin veil of protection within their own penalty areas, and opposing players can not run into them and attempt to dislodge the ball from their possession.

- **Offside:** The offside rule is designed to stop players goal hanging and camping out next to the opponent's goal. Players aren't allowed to do this. If they do, they are offside. A player is offside when, as the ball is played towards him, he has fewer than two defensive players, including the goalie, closer to the opponent's goal line than he is. An added complication is that offside only applies to a player who is active – in other words involved or immediately about to be involved in the play. A player who is wandering back nowhere near play is not offside. Offside does not apply to goal kicks, throw-ins, or corner kicks. Regulation mini-soccer doesn't have offside. (Because this rule is often misunderstood, it warrants its own section, later in this chapter.)

- **Unsporting conduct:** When the referee blows the whistle to issue a caution against a player, the opposing team restarts the game with an indirect free kick.

- **Double play:** When a player puts the ball into play, he can't touch it again until another player from either team makes contact with it.

Offsides

The most perplexing and misunderstood rule of all in football is offside. One of the most frustrating things in the game is seeing one of your players break free with the ball, ready to take a shot on goal, only to have the referee blow for offside. What is it? How does it occur? How can you help your players remember this confusing rule? This section takes an in-depth look at what offside is so that you and your players have a good handle on the rule.

The basic idea surrounding the offside rule is that attacking players can't position themselves ahead of the ball. The rule is in the books in order to ensure that players on the attacking team don't linger around the opponent's goal when the ball is nowhere near them in the hope of getting an easy goal if the ball is won somewhere on the pitch. When the referee blows for offside, the opposing team is given an indirect free kick, which is taken from the spot where the offside player was at the moment the violation occurred.

In order for a player to be given offside (see Figure 3-4), three things have to happen:

- ✔ **Beating the ball:** The attacker must be ahead of the ball when it is played to him. He can also to be level with the ball, but being just a half step ahead causes the referee to call the player back for offside. To be given offside, the attacker must be between the ball and the defending team's goal line.

- ✔ **Ahead of the defenders:** To be offside, there has to be just one of the opposing team between the offside player and the goal when the ball is played towards him. This player is usually, although not necessarily, the goalkeeper. If the player is level with the second to last defender, he is not offside.

- ✔ **Be involved in active play:** The attacking player must be actively involved in the game at the exact moment the ball is either passed or shot by his teammate. Being in the play represents one of those tricky areas in football where the referee has a lot of wiggle room for interpretation. Offside is usually given whenever the attacker in the offside position is moving to receive a pass, attempting to play the ball before a defender can get to it, or even blocking the vision of the goalie, among many other examples.

Conversely, there are many situations that exist where the offside rule does not come into play. For example, offside is not given if there are at least two defenders between the attacker and the goal line (see Figure 3–5). So, this can be the goalie along with one other defender. When a defender is level with the attacker, he is considered to be between the attacker and the goal, which nullifies any hint of being offside.

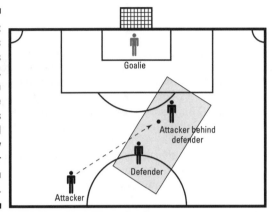

Figure 3-4: This attacker is offside, being both ahead of the ball as it is played and with only one player between him and the goal.

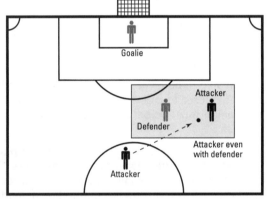

Figure 3-5: The attacker is onside here, being level with the defender as the ball is played.

Offside is never given at the defensive end of the pitch. Your players can only be given offside when they are in the opponent's half of the pitch.

The following are examples of when offside will not be given against your team:

- ✔ **Played by opponent:** Offside isn't called when the ball was last touched by an opposing player. A ball that ricochets off an opponent isn't considered to have been played by him. Now, if the kick that produced the rebound was delivered by a teammate of the offside player, then the referee blows the whistle for offside.

- ✔ **Receiving kicks:** Offside isn't called when the ball is received from a goal kick, corner kick, throw-in, or during the initial drop of the drop ball. The offside rule does apply, though, to direct and indirect free kicks, penalty kicks, goalie drop kicks, and throws.

✔ **Stepping off of the pitch:** Offside isn't given when the attacking player steps off the pitch before the ball is played, and he isn't a factor in how the opponent is able to play the ball. This happens to be one of those exceptions to the rule mentioned earlier in this chapter that players are only allowed to leave the pitch when they have permission from the referee. Once the player steps off of the pitch to avoid the offside decision, he can't return until his team loses possession of the ball, or until a natural stoppage in play occurs.

✔ **Defensive trickery:** Offside isn't given if the attacker is put into an offside position by a defender who intentionally runs off the pitch and leaves fewer than two defenders between the attacker and the goal line.

Part II
Building Your Coaching Skills

'I understand this new coach is also a drama
teacher at the local secondary school.'

In this part . . .

Parents can be a help or hindrance when it comes to their children and organised sport. In this part, we share secrets on how you can get parents on your side – and keep them there all season long. We also delve into what it takes to conduct training sessions that develop skills and keep your players excited about attending. Finally, we offer some tips to help match day go smoothly.

Chapter 4

Meet the Parents

· ·

· ·

A pre-season parents' meeting is a perfect starting point for the new football season. You can get everyone pulling in the same direction – rather than pulling against one another – for the benefit of the children. It's largely up to you to guide the parents, advise them, set a positive tone, and outline your expectations for their children – and them – during the season. The pre-season parents' meeting provides a forum for you to explain your coaching philosophy and discuss your goals and expectations for the upcoming season, as well as answer all the questions the parents are sure to have on everything from shinguards to post-match snacks.

The parents' meeting also lays the foundation for a smooth-running season, opens the lines of communication on a positive note, and encourages season-long dialogue among all parties. Plus, for many parents, this season is their first experience of having a child involved in sport, and they may find themselves in unfamiliar territory. The pre-season meeting can help to put their minds at ease.

If you don't hold this meeting, you are inviting all sorts of problems that you can prevent. Without this meeting, you may have an irate father screaming instructions to his child on the touchline during the first game of the season because he doesn't know that parents aren't allowed to do that. You may have a mother questioning why her daughter didn't get to play half the game, even though you haven't seen her at training in three weeks – a situation you can easily avoid if you let parents know about your rule requiring attendance at training in order to play in games. You don't want to risk opening the door to these uncomfortable scenarios, or others, by not scheduling a parents' meeting prior to the first training session of the season. It's simply not worth it.

Your meeting is the springboard to a fun-filled season. In this chapter, you find tips on planning the meeting, making a great first impression, and getting the parents to work with you all season long.

Introducing Yourself

How you interact with your young players – and their parents – has a pretty significant impact on how smoothly your season runs. The pre-season parents' meeting is your chance to explain all the team rules in a relaxed setting. Young athletes need to receive clear and consistent messages from their coaches and parents on everything from how much emphasis is going to be placed on winning this season, to how important displaying good sportsmanship is. If the team sees mixed signals between you and the parents, your message is going to be lost, and that's going to lead to unnecessary problems. Disciplining a child during the season for a team violation that was never discussed with the parents beforehand, for example, isn't fair and can turn into a catastrophe.

Approach the pre-season meeting with the same effort and enthusiasm you display when going for a job interview. Your first impression leaves a lasting imprint on the parents. No one expects you to be a professional speaker, but being able to clearly explain your thoughts on the topics you're covering demonstrates how deeply you care about the upcoming season and reinforces your commitment to each child you're coaching. Parents appreciate your initiative, recognise that you care, and feel much more at ease turning their children over to you to coach during the season. (Check out the 'Overcoming anxiety when speaking in public' sidebar later in this chapter for a few tips.)

Aside from getting your act together, you need to consider a few of the nuts-and-bolts meeting-planning details:

- ✓ **Location:** You can hold the meeting at your home, at the home of one of the parents, or at an assistant's home. Libraries or local village halls may also have meeting rooms available.

- ✓ **Timing:** Most parents juggle chaotic schedules, so finding time to get together with everyone can be difficult. Contact each child's parents to briefly introduce yourself as the coach and let them know the date, time, and location of the parents' meeting. Giving parents as much notice as possible may help them to rearrange their schedules in order to make your meeting. Plan on spending at least 30 minutes at this meeting, but no more than an hour.

- ✓ **Contingency plan:** Ideally, you want all parents to show up on your designated night, so stress the importance of everyone attending. If that isn't possible, you may want to have a contingency plan. Consider holding a second meeting on a backup night; going over everything on the phone or by email one evening; or, if all else fails, making arrangements to meet with the parents following the first training session of the season.

TIP

Overcoming anxiety when speaking in public

Public speaking strikes fear into everyone on occasion. Being properly prepared is the best antidote for conquering speaking nerves. Practise what you want to say to the group in the mirror in the days leading up to the parents' meeting. If you sense that you're really going to be uncomfortable, rehearse what you want to say in front of your spouse, a family member, or a friend.

Bring a notepad that contains everything you want to say to the meeting. Referring to it often throughout the meeting isn't a sign of weakness – it's an indication that you want to make sure that you cover everything for the benefit of the parents. You can also bring a flip chart with key points highlighted on it. A chart gives you something to divert your eyes toward to ease some of your nervousness throughout your presentation. The parents will also direct their attention to it, so they won't be watching you the entire time, which increases your comfort level.

The remainder of this chapter covers subjects that you may want to discuss with parents. As you can see, you have a lot of information to cover, but try to keep the parents actively involved and let them get to know you and one another. To accomplish this goal, include time for

- ✔ **Introductions:** Allow time during the meeting for the parents to introduce themselves and say who their children are, too. Although some parents may know one another, introductions are a good ice-breaker for everyone. Parents need to start socialising because they'll be seeing quite a bit of one another during the season.

- ✔ **One-on-one discussions:** The more comfortable the parents are with you, the stronger your relationship can be with them and with their children. If you have time following the meeting, talk to the parents individually and get to know a little about them.

Explaining your coaching philosophy

The most important topic you can address with parents is winning – more specifically, what your stance is on this very sensitive issue. Winning can be defined in a lot of ways. For young children involved in football for the first time, the score at the end of the game isn't nearly as important as having fun with their friends, getting exercise, enjoying the experience of participating in the sport, and using their newly developed skills. Countless studies indicate that children are far less concerned about winning – especially at the younger levels – than their parents are.

Your goal is to introduce the kids to the basic concepts of the game – like dribbling and shooting. You want to make it enough fun for them that they can't wait to get to training to work on their skills and they look forward to pulling on their team shirt when match day arrives.

By letting parents know your philosophy and how you're going to approach the season ahead of time, you give them ample time to find out whether this team is the appropriate setting or has the appropriate level of competitiveness for their child. This approach works out well for all concerned.

Emphasising good sportsmanship

Children are easily influenced by the behaviour of their parents and other adults at sports events. Youngsters who see parents yelling and criticising officials, opposing coaches, or even other players on the pitch, begin to think that this type of behaviour is acceptable. Part of your role is to stress the importance of good sportsmanship by your players at all times – and the same goes for parents.

If you get the parents to understand the importance of being models of good sportsmanship at all times – before, during, and after games – the youngsters should follow in their footsteps. Clearly explain that all comments to all participants (children, including opposing players; coaches; officials; and other parents) should be positive and encouraging, never negative or insulting.

A positive approach can be extremely difficult for some parents to follow. For many, it will be their first time back in a sports environment since their schooldays, and all sorts of competitive emotions can begin surging through them. Toss into the equation the fact that they're watching their own flesh and blood competing against other children, and it can become a pretty combustible mixture. In addition, many parents, without even being aware of it, perceive how well their child performs on the football pitch as a reflection of how good they are as parents. So, the more successful the child, the more impressive the parent looks in the eyes of other parents. (See Chapter 19, which discusses this mindset in greater detail.)

Just as you want to clarify the need for positive feedback, you want to be extremely clear with parents about what type of behaviour you won't tolerate:

> ✔ **Criticism of any sort directed at kids:** Football isn't fun when parents criticise their children for letting in a goal or making a mistake. This league isn't the Premiership, and negative comments affect the kids' enjoyment and detract from their ability to perform at their best.

✔ **Shouted instructions:** All the coaching needs to be left up to you. Remind parents that children are easily distracted and don't perform as well – or have as much fun – when they're being screamed at to go and get the ball.

✔ **Arguing with coaches:** You, as well as the opposing coaches, have enormous responsibilities to fulfil during the game and can't be bothered with criticisms regarding playing time or tactics. If parents have a problem with you, they can arrange to speak with you privately after the game.

✔ **Abuse of officials:** Yelling at a referee, no matter how bad the decision is or is perceived to be, is totally unacceptable at all times. Let parents know that dealing with decisions that go against your team is simply part of playing sport. Remind them that, over the course of a season, the decisions certainly balance out, and your team will receive its share of favourable ones as well. If the parents don't make a big deal about a decision, the kids won't even remember it by the end of the game.

Let parents know that you never want to reach the point where you have to ask them to leave because of inappropriate behaviour, but that you won't hesitate to do so if you feel they're negatively affecting the game. Leagues may have policies in place for the removal of spectators, and you need to be aware of what those policies entail. (See Chapter 19, which covers the importance of knowing your league's policies and offers solutions on how to deal with problem parents.)

Detailing how you determine playing time

Playing time can be a major source of grief for a football coach – if you aren't prepared. If you clearly spell out to parents your policies regarding this area of the game, you drastically reduce the chances of conflicts occurring during the season.

Dividing time equally

No one likes to sit on the subs bench, but sitting out is part of the game. A big part of your job, though, is to make sure that no youngster is stuck on that bench more than any of her teammates. At the higher ages of youth football, the bulk of the playing time goes to the team's best players. But for youngsters just taking up the sport, or kids who have only a season or two of experience under their belts, stick to spreading around the playing time as equally as you can. In the long run, everyone benefits from this approach, which is why many leagues have equal-playing-time policies in place. These policies ensure that every child who straps on shinguards, regardless of her skill level, receives as much playing time as her teammates.

Most parents will be comforted to know that you're doing your best to distribute playing time equally throughout the season, regardless of each child's skill level. At the lower age levels, a child who can kick a ball harder or run faster doesn't merit more playing time than another child who isn't nearly as skilled. Parents may grumble upon hearing this news, especially if they believe that they have a budding superstar on their hands and that you're hampering their child's development by surrendering her playing time to a less skilful teammate.

Rewarding players who practise

Frequent and unaccounted-for absences can create chaos when you're trying to put a team together to work cohesively as a unit. When you meet with the parents, stress how important it is that their child regularly attends training and that having children going AWOL during the week can create havoc with your training plan and wreck the team unity you're trying to build.

At some time during the course of the season, children are going to miss training sessions during the week but show up on match day ready for action. Let parents know that you adhere to a strict policy: Players who regularly attend training sessions receive equal playing time during games, but youngsters who show up for training only occasionally receive limited playing time.

Don't restrict a child's playing time if they have valid reasons for missing training, however. Let the parents know that the following reasons don't jeopardise the child's standing with the team and encourage the parents to call and let you know ahead of time if their child isn't able to attend training:

- ✔ **Injury or sickness:** Certainly, if a child is dealing with an injury (whether he suffered it during training, a game, or another activity), his standing with the team won't be affected when he can return to play. A child who misses training because of sickness shouldn't face any ramifications either.

- ✔ **Family vacation:** Parents typically have holidays planned well in advance, and they need to inform you of the dates their child isn't available as soon as possible. The last thing you want to do is show up for a game in the middle of the season only to find out that the three kids who play goalie are all on holiday. Consequently, you're left scrambling to fill that slot with a child who could have practised the position for weeks if you'd known of those parents' schedules ahead of time.

- ✔ **Family emergency:** Unfortunately, circumstances occur that are simply out of the parents' control. A death in the family or another family emergency may not allow them to contact you ahead of time. They may come up to you the following week at training and explain the situation. Be understanding in these types of situations and don't penalise the child for something that was out of everyone's control.

Be crystal clear when presenting your rules. Players who turn up for training play. Players who don't turn up, for unexcused reasons, get reduced playing time. You can be friendly – but firm – while presenting the rules. Let parents know that you make no exceptions, because it just isn't fair to the rest of the squad, and be willing to stand by your policy during the season. At some point, a parent will probably test you on your policy, and if you give in, you have to give in to everyone. Suddenly, your rules and policies carry no weight – and you're giving the indication that you have no control of the team.

'Who's playing goalie?' and other sticky positioning situations

In introductory or beginner-level football programmes, the playing pitch is smaller, the number of players per team is trimmed down, and the rules are modified. Often, games feature four-on-four or five-on-five, which helps to ensure that each youngster gets plenty of touches on the ball. This alternative is better than being stuck on a regulation pitch with ten other teammates where a child is lucky to kick the ball once during the game. At this level, football is often more about simply playing than positioning. Make sure that the parents receive this message at your initial meeting.

New players, regardless of their age, need to gain experience playing all positions. Take the time to help them develop their skills so that they can play positions confidently during games. Specialisation is only for older children, who have been playing football for years and are involved in highly competitive leagues. Older kids then hone their skills in one or perhaps two positions that they excel at. Don't treat your young players like the older, more experienced players.

By moving children around the pitch, you not only give them a complete introduction to the game, but also keep their interest and enthusiasm level high. If people do the same things day after day in their jobs, with nothing new to look forward to, they become stagnant and uninterested. New challenges create excitement and boost interest levels, and the kids reap the benefits.

The positions on a football team are as different as the youngsters who play them. Many of the positions require different skills, abilities, and personality traits than others (refer to Chapter 3 for more on the attributes needed in particular positions). Although you want to introduce players to a variety of positions, don't force a child into playing a position that she isn't ready for. (For example, at the first game of the season, you don't want to stick an extra-shy child in goal, where having all eyes focused on her may be traumatic.) Also, never position your young players with the intent of having a line-up that gives you the best chance of winning while forsaking the kids' development. If you focus on each player's progress, rather than just on whether the team wins or not, then everyone on your team ends up winning in the long run.

Let parents know that you're going to change the line-ups in order to get all the youngsters used to the different positions on the pitch. That means that even though the team worked really well together last week, you're not going to use that exact same line-up the rest of the season.

Putting Together the Paperwork

Virtually every football league and club requires that parents sign a series of permission-related forms before their child is allowed to participate. As coach, it may be your responsibility to obtain many of these forms and arrange for signatures. Beyond the league paperwork, you can make your job easier and keep your sanity intact by distributing your own team pack of information to parents, including lists of rules and contact information.

League paperwork

The following forms are typical of those that may be required. Although the content and style can vary from form to form, the purpose is generally the same:

- **Parental/guardian consent form:** This form states that the child risks getting hurt during training or games and that the league or club isn't responsible in the event of an injury.

  Many leagues and clubs have insurance. Be sure to ask about the insurance coverage at both the league and club and your own status under the policy. Coaching courses serve as a valuable layer of protection. In the unfortunate event that an incident occurs in which a child is injured and his parents sue, you can demonstrate in a court of law that you went through a coaching programme and did everything possible to properly prepare yourself for your responsibilities. Even if your league doesn't encourage coaches to complete a coaching programme, we strongly recommend that you complete one before taking the touchlines.

- **Medical evaluation form:** This form, signed by the child's doctor, basically states that the youngster is physically healthy and is able to participate in the sport. If the child has a certain condition, such as asthma or diabetes, it's listed on this sheet. (See the 'Meeting Players' Special Needs' section, later in the chapter, for information on working with kids who require special consideration.)

- **Emergency treatment authorisation form:** The child's parent or guardian signs this form, which lists the names of people to contact in the event that the child is injured and requires emergency medical treatment. The form may give the coach or other league personnel the authority to seek medical treatment for the child if no one can be reached.

Team packs

Distributing a team pack not only provides parents with convenient access to all the information they need this season, but also makes a great impression. Coaches who put in this much effort and go to such great lengths to include parents in every step of the season, are rewarded with the parents' respect, admiration, and assistance along the way. Include a page at the front that reinforces your coaching philosophy and reminds parents that they must be models of good behaviour in order to help you ensure that every child has a rewarding experience this season. In addition to that first page, include the following elements in your team packs:

✔ **A rules primer for parents:** Some parents aren't going to be familiar with the rules and terminology of football. You – and they – simply don't have enough time to go over the rules of the game in a lot of detail at your parents' meeting without the meeting dragging into all hours of the night.

Having a handy guide at their disposal greatly enhances each parent's understanding and enjoyment of the game. This guide doesn't have to be one of those essays you dreaded writing in school or college. Just put together a couple of pages on some of the basics of the game. Include a rough sketch of the pitch and indicate where each player is positioned; throw in a page on some basic terms that are used often during the season and what they mean; and include a page of the officials' hand signals and what they mean. (Refer back to Chapter 3 where information on hand signals is included.)

✔ **Special rules:** Be sure to include a page noting any special rules in effect in the league. Maybe the league has instructed officials not to play the offside rule in order to keep the game moving. Perhaps throw-ins aren't used at this level, and when the ball goes out of play, the official simply tosses it back into the pitch of play. Briefly alerting parents to any special modifications of the rules during your parents' meeting – and detailing them again in this pack – greatly reduces confusion at games and allows parents to fully understand what's taking place on the pitch.

✔ **Team sheet and contact information:** A sheet with all the kids' names, their parents' names, and their telephone numbers can be a pretty handy tool for parents. In the 'Defining supporting roles' section, later in this chapter, we suggest that you have the parents form a *phone tree* to quickly spread last-minute weather and scheduling updates for training sessions and games. And at some point during the season, parents may need to get in touch with other parents to arrange a ride to training for their child.

Assembling Your Parent Posse

Coaching youth football is an enormous undertaking, but you can make the job less stressful and time consuming by recruiting parents to lend a hand. They invest a lot of time and energy in making their child's football experience a rewarding one, and they're usually more than willing to pitch in to help make the season run smoothly. Yes, occasionally parents drop their children off and use you as a baby-sitting service for an hour or so, and some parents are more comfortable staying in the background, watching training sessions or games from the car. But for the most part, if you let parents know that you want them to be actively involved – and provide them with areas where they can lend a helping hand – they should gladly do so.

Choosing assistant coaches

To help ease your coaching workload, choose a couple of parents to serve as assistant coaches. With all those kids on the pitch, a few extra sets of eyes and ears to help direct the action are extremely beneficial to you and your squad. At training, assistant coaches can

- Run drills, which maximises your time on the pitch by allowing the kids to get extra repetitions and additional instruction
- Serve as goalkeepers during shooting drills or defenders during attacking drills
- Perform a variety of helpful tasks, such as chasing down loose balls during drills to keep training sessions moving, which is vital to keeping your sessions fun and productive.

Your assistant coaches can also be invaluable resources on game day. They can help

- Monitor your substitution rotation to ensure that all youngsters receive an equal amount of playing time
- Oversee warm-ups to make sure that each child stretches properly
- Orchestrate the pre-match exercises while you're meeting with the opposing coach and officials
- Alert you to any unsportsmanlike behaviour that you may not catch while fulfilling your other responsibilities during the course of the game
- Gather your players and speak to them in a calm, relaxed tone while you're tending to an injured child.

Choosing your assistant coaches is one of the most important decisions you make during the season, so do your homework before filling these key positions. You want to select parents who are best suited to support your philosophy and emphasise the fun and discovery you want to stress.

If you don't know most of the parents well, proceed carefully before asking who's interested in filling coaching positions. You may want to take a little time to get to know the parents as the first few training sessions of the season unfold. You don't want to make the mistake, for example, of choosing an apparently laid-back dad at your pre-season parents' meeting who turns out to be a yeller with a poor disposition when he arrives at the pitch. Pay close attention to see how parents interact with their children at training sessions and maybe even the first game of the season and gauge their interest in and enthusiasm for the sport.

Also, try to find a balance when seeking assistant coaches. Some overzealous parents may try to take over your training sessions and impose their own ideals, techniques, and philosophies on the youngsters. Meanwhile, others may require so much mentoring and assistance that it may actually detract from your valuable training time, and this can negatively affect the children.

Defining supporting roles

Some parents may not feel comfortable being on the football pitch providing instruction, but that doesn't mean they can't help in a number of other areas. Many parents want to be involved in their child's experience, and they can fill a number of roles to ease your stress and add to everyone's enjoyment of the season.

During your parents' meeting, you can circulate a list of jobs and responsibilities, which we cover in the following list, and have parents jot down their names next to those duties they're comfortable helping with. If five parents express an interest in being the team parent, do your best not to turn down their help and make them feel that you really don't need them after all. In this instance, have them all work together as a committee, or if no one signs up to be the fundraising co-ordinator, mention to them that you appreciate their willingness to help out and see whether anyone is willing to fill that role instead.

✔ **Team parent:** A great way to wrap up a training session or game is to gather the troops for a refreshing drink or tasty snack. Choosing a team parent allows you to keep your focus on coaching and skill development. The team parent can put together a schedule to let parents know which game or training session to bring snacks to. This role can also include organising an end-of-season pizza party or making arrangements to take the entire team to watch a local football match.

✔ **Telephone-tree co-ordinator:** When it rains all day, and an hour before training the sun pops out, parents are going to wonder whether training is still on. If you decide to cancel training, it can be extremely time consuming to call every parent. A telephone-tree co-ordinator is the parent in charge of putting together the phone list for such situations. In this scenario, you let your telephone-tree co-ordinator know that you've cancelled training and when you've rescheduled it for. The telephone-tree co-ordinator calls two parents on the phone list, those two parents each call two parents, and so on. In a matter of minutes, everyone knows that the session has been postponed.

✔ **Photo co-ordinator:** Team photos are great keepsakes for the children, who years from now will get – excuse the pun – a real kick out of seeing themselves and their friends all decked out in their colourful uniforms. Sometimes, the league co-ordinates directly with a local photography company; in most cases, however, team photos are left up to the discretion of the coach. In either case, having a parent fulfil the photo-co-ordinator position can be extremely helpful. Besides working with you to select a convenient time for the team photo, the photo co-ordinator can look into the possibility of having the photographer come out for a game or two to take action shots of the kids. Don't forget that a parent's consent form is required. At the end of the season, providing each child with a picture of himself or herself during a game is a great touch. (See Chapter 22 for greater detail on fun ways to conclude the season.)

✔ **Fundraising co-ordinator:** Running a football club is an expensive business: pitch fees, training ground fees, match balls, football strips, training equipment, it all adds up. Although some of your funding comes through *match subs* (the money players pay to play on match day) and directly from parents, team fundraisers can help to offset additional costs. Fundraisers can include the usual car washing, sweet sales, spaghetti dinners, jumble sales, boot fairs, or other fun activities that the co-ordinator comes up with.

✔ **Team trainer:** During the course of the season, children inevitably get the odd bump and bruise. Having a parent who's properly trained in first aid and has experience dealing with these sorts of problems is a big benefit for your team. Although all coaches should be trained in CPR and familiar with basic first aid, having parents who are skilled in such important areas is a real comfort not only to you, but also to the other parents.

✔ **Trophy co-ordinator:** Trophies can be a great way of celebrating a season. You may want to consider assigning a trophy co-ordinator, who can arrange to have small trophies or plaques to present to each child at the end of the season to mark their participation and celebrate their achievements. (See Chapter 22 where we explain this idea in greater detail.)

 ✔ **Football strip washer:** Someone has to wash the dirty kit after a game. It may seem a good idea to make each child responsible for their own shirt, shorts and socks, but if the team only has a limited number of strips, this can cause more problems than it solves. What if a kid forgets their strip, or is unable to play but doesn't let you know, or loses or damages their shirt? Better to have a volunteer who takes on the not-always-that-pleasant (especially in the muddy depths of winter) task of washing the football kit each week.

 ✔ **Match officials:** Some leagues rely on parents to fill roles as officials. And even those that don't may be unable to supply enough officials for every match throughout the season. Often, each team is required to provide one parent to serve as a referee's assistant or simply to monitor a part of the pitch for any type of major infraction. Whether this requirement is specified in your league or not, be sure to mention the possibility of needing to help out in this way during your meeting. Find out which parents are willing to fill these positions, if needed. Having their names jotted down eliminates one worry on game day. You don't want to be scrambling around minutes before your game looking for a parent volunteer when you could be spending the time getting your team ready.

 ✔ **Travel co-ordinator:** The travel-co-ordinator position is appropriate only for an older and more experienced team that may be participating in a lot of weekend away games in nearby villages or towns. The person handling this position is involved in sorting out team transport – organising a car pool, for example. Occasionally, a parent may fill this position at the younger levels if the team advances through several rounds of a local or regional tournament and qualifies to compete against other teams elsewhere in the county, or even in other parts of the country.

Going Over Equipment

Injuries are as much a part of football as grass-stained kits and goal celebrations. No matter the age or skill level of your team, every player who steps on the pitch is at risk of getting hurt. Although eliminating the threat of injury is impossible, you can minimise the number of injuries that occur – and their severity – by making sure that each child wears the proper equipment.

Don't let a child on the pitch unless she has the following equipment:

 ✔ **Shinguards:** Shinguards significantly reduce the risk of injury to the child's lower leg, which is the third most common area of the body injured in football, after the ankle and the knee. Encourage parents to purchase shinguards with padding that extends to cover the ankle bone, as well as socks long enough to cover the shinguards.

✔ **Water bottles:** One of your team rules may be that all children bring their own water bottles to training and games; otherwise, they don't get to play. Keeping kids hydrated is extremely important; not doing so can lead to serious health consequences and place the kids in unnecessary danger. Keep a large bottle of water on hand at all times so that the kids can refill their bottles. Remind parents to write their child's name on the bottle, too.

✔ **Sunscreen:** On sunny days, encourage parents to apply sunscreen to their children before they arrive for training and matches. Let them know that if you are continuing training or matches on weekends during the summer break you won't practise between the peak sun hours of 10 a.m. and 2 p.m. to minimise the team's exposure to the sun.

✔ **Sports bras and jockstraps:** Although you may not be entirely comfortable discussing such areas, they do need to be covered. Younger children don't need sports bras and jockstraps, but as children mature, strongly encourage them to wear these items. Have parents check with a reputable local sporting-goods retailer for additional information on proper fitting.

In addition to the must-have equipment players take to the pitch, briefly review the following pieces of equipment with the parents:

✔ **Strips:** Most clubs provide football kit in the form of shirts, shorts, and socks, for matches, as well as training bibs and maybe other training clothes. Parents need to supply footwear and also the appropriate clothes for training including waterproofs for the inevitable occasions when it rains.

✔ **Boots:** If your league allows boots with studs, as most do, make sure that the children wear normal shoes to the game and change into their boots after they get to the pitch. Car parks and pavements can quickly wear down the studs, plus it is difficult to walk across concrete with studs on. Most leagues say what types of boots children can and should wear during matches; blades may be banned for example, and an official will probably do a boot check at some point during the season, if not before every match. Make sure that you know what the league outlaws (refer to Chapter 2 for league policies) so that you can pass this information on to the parents before they go out and spend a big chunk of money on boots that aren't allowed on the pitch. Children just starting out in the sport are fine wearing a pair of comfortable trainers if the ground is firm enough and the league allows it.

To keep participation costs down, you can gain big bonus points with parents by suggesting that, for beginners at least, they don't shell out £50 plus for top-of-the-line boots. Mentioning this now may save problems later when one child shows up in fancy boots and the rest of the
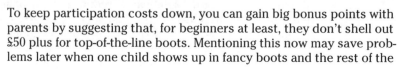

team is wearing trainers. This can be difficult for both the wearer of the expensive boots – it can make that child feel uncomfortable because he stands out – and the rest of the team members may suddenly feel that they're missing out on something. Although trainers are a good idea, especially when the ground is firmer, muddy playing conditions usually mean some kinds of studs are necessary.

✔ **Football balls:** Most clubs provide footballs for training and for matches. If resources don't allow for a ball per child, then you can ask the parents to have their child bring a ball to training if they have one. Have the children put their names or initials on the balls so that you can work out who owns the balls at the end of training.

Meeting Players' Special Needs

You may wonder whether you have what it takes to coach a child who has special needs. The answer is most certainly yes! Think about it. Every child on your team is remarkably different. You need to adapt in all sorts of ways and make countless adjustments to meet their needs. It's certainly no different when it comes to a child who may have a vision or hearing problem, attention deficit disorder, or asthma, diabetes, or epilepsy. (See Chapter 5, which discusses some of the conditions that your players may have in greater detail.)

During your parents' meeting, make sure to find out whether any of the children under your care this season have a medical condition that you need to be aware of, as well as whether you need to make any special accommodations. Often, a parent may not feel comfortable divulging that type of personal information in front of all the other parents, which is why setting aside time at the end of the meeting for one-on-one discussions is always a good idea.

Answering Parents' Questions

During the course of your meeting, the parents are probably going to ask you a variety of questions – and that's a good sign. You want active participation and interest throughout your meeting. Fielding questions throughout your discussion is a great indicator that the parents are deeply concerned about their children's well-being and genuinely enthusiastic about helping them to enjoy a rewarding season.

Be sure to set aside time at the end of the meeting to address any additional questions or concerns. Perhaps parents have questions that they're more comfortable asking in a one-on-one situation after the meeting concludes, so let them know that you're available to chat with them after the meeting or by phone at a time that's convenient for both of you. Also, if any parents ask questions that you can't answer during your presentation, be sure to make a note and let the parents know that you'll find out that information as soon as possible and get back to them with the answers.

Chapter 5

Evaluating Your Team

Successful business leaders understand the strengths and weaknesses of their employees and utilise their talents for the betterment of the company. The same type of approach applies to coaching a youth football team. True, your youth coaching experience isn't like the cutthroat world of big business. Yet, understanding the talent level of the squad you have inherited and moulding and cultivating it to the best of your ability helps define what type of coach you are and how much success your team enjoys in a season.

Your ability to relate to the kids – all of 'em – determines how successful you are in this endeavour. You are going to have youngsters on your team with enormously different levels of abilities, diverse characteristics, and wide-ranging wants and needs. This chapter takes a look at how you can go about relating to your team, evaluating its members, and getting them working together as a team.

The Art of Evaluation

If you received a job promotion and suddenly found yourself in charge of a new staff, one of the first things you would do is examine the skills of your new employees and work out whose talents best fit where. If you didn't, you probably wouldn't hang onto this position long.

The same goes for football. Although you wouldn't be in danger of losing your coaching responsibilities, you would jeopardise the impact you hope to have on your team this season. In order to maximise your effectiveness as a youth football coach and propel your players to reach their maximum potential, you must be able to evaluate their skills. Being able to accurately analyse what areas of their game may need bolstering, or even just a little fine tuning, is vital for long-term success and helping the kids to fully enjoy the sport.

Evaluating your players' skills

In school, it's a pretty straightforward approach when it comes to evaluating students and charting their progress. Teachers simply give kids tests to assess how well they have comprehended the material that has been presented. The process of evaluating is a little more challenging when it comes to your young football players. After all, football is a complex sport that requires a wide range not only of individual skills, but the ability to utilise these skills in a manner that benefits the team.

A youngster may be a great player in training, but if they are unable to transfer those abilities to the pitch during games they aren't going to derive as much enjoyment from the sport as they could. For example, you may have a truly gifted player who happens to be incredible with the ball. He is one of those players who can work the football with both feet equally well and he impresses teammates during training with his dribbling skills. But when the day of the game arrives, he turns into a different player. The impressive training skills he's demonstrated are long gone. So now what? By evaluating the player and watching him carefully you may find out that problems arise for him as soon as a defender puts any type of pressure on him. If you work with this player on one-on-one drills and get him accustomed to dribbling with a defender in front of him all the time, his ball control skills will come to the forefront and he is going to become a better player because of your evaluation.

Training drills offer a glimpse of a player's ability in a specific area of the game, but provide a rather limited view of the player's overall skills and abilities. When evaluating the skills of younger players, small-sided games of 3-a-side or 4-a-side are ideal. These types of training situation are great for gauging all aspects of their game and determining their strengths and weaknesses. Players get a lot of touches of the ball and are forced to control it in a variety of situations, as well as having to continually jump back and forth between attack and defence mode.

Here are a few tips to keep in mind when putting together evaluations of your players:

✔ **On the move:** Football is a game of continual movement and reaction. Players who are flat-footed or prone to standing still for any amount of time are going to be less likely to be able to take advantage of opportunities to attack when their team regains possession of the ball in an advantageous position; or vice versa, they may be a defensive liability when their team loses the ball and they are suddenly required to assume a defensive position. When evaluating a player's movement, be sure to take several factors into account in order to get a true sense of their ability in this area of the game. After they deliver a shot on goal, do they stand there and admire their shot or do they aggressively move forward in case of a rebound or a fumble? When they pass to a teammate, do they immediately become a statue afterward and watch to see whether the ball gets to them, or do they move down the pitch with the action and look to get free and receive a return pass?

✔ **Comfort zone:** How players respond to defensive pressure is a key factor to consider in your evaluation. Are they able to maintain control of the ball when an opposing player charges toward them? Can they manoeuvre the ball in a crowded situation? When they receive a pass do they look to gather it under control and move with it or immediately look to give it back to a teammate because they aren't comfortable dribbling it?

✔ **Capitalising on opportunities:** In the more advanced levels of youth football, a team usually have fewer chances to score a goal during the course of a game, because many of the players are more developed and highly skilled. With fewer opportunities to score goals, the ability to beat a player one-on-one on those occasions that are advantageous for your team is critical for its success. Do your players have the skills to negotiate their way past a defender and get a quality shot on goal? Can they work the ball with both feet, or do they rely too often on their dominant foot, which makes them easier to defend against? When they take shots on goal are they getting their full force behind their shots or is the ball barely making it to the goal?

✔ **Defensive tenacity:** The true mark of a well-rounded football player is their ability to excel both in attack and defence. A one-dimensional player who is only good when the ball is at their feet and they are attacking will have their defensive deficiencies exposed at some point, especially if they continue on into future levels of competition. Be on the lookout to see whether they attempt to make tackles to regain possession of the ball for their team when they are forced to play in defence, or whether they tend to pull back and rely on their teammates to take a more aggressive defensive approach.

✔ **Between the ears:** How much impact a player has on the game is influenced, to a great extent, by their mindset. Is he giving you his best effort at all times, or do you notice that his head tends to droop, his shoulders sag, and that he doesn't have quite as much spring in his step when things aren't going his way or when the team is losing? Do your players handle constructive criticism well and embrace your instruction and suggestions to improve their play, or do they withdraw and take your comments negatively?

✔ **Influence on the team:** What type of teammate the child is speaks volumes for what type of player they are. Are they a positive influence on the squad? Do they pump their teammates up when things aren't going well? Are their comments positive and supportive? Do they boost confidence levels or drain the team's enthusiasm? When they are not in the game, are they vocal supporters of their teammates, offering encouragement and providing useful guidance if they see an unmarked player? Or, do they tend to sulk that they are not in the game or simply do not even pay attention to what their teammates are doing on the pitch?

✔ **It's not just about results:** Simply because a child is your team's leading goal scorer and regularly notches goals, that doesn't necessarily mean she is a well-developed, all-around player. His goal-scoring prowess may be attributed to several underlying factors: His teammates are great passers and are always able to feed him the ball when he is unmarked; or perhaps he may simply have a more powerful leg than a lot of the other kids and his kicks are basically too difficult to stop. While such players' attacking skills are well-honed, they may have severe deficiencies in the defensive aspects of their play.

Your team's win-lose record isn't an evaluation of your team or the skills of each individual player. Take the time to evaluate each player and then help them strengthen those areas of their game that are lacking.

Identifying team strengths and weaknesses

During the course of the season, your team is going to be discovering and developing skills, as well as – hopefully – making great progress in how effectively they are working together on the pitch. But regardless of how talented your players are, or how experienced they may be, it's simply the nature of football that all teams are going to struggle with their play at some point along the way. Perhaps they'll go through a scoring drought, encounter problems working as a cohesive unit on defence, or lose confidence in their abilities after suffering a couple of close defeats in a row.

Being able to identify your team's strengths and weaknesses goes a long way to help mould them and getting the most out of them. If you're aware that your team's attacking abilities are lagging behind the skills it demonstrates on defence, make your training session time much more beneficial by devoting extra parts of the session to attacking rather than defending.

For example, if your team is struggling to score goals, it may be easy to jump to the conclusion that you need to spend more time during training working on shooting drills, when in reality that may not necessarily be the best solution. Perhaps the underlying problem is that your team encounters a lot of difficulty passing the ball out of their own half of the pitch, which translates into more time spent on defence and, consequently, fewer scoring opportunities. So, one way to remedy the situation may be to shift your focus in training sessions to passing drills that involve your defensive players. This subtle change may be all that is needed to erase some of your scoring woes.

In order to get a better perspective on your team and where its strengths and weaknesses lie, here are a few other helpful hints to consider:

✔ **Camcorder:** Consider having an assistant coach or parent record one of your games from one end of the pitch, or from the stands if there are any. Make sure that you get the parents' permission first though. The Football Association website has a number of permission forms that can be downloaded (see Chapter 23). Explain to the parents what you are doing and why.

As you have so many responsibilities going on during the course of a game, it's virtually impossible for you to be able to see everything that takes place on the pitch. Plus, at the more advanced levels of youth football when the playing area is quite large, sometimes your view from the touchline of what is happening on the pitch can be obstructed by the maze of players that you are forced to look through. Recording the game from behind the goal line or from up above provides you with an entirely different vantage point than you are normally accustomed to, and gives you a fresh perspective on the team's play.

This recording is for your own private viewing. Don't adopt a professional coaching mentality and use it to make your players watch recordings of games. Children involved in organised football need to be on the pitch working on skills, not in front of a screen watching a video.

✔ **Solicit outside advice:** If you have friends or acquaintances who are football coaches in another league, and they happen to have a lot more experience coaching the sport than you do, or perhaps they coach in a league where the players are more experienced, ask them to come and watch one of your training sessions. Another set of eyes is always helpful and they may be able to provide valuable feedback on areas of the game they believe you need to spend additional time on with your team.

Lining 'Em Up

Determining what positions your players are best suited for is sort of like putting together a giant jigsaw puzzle without a picture to go by. You've got all these pieces right in front of you – the kids – and endless combinations to consider. Your challenge is to not only find a position for each child that they are capable of playing and that provides the most benefits for the team, but one that they also embrace and derive lots of enjoyment from playing.

Assigning team positions

Selecting positions for your players is dictated primarily by their age and, to a lesser extent, their experience level. At the beginner's level, and certainly in mini-soccer, small-sided games like four-on-four and six-on-six are most common. These games typically take on a kick-and-chase-the-ball mentality. The ball moves and a pack of kids go after it. These types of game are great for introducing children to the sport and its most basic components. During these early stages of development, you often need to make the positioning of players take a backseat to simply getting the kids on the pitch running and kicking the ball. Assigning a 5-year-old the position of midfielder and trying to coach him in all the responsibilities that accompany the position would produce the same bewildered look as if you were attempting to explain to him the essence of astrophysics. It's just not realistic and leaves him with a bad experience.

As children get older and progress in the sport, expose them to all the different positions on the pitch. They should never be confined to just one position for the entire season. In order to fully experience football and everything that is involved in playing it, they need – and deserve – the chance to play everything from goalie to midfielder. Rotating youngsters through all of the positions during the course of a season gives them a wonderful sense of what football is all about, and keeps their interest and enthusiasm high as they are continually introduced to new challenges and different aspects of the game. By taking this approach, you will be creating all-round football players rather than just defenders or goalies. Assigning a child who's new or relatively new to football to a set position at the start of the season isn't going to be fun or any good for their development.

Also, don't typecast a player based on their physical appearance. Children who are slightly overweight are often delegated to play goalie because there won't be much running around required to play the position. Or, they aren't even considered for a position like midfielder because they don't have the 'look' of a player who can move with the ball and create scoring opportunities for her team. If a child gets typecast into one position early on she may never get the chance to fully enjoy the entire football experience. There may be a wonderfully skilled player just waiting to emerge, but if you don't give them the chance, they won't know how successful they could have been, and they may miss out on a wonderfully rewarding and truly enriching experience.

As children grow with experience and the level of play becomes more competitive, they'll become involved in regulation 11-a-side football matches. This is when you have to determine which players are appropriate for certain positions, and which provide the most benefits for the entire team. Should your most talented and experienced players be up front to help generate more goal-scoring opportunities for the team, or should they be placed in defensive positions to help protect the goal and limit the opposing team's chances to score? That is going to be your decision to make. No guidelines are set in stone for what qualities are best for any particular position. A lot of that is dictated by the style of play you have your team running.

The following are general considerations that you may want to take into account when determining some of the basic playing positions on the pitch:

- **Midfielders and forwards**: These positions require a steady amount of running so players must have the stamina – and speed – to handle their attacking and defensive responsibilities. Because midfielders typically get a large number of touches of the ball during the game, the more skilled they are in passing and trapping, the better they are able to take advantage of those touches in order to deliver the ball to their teammates. Forwards must possess good footwork and be accurate with their kicks to take advantage of scoring opportunities.

- **Defenders**: Quickness and the ability to read developing moves and react to them at the spur of the moment are the hallmarks of good defenders. Good heading skills are helpful in defending corner kicks, and a strong kick is an asset to clear the ball out of their area when under attack and to be able to get it to a teammate down the pitch.

- **Goalies**: It takes a strong individual to play in goal because a lot of pressure usually accompanies the position. Even though defensive breakdowns and lapses in judgement lead to many goals, because the goalie failed to make the stop, unfair blame is often directed toward him. Ideally, you would like your goalie to be technically sound, confident but not arrogant, and mentally strong so that he is able to concentrate on the game and has the ability to bounce back after surrendering a goal.

When delegating positions, remind each player that they have been chosen for that position because of the special skills they have and the ability they have demonstrated in training to really provide a great service to the team by playing that position. As the season progresses, you may recognise that a player you have in defence has really shown that they are quick to the ball and may be better suited to play as a midfielder. See Chapter 8, which discusses making mid-season adjustments to improve the team.

Finding roles for everyone

Regardless of how carefully you choose positions for your players and the great effort and lengths you go to in order to ensure that each youngster is assigned a position that they want to play, you're going to have kids who aren't going to be content with their positions. With only one goalie on the pitch, you're sure to have a handful of kids that want to play in goal. And out of all the kids that you've designated for defensive roles, you can be sure that one or two have had their hearts set on playing up front where they would have a chance to score more goals. So now what do you do?

One approach you can take to help kids get over the disappointment of not being able to play a position they had hoped to be playing this season is to take a trip to a professional football game, or a local game of a good standard. These can be outstanding educational experiences for the entire team. While there, instruct your players to closely monitor those players who are playing the same positions. When youngsters on your team watch how players at the more elite levels of competition play the position, they will have a better sense of its importance to the overall structure of the team. They'll also gain a better appreciation of how vital their role is to the team and they may even pick up a few pointers along the way that enhance how they play the position.

One of a coach's primary responsibilities is to recognise and value every child's contribution to the team, no matter how big or small the impact when it comes to wins and losses. Every child provides something to the chemistry of the team. Of course, with some kids it may be a little more difficult determining what that is, but just because they haven't scored any goals this season or made any outstanding defensive plays doesn't mean that they aren't a valued and appreciated member of the team. When youngsters are on the pitch giving it their best, or on the touchlines enthusiastically cheering for their teammates, it's important that their effort doesn't go unrecognised or unappreciated.

Every game and training session provides you with an opportunity to share your feelings and sense of pride with your team. Even though a child doesn't deliver match-winning goals, perhaps they have a never-give-up attitude that rubs off on the rest of the team. Other teammates may see this youngster constantly hustling after every loose ball and that makes them try that much harder. So, the child's work ethic has transcended the entire team and everyone is giving more than they thought they had in them. This won't show up in the statistics and if you don't take the time to recognise it then it may go unnoticed. If the child never hears this praise from you, then a great coaching opportunity and wonderful chance to build confidence and self-esteem in the youngster is lost. Remember, a child's value to the team must be measured by more than simply the number of goals they score.

Understanding and Interacting with All the Kids

One of the truly challenging aspects of coaching a youth football team is that every child that straps on shinguards to play for you is amazingly different in so many ways. You're embarking on a fascinating journey that should challenge your creativity, test your patience at times and challenge your ability to interact with all types of personalities.

You're going to encounter youngsters whose football talents, physical development and emotional characteristics cover an enormously broad spectrum. Some players are charismatic and outgoing, while others are shy and reclusive. You have kids who are passionate and live for football, and others that would rather be just about anywhere except on the football pitch with you. There are kids who are particularly talented, who already have a special flair for the game and are already excelling, and those who are clumsy, uncoordinated, and have difficulty running without tripping over their own feet. How you handle all these different types of kids plays a large role in determining just how much fun they have playing for you and whether or not they return again next season.

The shy child

Shyness is one of the most common characteristics you need to deal with with youngsters on your team – and it can be one of the easiest to handle if you are extremely patient and gradually work to lure the child out of their protective shell. Pushing too hard and too early in the season may scare them enough that they actually pull back and isolate themselves even further from the team.

One of the most common characteristics associated with shy children is that they go to extreme lengths to blend into the background and dodge attention. During training sessions, they avoid eye contact, they don't ask for help when working on skills, and they quietly move throughout the various drills while doing everything in their power not to draw attention to themselves.

 During your training sessions, rotate the kids who lead the warm-up and stretching at the beginning. Select the shy child along with a couple of other players to lead the team. This is a small step toward helping the youngster become comfortable in front of the team. By having a couple of other players up there with her, she won't feel isolated or gripped with fear that all eyes are on her. While helping a child overcome their shyness, you must proceed slowly and carefully. Pushing a child too quickly can have serious ramifications. It's going to be a deliberate process, but a truly rewarding one when you succeed in coaxing the child out of the shadows they have suffered in and open their eyes to all the wonderful opportunities and experiences that they have been missing out on up until now.

If a child's shyness isn't addressed during these critical formative years, it can have negative consequences on the rest of their life and restrict their ability to interact in all sorts of social settings. Shyness can compromise their abilities, paralyse their chances of ever excelling in the sport, and drag them down with feelings of despair. Coaches are in a great position to help shy children step out of these protective cocoons, discover an inner courage they never knew they had, and derive enormous pleasure participating – and interacting – in youth football.

The uncoordinated child

You are going to have kids on your team who aren't nearly as coordinated or skilful as many of their teammates. These are the ones that other kids may make fun of. These are the kids who struggle with the most basic football skills. While attempting to kick a football, they miss as often as they make contact. They stumble over their own feet a lot. They are unable to trap and control the ball coming to them or to direct a pass to an unmarked teammate. Basically, not a whole lot goes smoothly for them no matter how hard they try. Some children just aren't athletically inclined and it interferes with their self-esteem, as well as how they are perceived by others.

Regardless of these shortcomings, this doesn't mean that they aren't giving the game their very best. Some are going to become enormously frustrated with their inability to kick a football as well as their teammates do. Often, feelings of inadequacy settle in and further compromise their ability to perform basic football skills. Even after repeated demonstrations of how to perform a skill, they often aren't going to pick up on it as quickly as you would like. Be careful what words you choose and never allow a frustrated tone to come into your voice or be seen in your body language.

Helping a child improve their co-ordination takes a lot of practice. While most children embrace the physical activity that accompanies a sport like football, those who are wrestling with co-ordination problems cringe at the thought of playing in a game in which they are likely to struggle, fail, and ultimately disappoint their teammates, coaches and parents.

Encourage parents of such children to work with them at home. Stress the importance of having fun being out there kicking a football back and forth in the back garden, not on how well they are performing the skill itself. Make sure that the parents don't overdo the sessions. Have them keep sessions short and the praise flowing. Children who are unsuccessful tend to become frustrated and shy away from the activity. Children who see their friends performing at a level they believe they'll never reach are likely to become disenchanted with the sport, reluctant to continue participating and likely to adopt a more sedentary lifestyle that revolves around television and computer screens. Encourage them to continue being active, and never give them any reason whatsoever to think that you are the least bit frustrated or disappointed in their abilities. You can pull them through this difficult time in their young lives and years from now they may well surprise you in how they've blossomed into solid, co-ordinated football players with a good handle on all the basics of the game.

The child with the short attention span

Face it. When it comes to kids, short attention spans are as common as runny noses and skinned knees. The younger the child, the shorter their attention span is likely to be – and the trickier your job is going to be in the process. When coaching an outdoor sport like football, distractions are going to abound. Birds, airplanes, motorcycles, you name it, you are going to be competing with all sorts of things that vie for the kids' attention. That puts a greater responsibility on you to construct training sessions and devise drills that continually capture the kids' attention and keep their interest and excitement level high (see Chapter 6). The quickest route to losing a child's attention on the football pitch is to spend large amounts of time talking to them instead of keeping them on the move and actively involved in a wide variety of drills.

Make sure that you remember that a child whose mind continually strays may potentially have Attention-Deficit/Hyperactivity Disorder (ADHD), which usually appears before the age of seven. According to the various bodies associated with the condition, the most common characteristics of a child with ADHD are distractibility, which consists of poor sustained attention to tasks; impulsivity, which is an impaired ability to control sudden urges; and hyperactivity, which constitutes excessive activity and physical restlessness.

Youngsters with ADHD certainly don't want to be inattentive anymore than the child with bronchitis wants to struggle with coughing spells or the asthmatic child wants to gasp for breath. Children may be on medication (this is important information to be aware of when you meet with the parents prior to the season – refer back to Chapter 4), others may not be on any type of medication, and others, when you get right down to it, may just be having a bad day. The best remedy for working with a child that has ADHD is to dispense lots of praise for even the slightest improvements. ADHD youngsters are in constant need of praise and recognition, so when they follow your instructions or perform a skill in the appropriate fashion, pile on the praise.

The athletically gifted child

Every football team seems to have one, that one child whose talent and ability level exceeds everyone else's by a pretty substantial margin. This is the kid that kicks the ball harder than everyone else. His passes are constantly on the mark. He's the fastest player on the team and continually beats other players to loose balls. He scores goals by the hat-full. He frustrates opponents with his defensive tenacity. The game comes remarkably easily to him. Thanks to his size, strength, speed, co-ordination, and natural born talent – or a combination of these traits – this youngster gets the label of team star. He stands out. His teammates know that he's the best player on the team. The parents of all the other kids recognise he's the team's best player by far. You can certainly see how advanced he is compared to the rest of the team. So, how do you handle coaching this child?

One of the greatest challenges that accompanies coaching youngsters far superior to the others in skill development is providing them with drills that allow them to enhance their skills, while not compromising the rest of the team in the process. After all, this can be rather tricky because you don't want to isolate the children from their teammates when working on drills, but you also don't want them bored and unchallenged performing a drill that they are good at but the rest of the team is just picking up. By using your creativity you can concoct clever ways to help those kids just acquiring a skill, and the exceptionally talented children, all excel at the same time.

Say that you are working with the team on delivering a shot on goal with a moving ball. For youngsters just beginning to get their timing right, you need to slowly roll the ball directly to them. A youngster who is already highly skilled in this area of the game can still derive a number of benefits from this drill. You can increase the difficulty of the drill for this player in a number of ways, without drawing extra attention. You can roll the ball toward them with extra pace, which forces them to react quicker when delivering the shot. You can roll the ball a few feet wider than normal, which requires the player to move laterally before lining up the shot. Or, you can send the ball to the side of their less dominant foot, which gives them practice in using that foot in taking shots. As you can see, a little ingenuity on your part can go a long way.

If these players possess good attitudes and are not critical or condescending to their teammates, they have the potential to emerge as wonderful team leaders and positive role models. It's easy to fall into the habit of piling on the praise to these youngsters, who continually put a smile on your face with their ability to pass, shoot, and defend so well. Keep yourself in check and refrain from going overboard with praise. Too many accolades can have adverse effects on certain kids. They may begin feeling unnecessary pressure, which can inhibit their performance and derail their enjoyment of football. They may suddenly feel that, with all the attention being thrown in their direction, they have to shoulder more of the responsibility for the team's success, and failure. If they don't score a certain number of goals, they may feel personally responsible for the loss. Going overboard with the praise can also alienate other members of the team, who may begin to feel as though the talented player is the coach's favourite. If you allow this to happen, the team may harbour resentment towards you and the talented player and it can cause havoc with the team spirit and chemistry you are trying to build.

There's certainly nothing wrong with enjoying working with the highly gifted youngsters on your team. Just remember to maintain a proper perspective, and that these talented players are just one piece of the team puzzle. You have a squad full of other kids who need your help, support and guidance as well.

The child who doesn't want to be there

Children with chinks in their self-esteem armour often perceive sports participation as tests of personal worthiness. So, in their minds, it's often better to avoid the activity all together rather than risk failure, humiliation, and disappointment in their inability to perform to certain levels. These kids may have already written off football as a sport they can't enjoy, for of any number of reasons.

Perhaps they watched an older sibling participate and felt the pressure surrounding the activity to excel and really don't want any part of it, but their mum or dad has signed them up to play on your team anyway.

Maybe the child has played football for several years and has grown tired of it and simply needs a break. Maybe something happened last season that has affected their interest. Perhaps they had a problem with a teammate, a coach, or were hurt and are fearful now of suffering another injury. Talk to the child to find out the reason for their lack of interest. A lot of these reasons you can address, take care of and comfort the child, and restore their interest in playing again. Connecting emotionally with the child and helping them to solve their dilemma can do wonders for re-establishing their enthusiasm for playing.

The disruptive child

If you've got a dozen or so kids on your team, the chances are that you're going to have a child or two who is going to test the boundaries of what you consider acceptable behaviour. These are the kids that have a need for attention, and misbehaving is their way of soliciting it; or they are simply being raised by parents who haven't bothered to instil any manners in them. At any rate, they are going to be testing your authority, challenging your team rules, and taxing your patience at times.

Coaches often find themselves walking a tightrope when it comes to dealing with disruptive players. They are so overly concerned about being well-liked by everyone that they sacrifice discipline and ignore team rules that are broken in the process. Or, in an effort to keep the kids in line, they are exceedingly harsh, hand out punishment far too often and quickly turn the season into a boot camp that makes everyone miserable. Both of these approaches have disastrous consequences. Coaches have to find an appropriate balance between the two. Keep in mind that children can enjoy playing for you, and like you, while respecting your authority and abiding by your team rules.

Dealing with a disruptive child poses many unique challenges. First of all, you have to clearly outline to the team what type of behaviour you expect from them during training sessions and games. When a player crosses that line, you've got to address the situation immediately, while not embarrassing them in the process. We go into greater detail about disciplining children in Chapter 19.

If the best player on the team is allowed to get away with inappropriate behaviour, then you are sending a disturbing message to the rest of the team that this player is more important than they are and is above the team rules. In fact, you are elevating this player to a position more powerful than yours. Coaches who allow this type of insubordination to go on and avoid dealing with the problem usually do so because they are operating under a win-at-all-cost mentality and turn their backs on confronting any type of problems that can impact on the team's won–lost record.

As the coach, you need to take control of the situation immediately before it leads to team dissension and, even worse, to other players beginning to copy the antics of this player because they see that the coach is unwilling to discipline or punish the offenders. Quite simply, the only way that you are going to maintain the respect of your team, and be able to coach the merits of following the rules and respecting authority, is to punish the offending player and let the team clearly know that this type of behaviour is unacceptable and will not be tolerated. Be sure to remind your players that those who do not abide by the rules are making that choice themselves. Don't set the danger-ous precedent of making different rules for different levels of ability. (Jump to Chapter 19 to find out more about what types of disciplinary measures you can implement when dealing with disruptive youngsters.)

The child with special needs

All kids have a right to participate in sports like football, and that goes for those who have special needs. These needs can range from hearing loss and vision impairment to medical conditions such as diabetes or epilepsy. Youngsters with physical conditions that mean they don't have full use of their arms or legs also fall into this category. As a volunteer football coach, it's natural to perhaps question your own qualifications about working with a child who has special needs. But think about it. You're a coach and these are kids looking for your help and guidance. Just as you discover ways to suc-cessfully work with a child who has no co-ordination or is super-shy, applying the same approach works for a child with special needs, so you can safely include them without causing major disruptions to the team or the game.

In order for kids with special needs to participate in a sport like football, certain accommodations are going to have to be made. These modifications aren't designed to give the child or the team an unfair advantage, or to put the team at a disadvantage; they're simply used to help eliminate some of the obstacles that are preventing the child from participating in the sport, so that they can benefit as much from the experience as the other kids. You want to do everything you can to maintain the integrity of the game while also making it possible for these youngsters to be a part of the football experience.

During your pre-season parents meeting (refer to Chapter 4), you need to find out from the parents if any of their children have any conditions that you need to be aware of in order to meet their needs. If you happen to have a child with special needs, set aside time before the first training session of the season to talk to the family about their hopes and expectations for their child's participation. You want to open the lines of communication so that together you can come up with solutions that benefit everyone.

Keep in mind that this may be the parents' first foray into organised sport and they may be nervous and apprehensive about having their child partici-pating in the team. They are probably going to be turning to you for all the answers. Explore the endless possibilities that are out there. Work out ways for this youngster to be included and to be a valued and contributing member of the team.

For example, if the child has a visual impairment and has great difficulty seeing a white ball, perhaps playing with a different-coloured football would make all the difference. Or, if a child has a physical problem that doesn't allow them to run up and down the pitch, maybe they can handle all the team's throw-ins, or perhaps they can be the team's designated corner kicker. These are just a couple of examples of ways that children, regardless of their disabilities, can be included without compromising anyone else's safety or enjoyment of the game.

When these youngsters get an understanding of their role and how they fit into the structure of the team, then during training sessions they can work on specific skills and see improvement in these, just like their teammates.

If you are coaching a team of older kids, ask them for their thoughts and ideas on how the particular youngster in question can be included. Your players can be great resources for you and they may just surprise you with their creative suggestions on how to ensure that their teammate is a part of the action.

Regardless of the age or skill level of your team, having a child with special needs on the squad can also be enormously beneficial for your other players. Youngsters get a first-hand lesson on developing understanding, compassion and patience for their teammates, while also beginning to accept everyone for their differences. (See Chapter 7, where we discuss the importance of meeting with the opposing coach prior to games, to share any information regarding children on your team with special needs, and to find out whether any on the other team do, as well. By working together and making the necessary accommodations, you can help to ensure that these youngsters are an integral part of the team chemistry.)

The bully

You can probably recall the kids you went to school with who picked fights in the playground, pushed around the smaller and weaker children, and intimidated others with their mean streaks. They tormented, teased, and were totally troublesome. Bullies aren't limited to playgrounds and school hallways – they can show up on the football pitch with their intimidating scowls and over-aggressive play. Bullies thrive on attention and find pleasure in upsetting others. They also frequently feel weak and continually battle feelings of insecurity. There's no room on the football pitch for bullies or their intimidating tactics and physical play.

Kids that are picked on by a bully typically aren't going to complain for fear of making the situation worse than it already is. This means that you've got to keep a close eye on the interaction of the kids – not just during training, but what happens before training begins and afterwards. In school, bullies wreak the most havoc at break time, waiting for the school bus or in the hallways between classes – the common denominator being that it happens when adults are less likely to be around. In football, bullies often strike when coaches aren't paying attention, and kids are just mucking around waiting for training to begin. That's another good reason to have a training drill set up for the early-arriving kids (see Chapter 6). It eliminates the messing about before training that can injure a child or cause emotional distress.

If you are having problems with a bully, speak with the child away from the team and let her know that a change in her behaviour is in order for the good of the team. Let her know that you admire her tenacity on the pitch, but that her physical strength and motivation to overpower the opponent must be reined in a bit and used strictly within the confines of the rules of football. Not following the rules impacts negatively on the team and is counter-productive to what the entire team is striving to accomplish together. Tell the bully that you value her as a player but that bullying is not acceptable. If the child is simply picking on or making fun of teammates, address the fact that she should be encouraging and supporting them. After all, these are the guys she's going to be encouraging and counting on to pass to her on the pitch.

As a youth football coach, you have an obligation and a responsibility to do your best to bring out the best in your players as both football players and individuals. If the bullying is not addressed, it's as though you are condoning the behaviour. Be sure to point out that you know that she's capable of being a better teammate. Work with her to be a more positive influence on the team. Make the conversation a productive one by being friendly, yet firm. She may even pick up pointers from you on how to be a better person by how you deal with the issue.

The inexperienced child

Sometimes a child is a late arrival to the sport of football. For example, if you are coaching a 10-and-under team, one of your 10-year-olds may have never played organised football before, while the rest of his teammates may have been involved in the sport for several years. It's simply not possible to get the inexperienced child up to the skill level of his teammates in the relatively short amount of time that you are in contact with him. After all, there's no way to squeeze a few seasons' worth of training sessions, drills and game experience into a month or two. But you can still help the youngster to develop skills and be a contributing member of the team, without compromising the training time of the more experienced players.

For example, you can create a passing drill for four players in which the group is comprised of one talented child, two youngsters of average football ability and one child who is inexperienced in the sport. The less experienced player may struggle a bit, but with the positive encouragement from the talented player who can take on part of a coaching role, you can create a situation where everyone picks up skills, and the team bond is further cemented by everyone working together.

The ball hog

Having a ball hog on your team – one of those players who hangs onto the ball as though she is guarding her most prized toy – can create real problems for the entire team because it directly impacts on everyone's enjoyment of the game. Ball hogs typically aren't a problem at the younger age levels because most younger kids haven't played long enough to develop their skills to such a point that they can maintain control of the ball for extended periods of time. Ball hogs are generally found when kids begin to develop skills, their talent begins to shine through, and they realise they are getting pretty good. A player can earn the ball-hog label for a number of reasons, all of which you can help them discard by taking the right approach:

- ✔ **The player is unaware that she's a ball hog.** Quite often it can just be a case of the child not being aware that she was hanging onto the ball longer than she should. Incorporating a lot of drills into your training sessions that stress early passing, such as two-on-ones and three-on-ones, or training drills where the team must complete a set number of passes in a row before taking a shot on goal (see Chapter 6) is great for eliminating ball-hog problems. Any drills or exercises that force kids to work with, and rely on their teammates, can be instrumental in keeping the ball-hog syndrome from infiltrating your team and creating problems.

- ✔ **She's receiving conflicting instructions.** One of the more challenging scenarios can be that the youngster is receiving conflicting instructions from their dad or mum at home. It may be a case of the parent telling the child that they need to be more aggressive during games; or they are telling the child that they are the best player on the team and that they need to exert more control and dominate the game, and that they shouldn't relinquish the ball so often. Remind the parents that you appreciate their help teaching the kids by reinforcing *your* lessons at home. If a gentle group reminder doesn't get the message across, arrange a private meeting with the parents of the individual concerned.

✔ **The player is new to the sport.** The child may be new to football, or perhaps she has never been involved on a team before. It just may take extra time to get her accustomed to the team setting, helping her realise that she needs to utilise her teammates, and the importance of passing the ball for the benefit of the entire team.

✔ **She doesn't understand her position.** Take a closer look at how you are explaining the responsibilities of the various positions to your players, as well as the philosophies you are preaching to the team in respect of attack and defence. Do certain players tend to wander out of position, which is creating all these additional opportunities for them to get on the ball? Are your defenders creeping too far forward when the team is on the attack and forgetting their defensive responsibilities in the process, which gives them extra possession? Spending a few minutes clarifying the responsibilities of each position and touching on the fact that the team can only excel if everyone plays in position, may be all that is needed to quickly and easily remedy the problem.

✔ **The player has future ambitions.** Many times this type of youngster has aspirations of playing at a higher and more competitive level of football in the future. These thoughts may be fuelled by what her parents are telling her at home, or by a genuine interest herself in excelling in the sport. Regardless of where the motivation is coming from, talk to her and let her know that when she begins playing at the more competitive levels of football, the players that she will be going up against will have the same skills – and perhaps more – than she does. That makes the ability to distribute the ball to teammates even more important, and if she doesn't hone those skills now, she'll be a liability on her next team.

You should also ask yourself whether you're the problem. Take the time to really examine your training sessions, as you may be fuelling the problem yourself. During drills, are you allowing kids to unnecessarily hang onto the ball for extended periods of time while ignoring their teammates? Are you enamoured with the stellar play of certain individuals who mesmerise you with their dribbling skills as they negotiate their way down the pitch during training, while their teammates stand idly by? If so, then the ball hogs are certainly going to carry over this style of play to games. Continually stressing the importance of teamwork during training, and pointing out to players who have shown a tendency to hog the ball that they should have passed the ball to a teammate, helps to eliminate this problem from showing up during games.

You also may want to alter your training drills. Play keepball. These are games during training where the purpose is to maintain possession of the ball, not score goals. This isn't a destructive approach to coaching football. By doing so, the entire team discovers how to pass the ball, receive passes, and make space in order to take advantage of the defence. You can even make a rule that each player on the team has to touch the ball before a player can touch it a second time on each change of possession. If not, they lose possession of the ball to the other team. This type of drill ensures that everyone is involved in the game and forces players to find ways to get the ball to teammates who haven't had a touch yet. Alternatively, insist that each player only takes three touches or less on the ball. For more advanced kids, this can be two touches.

Regardless of the reasons behind the emergence of a ball hog, it's imperative to deal with it swiftly because it affects everything from team morale to each child's overall enjoyment of the sport. Letting the problem linger has long-lasting repercussions. Allowing the player to continue hogging the ball game after game sends them a distorted message about how to play football, as well as frustrate and alienate their teammates in the process.

It's essential that you coach players in the essence of teamwork to ensure that no single player is monopolising the ball at the expense of his teammates. While dealing with this, don't make it a public display. The last thing you want to do is embarrass the player in front of his teammates and, in the process, make him suddenly afraid to take any shots or dribble the ball for any length of time, for fear of being reprimanded again. A ball hog doesn't need to be disciplined; they simply need coaching and guidance on how to work more effectively as a team. You don't want to detract from their aggressive play or drain their passion for playing the game. You do want to make them aware that in order for the team to reach its potential, every child has to play an instrumental role.

Also, stress to the player that the more they bring their teammates into the game, the more effective a player they will be as they advance in their football career and play at more competitive levels. Talk to them about becoming a well-rounded player who can not only deftly control the ball and score goals, but who can also thread pinpoint passes through a maze of defenders. Good football players have a penchant for playing all aspects of the game well.

The average child

You're going to have all types of youngsters on your team, from the ball hogs and bullies to the behaviourally challenged (see preceding sections). Yes, some kids are self-motivated, while others rely on you for motivation and inspiration. They may be involved to quench their competitive desires, to

simply get a better grasp on skills of the game or merely for the social interaction and camaraderie of being part of a team. Some kids are going to be
extremely coachable and receptive to all of your instructions and feedback,
while others may not be quite as receptive. Some kids are going to be skinny,
short and not nearly as physically developed as their teammates; and others
may be overweight and taller than others their age.

For the most part, the majority of your players are just going to be your regular, everyday kids who enjoy playing football and being with their friends.
They're not going to be super talents destined for professional football or disruptive influences creating havoc with the team's chemistry and your blood
pressure. They're simply going to be average kids showing up with smiles
and shinguards to play for you, pick up skills from you, and grow under you.
A lot of the kids may just be involved because their friends are playing and
they want to be spend time with their friends. Some kids – through their
involvement with you this season – should develop a real love and passion
for the game and continue playing it for years to come. Others will be content
to try a new sport next season, but now have a handle on the basics of the
game if they ever choose to return to the sport in the future.

Chapter 6

Running a Great Training Session

*N*othing wipes the smiles off the faces of a young football team quicker than dull training sessions where the same tiresome drills are used all season long. As the coach, You're the one who has to keep the interest and excitement level high, every time your youngsters step on the pitch.

Creative training sessions that children anxiously look forward to attending week after week pay big dividends in the kids' skill development, speed up the process of discovery, enhance their overall enjoyment of the sport, and translate into plenty of that all-important fun in the process. During your training sessions, you must constantly challenge, encourage, and entertain your youngsters. You must be creative in your planning, enthusiastic in your instruction, and overflowing with your praise. Training sessions must also be carefully crafted days beforehand rather than at the stop light on the drive over to the pitch; every drill must serve a specific purpose rather than just fill a chunk of training time; and every training session must be designed with the intention of helping youngsters progress in all areas of the game.

Of course, the day of the game is what all kids naturally look forward to the most. The trick is turning your training sessions into equally fun-filled outings that generate the same type of interest. Sound planning for training that maximises your time with the kids is the foundation of any successful youth football season.

Coming to Training Prepared

Just as you expect your players to arrive at training with the right equipment and their water bottles, your players expect you to be prepared as well. Besides doing your homework and outlining the drills you want to use and the skills you want to focus on, your responsibilities extend beyond that to not only arriving at the training venue with your training plan, but with all the necessary equipment needed for a great training session.

Bringing balls and cones

What is a football coach's worst nightmare? Well, besides dealing with an over-involved parent, (which, by the way, I discuss in Chapter 19) it's not having enough equipment for training. If you don't already have enough footballs, your best bet is to let parents know at the parents' meeting (refer to Chapter 4) that it would be extremely helpful if their child brings a football with them to training. For the most part, for children involved in a youth football club, the club should supply the balls.

In order to make your training sessions the most effective, you always want to have at least one football per child. If the children are bringing footballs, you can pretty much guarantee that at least one child forgets his ball at just about every training session, so make sure that you bring along a few spares.

You don't need shiny new balls to coach kids. You don't need to have the latest match ball by a well-known brand name. Practice balls get a reasonable amount of wear and tear, and need to be highly durable, especially as they may be used on rough all-weather surfaces, so the high performance match balls are not really suited to training sessions anyway. But make sure that the ball holds air and is the proper size and weight for the age group you are coaching.

In the worst case scenario in which you only have enough footballs for a handful of players, you need to adjust your training plan accordingly. Obviously, planning a bunch of one-on-one passing games isn't going to be making the most beneficial use of your training time if you don't have enough balls to go around. Instead, you may have to make minor adjustments, such as going to a two-on-one passing drill with a defensive player included. While this slightly cuts down on the number of touches of the ball a child gets during the course of the session, it won't be a significant reduction.

Small plastic cones are perfect for marking off areas of the pitch that you want to conduct a drill in. If these aren't already provided, you can purchase a cheap set yourself at your local sporting goods retailer, or you can get creative. Old towels or t-shirts can work just as well to mark off the playing area, as well as many other items. Just make sure that whatever items you choose to mark off an area don't pose any injury risk to the child.

Packing your first-aid kit

One aspect of preparing for training includes an area of the game that a lot of coaches fail to give proper consideration to, and that's having a properly stocked first-aid kit. Lugging a first-aid kit with you to training sessions and games all season long may seem like more trouble than it is worth, but the first time you have to deal with an injury you see its enormous value – and importance. First aid kits are often league requirements. Certainly, it would be great if you never had to open the kit all season long, but injuries are a part of football (see Chapter 18). Make sure that you are prepared, rather than taking the unrealistic approach of simply hoping that nothing ever happens to your players.

Taped inside your first-aid kit should be your list of emergency contact numbers that the parents filled out and returned you prior to the season, as well as details of any particular medical conditions your players may have. (See Chapter 4 for more on these forms.)

Most clubs issue each coach with a first-aid kit. If not, you should address the issue with the club as you must have one. If your team is recreational and not part of a club, you need to supply a first-aid kit yourself. You should never conduct a training session or go to a game without your kit. You can use a tool box or any other type of container to protect your supplies, but it must be waterproof.

The basic essentials that should be in every coach's first-aid kit are the following:

- ✔ Sterile eyewash and pre-packaged sterile eye pads, in the event that debris or anything else becomes stuck in the child's eye

- ✔ Emergency tooth preserving system for a tooth that gets knocked out

- ✔ CPR mouth barrier/vent guard in the event that you or another parent needs to perform mouth-to-mouth resuscitation on a child

- ✔ Insect repellent for evening training sessions and games when those pesky mosquitoes make an unwanted appearance; sunscreen; antiseptic spray or wipes to clean out cuts and abrasions; triangular bandages, size seven and eight dressings, and other assorted size bandages to cover cuts or other wounds

- ✔ Disposable latex gloves to wear while administering to bloody cuts and other injuries

✔ Instant ice-dressing pack, plus freezer-type bags, which are great for holding ice packs

✔ A pair of scissors, water spray and carrier, tweezers, a nail clipper, and a bee-sting kit

✔ Prescriptions as needed. For example, if a youngster has asthma, it would be a good idea to keep a spare bronchodilator in your first-aid kit in the event that the child forgets his, or perhaps his parents are late arriving to a training session or game and the situation calls for it.

A few other tips to keep in mind when it comes to your first-aid kit:

✔ **Be realistic.** Stock a reasonable amount of supplies in order to treat more than one youngster at a training session or game.

✔ **Keep tally.** If you had to use a few bandages during a game to treat cuts, be sure to restock those supplies right away so that you aren't caught off-guard at your next training session when the situation calls for a bandage and you aren't prepared.

✔ **Have it readily available.** Make sure that your supplies are clearly marked and in a sensible order. If a situation arises where you are dealing with an injury and you ask the parent to retrieve a supply from your kit, you don't want to waste any unnecessary time with the parent unable to tell what is what. Freezer-type bags work well for keeping supplies in order.

First Training Session: Kicking Off the Season

Delivering an important presentation to the boss; meeting your future in-laws for the first time; getting a call from the Inland Revenue Service about your recently submitted tax forms; and conducting your first football training session of the season. All the above can all be pretty nerve-wracking experiences, but they don't have to be. Well, at least running a football training session doesn't have to be anyway.

If you have never coached a youth football team, chances are that it may seem pretty daunting – and even a lot more difficult than you expected – when you arrive at the pitch for the first time and you've got 15 sets of eyes suddenly staring up at you for guidance, instruction and motivation. Even though you may have brought all the equipment the kids need, and you have a clipboard at your side and a whistle dangling from your neck – if you haven't come armed with a training session plan that has been carefully crafted – you've got big problems.

There's a lot at stake when you take the pitch for your training sessions. While the first training session of the season sets the tone and provides kids with an indication of what is in store for them, each and every training session you conduct is enormously important in each child's overall development. These outings, if they are well constructed and efficiently run, go beyond coaching and developing basic football skills. They also promote positive attitudes, efficient training session routines, team chemistry, healthy fitness habits, increased knowledge of the game and reduced chances of injuries occurring. Now, that's a pretty impressive list.

Greeting the team for the first time

Just like in the pre-season parents' meeting (refer to Chapter 4), first impressions are oh so important for establishing the proper frame of mind for all the kids involved. A smile and a friendly pat on the back from you as you meet your young players as they arrive for the first training session of the season helps build a comfortable foundation and goes a long way towards establishing those special coach-player bonds that can make a season so rewarding. When you show up to start a new job, you aren't left standing off to the side wondering if anyone is going to come up and talk to you or welcome you. So don't leave arriving youngsters stranded and forced to linger on the side of the pitch. Be sure to get there first so that as kids climb out of the car, usually with their parents, you are there with a friendly smile to welcome them.

With older players, you should greet them with a friendly handshake and welcome them to the pitch. Talk to them about how long they have played football, what team they played for last year, what coach they played for and how their season went. If they get a sense of your genuine enthusiasm for coaching them – and how you are sincerely interested in them – the seeds of a relationship based on mutual respect are planted, and then grow stronger and stronger as the season moves along.

If you're coaching a team that has some experience playing football, you can help the kids start to become familiar with each other by having players pair up as they arrive and loosen up passing the ball back and forth to each other. Until players get to know one another better, they are often reluctant to go up to each other and often just stand around waiting for the start of training. As you're greeting the players, introduce them to another player and let them know they can get started warming up and that the training session will be starting in a few minutes. This gives you a nice head start on building team chemistry as the players begin getting comfortable with their new teammates. It also gives you a sneaky peek at the experience and talent level of your team. By watching the players in these few minutes, you can also get a sense of how well they pass and receive the ball, and how comfortable they are with the ball in general. You may realise that the drills you've put on your training session plan are too easy or too difficult for this group and that adjustments are in order.

At all your subsequent training sessions, have a drill or fun game that the players who arrive early can do with a teammate. At the end of the training session, let kids know that when they arrive before the next training session that you want them to pair up and work on their passing and receiving skills, for example. Turn it into a fun contest to see which pair can complete the most number of passes in a row. You'll be surprised how many kids show up ahead of time, allowing you to start training right on time with kids enthused to get going. That's a great environment for quality improvement to take place.

Making coach and player introductions

Just like a child's first day of school, their first football training session can be a stressful time in their young life, particularly if they have never played the sport. After all, they have new kids and coaches to meet, instructions to follow and skills to discover. They are in unfamiliar surroundings so anything you can do to alleviate stress and make them comfortable should go a long way toward getting things off to a smooth start.

The first step in that direction is to formally introduce yourself, as well as any assistant coaches if you have already selected them, to the entire team. (Refer to Chapter 4 on the importance of proceeding cautiously before selecting parents to fill these important roles.) A school teacher wouldn't throw a reading assignment at the class on the first day of school without first introducing themselves, and the same approach applies to coaching a sport like football.

When meeting with your team, keep the following in mind:

  ✔ **Gather the team in a part of the training ground that has the fewest distractions.** If you are standing with your back to another training session or game that is taking place, some of your players will almost certainly be more interested in what is taking place behind you than what you are saying. So choose a spot that enables you to introduce yourself to the team and get a few main points across before beginning training.

✔ **Be mindful of where the sun is when getting the team together.** The last thing you want to do is to have a dozen youngsters squinting to see you because they are staring directly into the sun. Whenever possible, you should be the one facing the sun. Remember, paying close attention to the smallest details can make a giant difference in the impact you have with your team.

✔ **When speaking to the team, particularly children aged 8 and under, get down to their level so you can talk directly to them.** Standing up while the team is sitting in front of you isn't conducive to them listening and absorbing the best, especially if they have to strain to keep their head up to focus on you. Speak to them at eye level and your talk will be more beneficial. Sit cross-legged with your players gathered in front of you, or talk to them while bent down on a knee. Your discussion will go much more smoothly and be so much better received using this approach.

✔ **Let the kids know that they can call you 'Coach' or 'Coach Jim'" or whatever else you are comfortable with.** The kids are going to be curious about whom they are going to be spending the season with. Also, share a few quick titbits about yourself and if you have a son or daughter on the team, introduce them. This also serves as a good lead in for the other members of the team to introduce themselves.

✔ **Make introductions a fun game by trying to guess their name.** Many children are naturally going to be shy and may even be afraid to say their names to the group. Throwing out crazy guesses gets the kids laughing and put them at ease when sharing their name.

✔ **With older kids who are more experienced, you may also want to share a little more detailed information about your coaching background.** Kids are naturally going to be interested in who they are playing for this season, and if they have been involved in the sport for years they will want to know what type of experience you have of being on the sidelines.

✔ **As with any team discussion, the shorter the talk the better.** Short attention spans abound in the younger age groups, so the less time that is spent listening to you and the more time that is spent running around on the pitch, the better for everyone involved.

To help the name remembering process, give each of the kids a name tag to wear during the first couple of training sessions. This gives you the opportunity to remember each of their names more quickly, and it allows the youngsters the chance to get to know who their teammates are much more easily as well. Put a name tag on yourself, as well as your assistants too, to help promote team unity. When they pass the ball to each other in passing drills, always make sure that they call the name of the person they are passing to.

You can also help youngsters get to know each other by selecting a couple of kids to lead warm-ups at each training session. By rotating the players leading the callisthenics each training session, you ensure that the children get to know one another pretty quickly.

Knowing the skills to focus on first

It can be a pretty overwhelming environment for a young child whose only sports experience up until now may consist of playing ball with a sibling or maybe a neighbourhood friend down the street. This means that you've got to ease them into training and introduce them to the most basic of skills those first few weeks of the season to give them a sense of what is required to play this sport.

If you are coaching at the beginner's level, your job description is basically already filled out for you. With kids at this age who are unfamiliar with the sport – and some may have never kicked a football in their life but have been signed up for football by mum and dad – your initial focus is going to be on the rudimentary skills that every young player needs to acquire. The most important skill to begin with is explaining how to kick the ball in the general direction they are aiming. Clearly, this is essential for being able to derive any sense of enjoyment and accomplishment from the sport. Eventually, you can slowly incorporate other aspects of the game, such as passing and receiving.

With older kids who are probably going to have a decent grip on many of the basics of the game, you want to shift the focus to ball movement and retaining possession. Being able to efficiently work the ball down the pitch as a unit is vital at this juncture in their development.

Putting smiles on their faces

The quickest route to putting smiles on the children's faces and a spring in their step is getting them involved in fun-filled drills that lead to not only skill acquisition but laughter. During your initial contact with the team, keep the drills simple, straightforward, and, of course, fun. The last thing you want to do is throw out complex drills that confuse and overwhelm children and cause them to question whether they want to come back for the next training session.

Use your imagination. Be resourceful. Don't limit your creativity to simply having players dribble a football through cones that have been arranged in a straight line – boring! Children are going to look forward to a drill like that about as much as they would a trip to the dentist. You are certainly capable of doing much better than that for your team. See Chapter 10 for some basic drills.

For example, instead of conducting that boring dribble-around-the-cone drill just mentioned, consider this approach instead. Take a look at your surroundings. Are there trees and bushes within sight? Why not use those as the obstacles that the kids have to dribble around. You get a much more enthusiastic response from the kids when you point out that they have to dribble the ball around that big tree over there and then negotiate that mound of dandelions to the right of the tree and so on.

You can even use this drill with the older and more experienced kids by turning it into a fun little competition. By creating a random obstacle course involving trees or anything else in the area, see which kids can manoeuvre through your course the fastest. Another twist is to go through the course first yourself while the team times you. Then, see how many players can outperform you.

Issue a challenge to the team that if half the players can beat your time you will – as punishment for losing – have to do something of their choosing, within reason, of course. This can be anything from having to wear your clothes inside out at the next training session to singing a song of the kids' choice. Conversely, you get to decide what the team has to do if they fail to come out on top. While it may be easy to opt for having the kids run a lap around the pitch, it's best to stay away from that. (Instead, find alternatives for the traditional running laps that have been used through the years. Having players run laps as punishment is not a good idea because that sends the message that conditioning drills are thought of as a negative, when on the contrary, they are extremely important.) This drill also serves as a great bonding exercise for the entire team because the players are encouraging and supporting each other and cheering one another on as they go around the course.

Take plenty of innovative approaches to turn your training sessions into lively and energetic sessions that promote discovery and skill development. Use the Internet or visit your local library to read up on the different types of drills that are out there. The key is to not restrict your thinking to what you read, though. Take any drill that you come across and look for ways that it can be tweaked for more discovery and fun to take place.

Inject your training sessions with a whole new level of excitement by getting mum and dad involved. Often, parents drop their child off at a training session and run a few errands. Or they sit in the car nearby and balance their chequebook, catch up on their reading, or strike up conversations with other parents. Why? Because no one asked them to get involved. You can liven up your training sessions, and boost the enthusiasm of the kids, by getting the parents out on the pitch with the team. Football just happens to be one of those truly special sports where special parent-child bonds can be forged by participating together. You can orchestrate the proceedings to make this happen.

Here are a few approaches that you can incorporate into your training sessions to promote fun and build skills, while also helping parents and their youngsters connect on a whole new level.

- **Kids versus parents:** This gives the youngsters on your team the chance to put what they've found out in training to use in a game-like setting, and they enjoy doing it against their mum or dad, or their friend's parent. This works great for kids of all ages and abilities. It definitely gets the competitive juices flowing in the older kids, as well. They embrace the chance to showcase a dribbling move to manoeuvre past their dad, or to deliver a pass to a teammate that leaves a mum flat-footed and impressed at the accuracy of their child's kick. Let parents know of your plans ahead of time so that they show up in the proper attire and shoes because otherwise you are going to have a pretty tough time convincing a mum in her business suit and heels to join the action on the training ground. You can build the excitement level and get your team anxiously looking forward to the next training session by letting them know during your post-training chat that they will be taking on the parents at the next training session. Don't be surprised when you see a lot of early arrivals at your next training session because it is bound to generate plenty of excitement.

- **Parent in goal:** Nothing livens up an ordinary shooting drill more than having the kids try to score when a parent is between the goalposts. You can turn it into a fun contest by having each child take five shots against their parent and see who ends up with the most goals. You can even switch the drill up by reversing positions and see how the parents fare trying to score against their youngster.

- **One-on-one:** Doing one-on-one drills between kids and their parents is a great way to boost the energy level during a training session that may be lacking intensity or enthusiasm. If you are doing a passing drill, have the child work with their parent and see how many successful passes each pair can make. If you're doing a drill working on attacking skills, have the child work on manoeuvring the ball past their parent while maintaining control of it.

Are you looking for other fun ways to entertain your young squad? Think back to your own childhood and the games you enjoyed playing at school or with neighbourhood friends during the summertime. Take those games and devise ways to work a football skill into them. You won't find this as difficult as you may think. To help you get those creative juices flowing, here are a few variations on a few classic kids' games:

- ✔ **Piggy in the middle:** Break the team into small groups of three. Each trio gets a ball and the object is for the two designated passers to keep the ball away from the defender in the middle. This drill has it all. Players get practice on their passing, receiving, and ball control, and the child in the middle gets to work on their defensive skills. Whenever the player in the middle is able to intercept a pass and win possession of the ball, they become one of the passers and the player they stole the ball from moves into the middle.

- ✔ **Stop and go:** This game helps your players develop quick reactions and improves their balance. Give each player a football. Position yourself 50 metres away from the players with your back to them. When you yell 'go', the players begin dribbling toward you. When you yell 'stop', you quickly turn around and whichever players you catch still moving with their ball are sent back to the starting line. Continue with the drill until you can see which players can successfully negotiate their way down the pitch without being stopped by you.

Make sure that you are creative with the older and more experienced kids. These youngsters who have been playing the sport for a few years are going to embrace any opportunities to showcase their skills against the other players on the team. The competitive juices start flowing at around age 12 and older, so any way you can come up with to meet their thirst for challenging competitions is an aid to their development and the team's overall progress. Here are a few ideas that you may want to incorporate into your training sessions.

- ✔ **Keep away from the coach:** Youngsters love chances to compete against – and beat – their coach. So here's a fun opportunity for them to try. Mark off a playing area with cones and give each youngster a ball. The purpose of the drill is for each child to try to keep control of their ball while the coach, and the assistants, try to kick the players' footballs out of the playing area. Such drills are ideal for getting a handle on ball control and shielding techniques, as well as a great confidence booster when they are able to hold off the coach. Another benefit that can be gained from this drill is that youngsters should gain insight into what the defenders did that gave them the most trouble or that caused them to lose possession of the ball, which they can employ when they are defending in a game.

Creating a Training Plan

A well-constructed training plan may take, dare we say it, a little practice on your part to get down. But after putting together a couple of them, you should get the hang of it. Putting together a quality training plan – and then being able to execute it – is sort of like putting together a giant jigsaw puzzle. You have all these pieces in front of you in the form of the skills you want to coach in and you probably have at least a general idea of the drills and techniques you want to use to do this. All you need to do is find the right spot to fit them all in and determining their most useful order during the allotted time you have with the team each week during the season.

Jotting down what skills you want to work on initially – and what you want to accomplish in those first couple of weeks of the season – helps jump-start your thought process and get you started along the way to mapping out useful training session plans. Once you've put those skills down, go ahead and break your session down even further into how much time you want to devote to each area. If you are able to train your team twice a week for an hour at a time, then you know that you have two hours this week to work with the kids and can break down how much time you want to spend on different aspects.

Devising your training session plans before practising with the team is a good idea. You certainly don't need to outline every aspect and drill of every training session you are planning to conduct this season all at once. That would be counter-productive because as your players develop skills and discover new ones, you need to be constantly changing your training sessions to accommodate their improved level of play. (See Chapter 5, which covers this aspect of evaluating your team and making the necessary adjustments in your coaching.)

When selecting drills, you want to avoid using those that turn out to be too easy for the kids, as not much skill improvement can then take place. You also want to steer clear of drills that are too difficult, which not only limits the amount of improvement that can take place, but also frustrates youngsters when they are unable to enjoy any level of success.

When selecting drills, consider the following:

- ✔ If you can't explain the drill in 15 seconds or less, it is probably far too complicated for this age level.

- ✔ By using variations of games like Piggy in the Middle (see the 'Putting smiles on their faces' section earlier in this chapter), these won't require much explanation on your part as the majority of kids have all played these games and know what they are all about.

✔ Don't waste a lot of training time setting cones up for each drill. You can also cut down on the amount of time you spend moving cones by using different drills that can be held in the same area you have marked off.

✔ Be prepared. It can't be said enough that preparation is vital for a smooth-running and effective training session. Even though you feel prepared because you have your training session all mapped out, some-times a drill or game you designed that you were sure was going to be a hit simply falls flat. So now what? Hopefully, on your training session plan you have a couple of back-up drills listed that you can resort to, if needed. You get a sense early on in a new drill whether the kids like it, and whether the drill is accomplishing what you intended. If not, you've got to be ready to make the switch and go with something else.

✔ Try to cut down on the number of elimination type drills that you work into training. These drills tend to knock out those lesser-skilled players who would actually benefit the most from additional repetitions. If you do conduct an elimination drill, as soon as players are knocked out you should have another drill set up for these players to participate in. The last thing you want is for youngsters to be eliminated from the drill and then standing around watching the team's most talented players carry on playing.

✔ When designing drills, try to make them game-like in nature. For exam-ple, if all your shooting drills involve kicking a ball into an empty net, when it comes to a game situation and a player is winding up to take a kick and all of a sudden now they're seeing a goalie standing in their way, which may throw them off because they haven't practised that before.

Putting it all together

After you have worked up a few drills that you want to use (see preceding section), it's time to put it all together. A sample one-hour training session for a team of 11- and 12-year-olds may look something like this:

✔ **Ten minutes:** Stretching and a light jog around the pitch to loosen up.

✔ **Five minutes:** Partner Passing. Pair the team up with a partner and spread out on the pitch. Start them five yards apart and each minute move them back a few yards so that they can work on passing and receiving from a variety of distances. During the last 15 seconds of the drill, have them pass and receive the ball with their less dominant foot.

- ✔ **Ten minutes:** 2-on-1 passing with a defender. Break the team into groups of three and scatter them around the pitch. The two attacking players attempt to pass the ball back and forth and keep it away from the defender. As soon as a player intercepts the ball, they take over as an attacking player and the player whose pass was intercepted assumes the role of defender.

- ✔ **Five minutes:** Corner kicks. Break the squad up into four separate groups and position them at the four corners of the pitch. Have an assistant coach or parent with each group to help retrieve loose balls to keep the drill moving.

- ✔ **Five minutes:** Penalty kicks. Remember to stress proper technique and following through at the target because kids often struggle with their technique in this area.

- ✔ **Five minutes:** Trapping with the chest and thigh. Before the drill begins, give a brief demonstration of how to do it.

- ✔ **Fifteen minutes:** Working on shots on goal/long passes. Break the team into three groups. Two groups work at each end of the pitch on making accurate kicks on the goal, while the other group works in the middle of the pitch on delivering long passes to teammates. After five minutes, rotate the groups.

- ✔ **Five minutes:** A game in which the team must complete three passes in a row before taking a shot on goal. Divide the team up, making sure that each side has roughly the same number of talented players so that one team doesn't dominate. During the last minute of the game, throw another ball into the mix. Having two balls going at the same time increases the excitement and concludes the training session on a positive note.

As you can see in the preceding sample schedule, this training session has a little bit of everything, which is ideal for maintaining interest and keeping the kids' enthusiasm high. Spending a lot of time on any one area won't bog down the training session. Training sessions like this where the skills and the drills are constantly changing keeps the kids' interest and doesn't allow any time for them to become distracted and lose focus.

You may wish to jot down little reminders for yourself. In the preceding sample, the coach has made a note to himself to remember to stress to the team the need for proper technique with their penalty kicks. Also, as this is only the team's second training session working on trapping with the chest and thigh, he's made a note to spend a moment going over how to perform the drill as a little refresher before turning the kids loose on their own.

Of course, you can be flexible with your schedule and adjust it according to how the training session is progressing. For example, during the 2-on-1 passing drill you may see that a number of players are really struggling. So, you may want to run this drill another couple of minutes and just reduce the amount of time you spend in a game at the end of training. Your training session plan doesn't have to be carved in stone, but use it as your guide to helping your team progress during their time with you.

While the basic elements of a good training session plan should remain consistent, the drills you do and the way you approach coaching them can constantly be changing to keep pace with the demands and improved play of your youngsters. Evaluate your training session later that evening while the day's events are still fresh in your mind. This helps you determine which skills should be taught in a different manner, which drills the kids liked, and which ones should perhaps be discarded all together.

You can even keep a training notebook – your own personal diary of the season – in order to best monitor progress and keep track of all sorts of important factors. Make note of what training objectives were achieved and which ones should be followed up at the next training session. Did the kids have fun during the drills? If there was a drill for passing that the team really seemed to enjoy, highlight it in your notebook and use it again at some point during the season. Conversely, if there was a drill that just didn't create a whole lot of enthusiasm among your troops, or that didn't produce the desired results you were looking for, you are probably not going to want to run that one again in the future.

Figuring out how long and how often

Sometimes coaches have a tough time curbing their enthusiasm. After all, when you see kids acquiring skills and improving – and hopefully having lots of fun in the process – it can be tempting to naturally want to spend more time with them during the week than they actually want to spend with you. The league should have suggestions or even rules regarding how often and how long a coach may practise with their team. Make sure that you check, as you need to be aware of any such policies before you can begin to create training plans for your team. If the league doesn't have any policies in place, exercise your best judgement when devising the team schedule.

With youngsters just starting out in the sport, you want to give them an introduction to football and show them basic skills that they can build on the following year, if they choose to continue with the sport. You don't want to overwhelm them by cramming their weeks full of training sessions and games. One training session a week, for an hour, is plenty for children at this level who also generally have one game a week to play in. As they get older, you can bump it up to a couple of training sessions a week they have just one game on the schedule that week. Only at the older and more advanced levels should your training sessions last longer than an hour.

Thinking about practice games

Practice games are a great way to give kids a taste of what playing in an actual game is like. But you should be careful not to overuse them at the expense of skill development drills. Practice games reduce the number of touches that a child gets with the ball, so they should never be the foundation of your training session. A few minutes at the end of training just to get the kids accustomed to performing the skills they have been practising in a game-like setting is fine.

Rather than conduct a full-scale game, if your team is large enough, you can break them into four smaller teams and run two games simultaneously on each half of the pitch. This increases the amount of touches of the ball a child gets. Also, with a small-sided game, each child is more likely to have to perform a variety of skills. In a full-scale game, they may only get a chance to be a forward and score a goal with so many players involved. But, in the small-scale game, they are more likely to have to play in defence and try to win the ball, or make a pass to a teammate going down the pitch.

You can also get really creative and turn an ordinary practice game into an exciting one simply by adjusting the rules here and there to mix things up for the kids. Not only do you increase the fun, but you also enhance the skill development of your players and leave them begging for more at the next training session. Here are a few ways that you can improvise on those traditional practice games:

- ✔ **Passing points:** Sometimes getting the message across to children that passing is an important part of the game can be a little difficult. After all, kids love kicking and scoring goals, so the skill of passing to a teammate often takes a back seat on their priority list – but not in this practice game. The way this practice is set up, a team that successfully completes a designated number of passes in a row while maintaining possession of the ball receives a point, the same as if they had scored a goal. The younger and less advanced the players' skills are, the fewer passes they must complete. This way, passing, receiving, ball control and possession – all-important skills – become as important as scoring goals.

✔ **Lefty-righty:** During games, players are forced to make passes and receive passes with their weaker foot, as well as even take occasional shots on goal with their weaker foot as the situation dictates. Developing this skill can often be overlooked during the course of training sessions, when players are naturally going to use their more dominant foot whenever possible to pass, kick, and receive balls. A good way to break them of that habit is to conduct a practice game where all touches on the ball must be made with the youngster's weaker foot. Or you can conduct a regular game but award a bonus point for a goal scored by a player using their weaker foot; or a bonus point for a pass made by the less dominant foot that resulted in a goal. Making these slight adjustments gradually helps the players become more comfortable and accustomed to using both feet and enhance their overall enjoyment of the game.

✔ **Football mania:** Getting kids a lot of touches on the ball is one of the biggest training objectives for all football coaches. Lots of touches lead to skill development. Holding a practice game in which two or three footballs are in play at the same time can be beneficial for several reasons. Foremost, young kids will love the action-packed game with plenty of balls bouncing around to keep their attention. Secondly, with the additional balls in play, your players get the chance to experience two and three times the regular action they would see in a typical game. It also builds their timing, enhances their co-ordination and improves their reaction skills. Bottom line, a multi-football game provides endless benefits, and leaves the kids smiling at the conclusion.

Ensuring lots of touches for each child

Monotonous training sessions that children have to be dragged to by their parents will be the downfall of your season and a roadblock to their development and interest in the sport. By constantly keeping a ball at their feet, you keep a smile on their faces. Here are a few ways to ensure that every child gets lots of touches of the ball at training:

✔ **Always break drills down into the smallest number of players possible.** Use your assistant coaches, recruit parents, do whatever it takes to make sure that children never have to wait in line for too long to participate in a drill.

✔ **Scale down your practice games.** Always have a couple of smaller games going than one big game where children don't see the ball quite as often. (For more on practice games, see the preceding section.)

✔ **Re-examine your drills.** Keep a close eye not just on the kids, but your drills, as well. See whether the kids are getting a lot of time with the ball. If not, you probably want to revise the drill or eliminate it from your future training sessions.

✔ **Keep your explanations short.** Give short demonstrations while introducing a new skill or going over a drill. The longer you spend talking, the less time the kids have to play.

Letting kids help select training session drills

As you negotiate your way through the season, make a note of those drills that the kids really seem to enjoy and that seem to be the most beneficial for them. For young kids, you can give each of the drills a fun name that gets their attention. For example, using the name Purple Bear carries a lot more meaning to them than simply calling it the 2-on-1 drill.

As the season progresses, you may want to consider setting aside a segment of your training session each week for each child to select their favourite drill for the team to do. This is a great way to include all the kids in the training session and really make them feel a part of what is going on. It also gives you a good idea of what types of drills the kids like. Obviously, you may want to discard or rethink drills that no child picks if you continue coaching this age group.

You can even ask older and more advanced kids if they would like to use drills that they may fondly remember from other coaches they have played for over the years. Don't think that you're wrong to incorporate another coach's drill into your training session. If the kids have fun, and the drill's effective in getting them to work on a particular skill, find room for it in your training sessions.

Setting the tone

The tone you set at the first training session of the season – and carry throughout – should be one built around praise, encouragement, and positive feedback rather than criticism, harsh instruction, and negativity.

You set the tone for your training sessions by your mood and attitude. If you played football growing up, or any sport for that matter, you can probably recall those days when you showed up for training and the coach was in a foul mood. What did you do? You and your teammates grumbled to each other about what a miserable afternoon was in store for you. How much fun and discovery do you think those sessions produced? Probably none at all. In order to have the most effective training sessions, you have to arrive in a positive mood every day. Regardless of what is going on outside your life as a football coach, you've got to portray a positive attitude to your players. That means keeping your head up, walking with a spring in your step, and wearing a smile on your face. You won't even have to say a word. By using this approach, your players should recognise from your body language that you are in a positive mood, and this translates into the team starting training off on the right foot.

As the leader of the training session, you wield all the power when it comes to influencing whether training is going to be something your young players look forward to or dread. Good attitudes are infectious. Do your best to spread yours around for everyone to soak up.

Get the coach is a great drill to get young kids to loosen up at the first training session and start to get them comfortable with you. Give each of the kids a ball. The idea is for them to touch you while maintaining control of their football, while you do your best to dodge all the youngsters coming your way. It gets the kids running around, laughing and having fun right away, which is what you want to start off the season on a high note. Plus, it actually doubles as not just a team ice-breaker, but a skill-building drill as well because the kids reworking on moving with the ball and controlling it, without even realising it.

Keeping things consistent

Kids are going to benefit the most from training sessions that are run in the same manner all season long. If they know what to expect, they are going to arrive at the pitch prepared and ready to participate. If they are caught off guard because you have deviated from how you've run training sessions in the past, then you are probably not going to get their best effort.

Doing the same stretches and warm-ups each training session provides kids with a nice routine before they get into the heart of the session. Instead of pairing up the kids to work on their passing back and forth or their ball receiving, encourage any parents who are willing to take part in this part of training with their child. By doing this you can help the parent, who may not be familiar with football, find out the proper techniques of a skill so that they may work with their child at home during the week. If the parents are interested, you may even want to give them additional drills that they can do at home with their child to work on various skills.

Making Training Time Beneficial

Everyone cringes when stuck in a lengthy grocery store checkout queue to purchase a simple loaf of bread and milk. One of the last things you want to do is to put your young players through that on the football pitch. In order to maximise your training time with the team, your top priority should be to minimise the standing around time. Standing in a queue is acceptable at amusement parks and cinemas – not on the football pitch.

Waiting around drains the fun out of a training session and is a real deterrent to discovery and skill development, which are the basis of a productive training session. Be sure not to have too many lulls between your drills, too, which can bring the momentum of the activity to a screeching halt. You want the energy and enthusiasm of one drill to carry over into the next. This not only maximises every second of your training session, it doesn't allow kids to become bored or their attention to drift to what is happening on the pitch across from them or what their little brother is doing on the sidelines.

Remember, when players and balls are on the move, skill improvement is taking place. When players look like statues, improvement stops. Avoid long lines, mind-numbing laps, and long-winded lectures. It's all up to you whether children arrive at your training sessions with a bounce in their step or their shoulders slumping.

Make sure that you praise every player during the course of your training session. Children know when their efforts haven't been appreciated. You never want a child to leave the training ground without ever hearing a single word of praise or recognition for their efforts. If you have to, have your squad's names written down on your clipboard and as you move throughout the training session, each time you give positive feedback to a player simply mark an X next to their name. This way you can easily monitor how your praise is being divided up and you won't commit the coaching sin of failing to recognise a child.

Recognising the high points

Children love and relate to contact. A high-five is a great way to acknowledge a special move or improvement of a skill. Be creative. Do low-fives, where you and the player have your hand as low to the ground as possible. Kids eat this up and really focus on performing a drill or skill the right way if they know you are waiting there to slap hands with them. As a coach, when you go out of your way to acknowledge a player, that player is going to go out of their way and give it their very best to continue receiving that praise. Now, that's a winning situation for everyone involved.

When skills are performed the wrong way, never shout negative comments. Reserve that tone of voice for when you really need it, such as for a discipline problem (see Chapter 19). A negative voice often makes the child afraid of making another mistake, which handcuffs their ability to play the game. Mistakes are a part of football and if children feel that you're allowing no room for errors, they are going to be less likely to want the ball for fear of making a mistake.

Let players know what improvements need to be made in their game and, most importantly, how to make those corrections successfully and consistently. If the majority of your comments centre on dissecting what they are doing wrong, you are contributing to why they are not performing up to their capabilities and fuelling their fear of failure. Young players want to please their coach and avoid the negative consequences of failing. Consequently, they begin to think too much about what they are doing to avoid a possible mistake rather than just going out and performing and doing their best.

Your youngsters will enjoy participating for you if positive reinforcement and praise dominate your interactions with them. You need to remember that establishing a positive environment is one step in creating a place where athletes like to be involved. You can be demanding while being positive. You can offer constructive criticism and still be encouraging. Good coaches find the balance between the two to help their young players reach their full potential.

By all means, point out things that a child isn't doing well, but be sure to sandwich the comment around positive feedback, as well. For example, 'Sandy, that was excellent how you planted your foot, but I noticed you were looking down at the ball when you kicked it rather than looking up to see who was unmarked. And I loved how you followed through on the kick. That's the way to put all your power behind it.' This way, the child picks up a tip from the coach that she needs to be more aware of what is happening on the pitch around her and her self-esteem gets a nice boost because the coach recognised how well she kicked the ball.

We all love to get recognition for a job well done. When the boss points out that we did something well – particularly in front of our peers – it means a lot. Vocal acknowledgement yelled out for the entire team to hear can really have an impact on a youngster. That type of praise is equally powerful – if not more so – in the mind of a developing child who is probably unsure of their skills and maybe questions their ability.

Give specific, performance-based feedback to players rather than general comments lacking performance-related information. Comments such as 'go on son' and 'that's it' probably aren't going to mean a whole lot to a child. Zero in on exactly what you're applauding the player for. Saying something along the lines of, 'that's the way to follow through on your shot' packs much more punch and is more likely to stick in the child's head every time they prepare to take a shot.

With kids who already have a basic knowledge of how to perform skills, you still want to praise them for performing skills the proper way, but you don't want to go overboard where you begin to lose credibility with the team. You don't want to overlook errors just for the sake of avoiding bringing it up with a player. After all, part of your job is to spot errors, and rather than dwell on them, work to help the child correct them and become more efficient in that area of their game. Children who are showered with excessive praise for performances that they know border on mediocre or are not their best, may begin to tune you out. Also, their respect for you and your knowledge of the sport may drop down a level or two, and that's tough to get back during the remainder of the season.

Building skills

The sport of football is truly unique because it requires a wide range of skills that use assorted body parts like the head, chest, thigh, shin, and all areas of the foot. During your training sessions with younger children, you are introducing them to some of the basics of the game: kicking, passing and receiving, dribbling, tackling, and goalkeeping. As they start to get a handle on those drills, you can begin to give them a feel for other areas of the game, such as trapping and heading.

While skills such as throw-ins, corner kicks, penalty kicks, and direct and indirect kicks usually aren't always used in leagues at the younger levels, you may want to briefly introduce your team to these concepts later in the season once they have a pretty good handle on other basics of the game. This helps to prepare those kids who are planning to continue on with the sport next season.

Helping those who need it

Even if a child is struggling to pick up a certain skill after repeated tries, be sure to acknowledge their effort. Eventually they will make improvements in this area of their game. In the meantime, the fact that they never give up and are constantly working, even when things aren't going well, are great attributes that are not only going to benefit them during their football career, but also carry over into their every day adult life. Reward effort as much as outcome. Repeated effort, especially in the face of failure and adversity, is one of the most important ingredients for future success.

If a youngster just can't quite get a handle on a skill, instead of telling them what they are doing wrong, show them how they can correct it. Demonstrate to them yourself, and then let them copy your move. It may be tempting when you spot a player doing something wrong, to tell them to watch Jimmy do the drill. This immediately sends the message that Jimmy is better than they are, so rather than helping the player improve this particular skill you have damaged their self-esteem. Take the time to show the player exactly what you mean and acknowledge even the slightest improvement the next time they perform the drill to keep them headed on the right track.

Do your best to avoid the paralysis by analysis that you have probably heard of before. Basically, you want to avoid giving the child so much instruction and information that their brain goes into overload and they aren't able to perform even the most basic skills. Instead of helping them improve, you actually push them back further in their development.

When a child makes a mistake, remind them what the proper way is to perform this skill. This reminder should be a positive approach rather than a negative comment. For example, it is far more beneficial to say, 'Remember to follow through with your leg toward the target when you kick,' than to say 'you didn't follow through again,' or 'I told you to follow through last time, how could you forget?'

Ending on a Positive Note

Ending your training sessions on a positive note sends the kids home happy and, just as important, have them anxiously looking forward to the next training session. How do you do that? Saving your best drill or practice game idea for the final minutes of training is one of the most effective coaching tricks around for concluding on a high note. Think of it as like when you go out to dinner. You start with an appetiser, and work up to the main course that you have been looking forward to. Basically, you save the best for last. So, view the final session of training as the main course. While you certainly want all your drills to be fun, using those that generate the most excitement and enthusiasm at the end of the session ensures that everyone goes home happy.

Before you turn the kids loose to their parents, have a quick team talk. Because the kids have just had a really good time and their spirits are going to be up, this is a great opportunity for you to give their confidence another boost.

Talk to the players about how proud you are of them for working so hard and doing their best. Point out that you are seeing steady improvement in their play and how impressed you are about how quickly they are picking up new skills. You should usually speak in general terms about the entire team at this point. If you recognise just a few players for their outstanding training, you run the risk of alienating those children who may have turned in their best effort of the season but yet head home somewhat disappointed that you didn't acknowledge them.

Sometimes you should single out a player or two. Perhaps a youngster who has really been struggling with his passing skills did really well in the passing drill today. Pointing out what a great job that player did while you are praising the entire team is a great way to boost the spirits of a player who isn't enjoying as much success as most of his teammates. Use your best discretion. As you get to know the kids and spend time around them, you get a sense for what is best.

This post-training session chat is not the time to go over an area of the game that a lot of players may be struggling in, or to rehash a drill that didn't go well because some of the kids weren't focused or for whatever reason were having problems executing. You never want to send kids home feeling that they disappointed you or failed to perform up to expectations. Even in those training sessions where nothing seems to go right – and there are days like that during the course of every season – you've got to find a nugget to praise and build on for the following training session. Even complimenting them on how they are chasing down loose balls is good, since those are great qualities you would love to have ingrained in every player.

Serving as a role model

As a youth football coach, the training sessions you devise are going to have a direct impact on each child's development and enjoyment of the sport. While you may not have given this much thought, while you are at training you are in a unique position to impact more than just each youngster's ability to kick a football or deliver an accurate pass. By becoming the coach, you have stepped into a special and important position of role model, coach, and friend all rolled up into one. The players on your team are going to look up to you for leadership, guidance, and perhaps even advice in areas that don't encompass the actual sport of football itself. By taking the time to observe, listen, and talk to your team about other areas of life, you can make a positive difference for them.

With older children, you can use events in the news as coaching points. Perhaps a well-known athlete that the kids are familiar with who has been suspended for using performance-enhancing drugs. You can ask the kids what they think about this. Get their thoughts on if they think this is cheating and if they are disappointed that she was using illegal substances to gain a competitive advantage. Getting the kids to talk to you about the issue, instead of you always instructing them, can be a great way to get good dialogue going. And during an

appropriate time in the conversation, you can share your views on the issue and use it to reinforce the importance of children staying away from these harmful substances.

- ✔ **Performance-enhancing drugs and supplements:** Many youngsters may be interested in taking these substances because of their desire to become bigger, stronger, and a better football player, without really understanding the health consequences of their actions. Talk to your team about the dangers of using performance-enhancing drugs and supplements and stress that they can receive the same benefits through hard work and dedicated practice, which is also a much safer route.

- ✔ **Tobacco:** The dangers of using tobacco are well documented, but those messages may not be getting through to youngsters. Studies indicate that an increasing number of secondary school students use some form of tobacco. Talk to your players about the dangers of using any forms of tobacco and how it not only affects their health, but also hinders performance. A warning is sure to carry a little more weight when a child begins to think in terms of not being able to run down the pitch as fast as another player, for example.

Finally, spend just a few seconds going over the schedule for the week. Double check that everyone is coming to the next game, and update any schedule changes that may have developed due to postponements or other factors. Thank them for listening to your instruction and working hard, and call it a day.

Chapter 7

Match Day

*Y*ou've spent the week conducting training sessions, working on skills and providing instruction to your players. Now, match day has arrived, and it's time for the team to put all the skills you've coached them into good use. It also means that you suddenly have an entirely new list of responsibilities that you may not have been aware of when you took up the coaching reins this season. You've got opposing coaches and referees to meet, a football pitch to inspect, and a starting line-up to create. You have warm-ups to oversee, a pre-match team talk to deliver and half-time adjustments to be made. You've also got substitutions to monitor, instructions to communicate, and a post-match talk to give to wrap up the day.

Being on the sidelines for a youth football game requires you to be not just a coach, but a supporter, tactician of the game, a master motivator, and a constant model of good sportsmanship all rolled up into one. Yes, it's a big responsibility but certainly one that you are equipped to handle. You've spent large chunks of time preparing your team to run out onto the pitch. This chapter prepares you to handle Match Day as well, and all that comes with it.

Understanding Your Pre-game Responsibilities

Match day may be an entirely new experience for you, just as it is to many of your players. You may be somewhat surprised to find out that your match-day tasks extend beyond tactics, substituting players, and providing enthusiastic support from the sidelines. Before your team runs onto the pitch you've got a few tasks to fulfil. The following sections guide you through your pre-game responsibilities.

Don't forget to arrive at the match early. You want to make sure that you leave plenty of time to inspect the pitch and meet the opposition. An hour or so before kick-off is a good amount of time to aim for.

Inspect the pitch

Before you allow your youngsters to take to the pitch you, and your assistant coaches, should carefully inspect the entire playing area. Keep an eye out for hazards such as broken glass, loose rocks, a raised sprinkler head, a loose piece of turf, or anything else that could injure a child during the course of play. Don't rely on the opposing coach or a member of the league's grounds crew to do this. Remember, every player participating in the game is your responsibility and every step you can take to help ensure their safety and well-being is going to benefit them. Many pitches are public areas so take a plastic bag to remove any dog's mess.

Often games are played one after the other at a local facility, but don't skirt the pre-game pitch check just because another game was just played there and you think that everything is fine. You don't know if anyone else has done a check of the pitch throughout the day, and it never hurts to have another set of eyes take a look anyway. Plus, with the pitch getting plenty of use, you never know whether someone has torn up a chunk of grass that may trip a young player if not properly replaced before the game begins.

Meet with the opposing coach and officials

It is always a good idea before the game starts to head over and shake the hand of the opposing coach. A trip to the other side of the pitch displays a sign of good sportsmanship. It also sets a good example for the players on both teams, as well as for all of the other spectators.

During this chat, inform the other coach if any of your kids have any special needs and find out if any of his do as well – and then make the necessary accommodations or come up with suggestions that are fair for everyone involved. If one of his kids has a vision problem, for example, and has a problem seeing the ball coming right at him, perhaps you can suggest that, if it hits the child in the hands and the team doesn't gain an unfair advantage from it, the official should just let play continue. Let the coach decide, but by demonstrating that you are willing to ensure that each child on both teams has a fun and rewarding experience, you set the tone for a great day of football and further reduce the chances of problems arising during the game.

Meeting with the referee officiating your game is another example of good sportsmanship. When you introduce yourself to the officials, let them know that you would like to be informed if any of your players say or do anything that is unsportsmanlike. The same goes for any comments from parents or other spectators, as well. Remember, you want to do everything you can to work with the officials – not against them. Just because they are wearing a black shirt doesn't mean that they aren't doing their best for the kids, just like you are.

During your meeting with the referee alert her if any of the children on your team have any special needs, such as a hearing or vision problem. If the official knows this information beforehand, she can make the proper adjustments. For example, if a child has a hearing problem and may not hear the official's whistle being blown during the game, the official can make a hand signal to the child to let her know the whistle has been blown and play has been stopped. Being considerate to all children and meeting their needs is a big part of being a top-quality football coach.

Holding a Pre-game Team Meeting

Conducting a pre-game team talk is an important piece of the match-day experience for youngsters. Letting kids know what is going to be taking place right up until kick off is enormously beneficial to them. Here are some tips to keep in mind when holding this meeting:

- ✔ **Meet with the team away from the parents:** Choose a spot to gather the team that eliminates as many potential distractions as possible. Children, especially younger ones, have extremely short attention spans and are going to be easily distracted by everything going on near the pitch. If, from their vantage point in the pre-game team talk, they can see their mum or dad, or any other family members who have shown up to watch the game, they aren't going to be listening to what you are saying. Such distraction dramatically limits the effectiveness of your talk. Also, avoid being near the other team. Kids naturally want to see who is on the other team and watch them warm-up and compare their abilities to their own, which is another distraction that you don't need to contend with during this time.

- ✔ **Keep your talk brief:** Your talk isn't the time for a long-winded state of the team address. Remember, kids have short attention spans, their minds are going to wander and they are going to start squirming if you turn this into a one giant speech. You are best off keeping your talk with younger kids to five minutes or less. The last thing you want to do is defuse the players' energy and enthusiasm for the game by delivering a lengthy talk.

✔ **Relax:** Speak to the team in a calm and relaxed manner. If you appear nervous or uptight, your players are going to be more likely to develop those same feelings, which can infringe on their performance. If you are laughing and joking, the team can feed off that and they should approach the game in a much more relaxed manner.

✔ **It's all about having fun:** Stress that the most important thing is for everyone to do their best and to have fun. If the kids genuinely believe that, it frees them up to play better. They also won't be fearful of making a mistake or losing a game.

✔ **Good sportsmanship matters:** Remind them to display good sportsmanship at all times; to show respect toward officials, regardless of what decisions are made; and to shake the hands of the opposing team at the end of the game, regardless of who wins. Don't replicate the many examples of bad sportsmanship your kids see in youth sports these days. You have an opportunity to make your team a model of good sportsmanship in your league, and one that others strive to emulate.

✔ **Brief recap of warm-up:** Spend a brief moment going over the pre-game warm-up to refresh the kids' memories on the order of the stretches and drills.

✔ **Team cheer:** For the younger children, one idea is to conclude the talk with a team huddle, or have everyone put their hands together with a chant of '1-2-3...(insert name of team)!' or '1-2-3 Together!' Besides being symbolic, a chant is a final helpful gesture that reminds all the players that football is a team sport and that everyone must work together.

During your talk with the team, make sure that everyone has all the necessary kit – typically shinguards at the younger levels. Also, in more advanced levels of play, make sure that each child has brought boots with studs that meet the league regulations. Children should never be allowed on the pitch without all the proper safety equipment (refer to Chapter 4). Also, check to make sure that everyone has their water bottles. A good team rule to enforce is that every child must bring a water bottle to all training sessions and games.

Fire up your team with an inspirational talk

A big part of coaching comes down to motivation. In order to get the best out of your players, you've got to inspire them to want to get the most out of their ability every time they step on the pitch. Such inspiration can be a pretty challenging endeavour. A motivational talk can be a great tool to get everyone fired up and excited about performing their best in the game – if it is structured the right way.

You already know that the kids on your team are all vastly different in their emotional make-up, and this is magnified on match day. Some are already going to possess that inner drive and are going to arrive at the pitch anxious to get under way and compete against their peers. Others are going to be excited simply because it's the chance to wear a cool football strip and see their friends. And there are those youngsters petrified that they are going to have to kick a football while all sorts of unfamiliar faces are watching every move they make very closely from the sidelines.

So, how do you approach this motivational talk? Well, it isn't the time to deliver any 'Win one for the coach' speeches or to repeat a spirited talk one of your old football coaches may have given to you and your teammates years ago. It is the time to get everyone to focus as a team and work together. If you handle your motivational talk the right way, you should find that your players are hanging on every word and embracing what you have to say. If you can accomplish this, the focus and positive energy should spill over onto the pitch, where it can really pay big dividends for you and your team. Here are some tips to consider regarding your pre-game team talk to help ensure that your words pack some punch.

- ✔ **Be positive:** Touch on areas of the game that the team has shown progress in during the week and let them know that you are looking forward to seeing them put those skills into action today.

- ✔ **Avoid pressure phrases:** Stay away from saying things such as, 'Let's score five goals today', or 'Let's hold them to two goals'. While these phrases may seem motivational in nature, keep in mind that children can only give you their best effort; they can't control the outcome of games.

- ✔ **Focus on your team:** Talk about your team, your players and how confident you are in their abilities. It's not going to do you, or your team, much good to discuss the strengths and weaknesses of a team they may know very little about. Positive reinforcement of their own skills gives them that extra boost of confidence to perform up to their capabilities.

- ✔ **Stay away from clichés:** Overused sports clichés such as 'no pain, no gain' are laughable, not motivational. You don't need to resort to these types of sayings to get the most out of your players. Speaking from the heart with genuine passion serves you and your team far better in the long run.

- ✔ **Look back:** Reflect back on your playing days in youth sport. Whether it was football, or some other sport, you probably remember some of the speeches that you heard prior to games. Some were no doubt wonderfully good, while others were beyond awful. Draw from your playing experiences. Steal from the good speeches, and stay away from the bad ones. If you didn't participate in sports as a child, that certainly doesn't mean you aren't qualified to give a motivational talk. Speak from the heart. Put yourself in those small football boots of your youngsters.

Think about what you would want to hear from an adult if you were in their position. What would get you excited and pumped up ready to play your best? Incorporate those thoughts and ideas into your talk and you can't lose.

Assign positions

Before you even get to the pitch, you should have your starting line-up mapped out, as well as your substitution rotation firmly in place. Having a plan helps ensure that everyone gets an equal amount of playing time. If you don't plan this out ahead of time, once the game starts it is virtually impossible to keep track of how much time and which position each child has played. Remember, every child on the team signed up to play, not to sit on the bench and watch. You may want to delegate to an assistant coach the responsibility of monitoring playing time to ensure that it is equally distributed throughout the game.

Take a moment to go over the line-up with your players. By announcing who is playing where ahead of time, the players won't be caught off guard or surprised once it is kick-off time. Letting them know the line-up well in advance also gives them time to mentally prepare for their responsibilities.

Keep instructions simple

Children are naturally going to have a lot on their young minds when they arrive at the pitch. They may be wondering if they know any of the kids on the other team, if Grandma brought enough film for the camera, and what kind of snacks they're getting after the game. If you're coaching a team of older and more advanced kids, they may be looking to turn in an impressive performance to help the team win the game. So, you want to simplify everything you do when it comes to instructions. The less technical the better. The following are a few tips to keep in mind when it comes to keeping those instructions simple:

- **Don't overwhelm:** It is not a good idea to overload the team with a lot of discussion about game strategies or fancy formations. This simply isn't the time or place to pile on the instruction. Also, never introduce anything that hasn't already been covered several times during the course of your training sessions.

- **Avoid confusing phrases:** Football has a unique language all its own, so stay away from using phrases and terms that kids are unfamiliar with. If you haven't spent any time during your training sessions discussing marking, for example, then it's hardly realistic to expect a youngster to comprehend if you yell out that term to them in the middle of the action.

✔ **Be specific:** Children relate best to specific instructions that are easily understood and implemented. Using general terms like 'get back in defence' are often confusing and unproductive. A specific remark, such as 'Jimmy, cover number eight going down the line' can prove to be much more beneficial.

✔ **Sidestep repetitiveness:** You don't want to sound like a broken record saying the same things over and over. Otherwise, your players may begin to ignore you. For example, continually shouting 'go, go, go' every time one of your players breaks free with the ball doesn't serve any purpose other than to get on the nerves of your players. Vary your comments. Avoid giving the same instructions. If you find yourself repeating the same instructions, you may want to take a close look at spending more time on that skill in your upcoming training sessions because that may be a sign that the team needs additional work in that area.

✔ **Cover pitch conditions:** During your pre-game check of the pitch, you may have noticed some uneven spots, or a part of the pitch that may have some rough patches that can make passing more difficult. Make sure that you inform your players of these areas as they can impact the game or a player's ability to dribble the ball. Even if the pitch is in great shape, pay attention to the length of the grass. A closely trimmed pitch plays faster than a pitch that has longer grass. If the grass is long, make sure that your players are aware that they have to put a little more force behind their passes to get these passes to teammates. The pre-game warm-up, discussed in the next section, also helps them get accustomed to the conditions that they may not have any experience playing in.

In the more advanced levels of football, the conditions of the pitch can have a larger impact on the game. Wet or rainy conditions translate into a faster-paced game as the ball travels across the grass much quicker than usual. A wet ball is more slippery and a little more difficult to control. Wet conditions can create havoc with timing on passes to teammates, as well as make trapping and tackling a little trickier. Taking just a few seconds to relay that information to your team helps them get into the proper mindset as they take to the pitch for their pre-game warm-up session.

Conducting Your Warm-Up

A good pre-game warm-up is comprised of activities that get kids' bodies loosened up, gradually elevate their heart rate and prepare them for competition. Your aim during the pre-game warm-up is to prepare kids for competition, which is the best route to ensuring an overall good performance by the entire team. Youngsters taking to the pitch with muscles stretched and bodies loose have a reduced chance of suffering an injury, are more mobile and quicker to the ball, and are more likely to perform at a higher level.

The older the child, the more susceptible they are to muscle pulls and strains. A warm-up is about getting kids to perform at their optimal levels. During the warm-up, you want to create a positive environment that has players confidently performing skills and enthusiastically looking forward to the game. Warm-up is less about coaching and more about preparing kids. Throughout your dealings with the team, you want to send positive messages through your words, facial expressions, and body language. An upbeat, positive attitude creates a positive and upbeat tempo that is conducive to a great warm-up.

In many youth football clubs, you may only see the kids once a week for a one-hour training session between games. So, it may be four or five days since your last training session. With the hectic schedules many families have these days, a lot of the youngsters on your team probably haven't even touched a football since you saw them last. So, a good pre-game warm-up helps to reintroduce them to some of the skills that you worked on at your last training session and get them reacquainted with the feel of running and kicking a football.

Keep the following tips in mind when putting together your pre-match warm-up:

- ✔ **Keep the drills light:** You want the kids to get loosened up gradually. Remind them to go at no more than half speed in the beginning. You don't want them going full speed throughout the entire warm-up so that by the time the game begins they are gasping for breath.

- ✔ **Cover all the muscle groups:** You want the pre-game warm-up to involve all the major muscle groups that will be used during the game. That means stretches for the hamstrings, calves, neck, and back. You don't want to wear these muscle groups out so that the exercise hampers a child's productivity. You simply want them to get these areas of the body warmed up and prepared for the game.

- ✔ **Confidence boosters:** While the team is stretching, this is a good opportunity for you to work your way around to all the players and provide a little extra encouragement. A pat on the back, a wink of the eye, or a general comment about how you are looking forward to watching them play today gives kids that extra little shot of confidence that can make a big difference in their play and how much they enjoy the game.

- ✔ **Involve all the skills:** Besides getting your team loosened up, you want to get them comfortable performing all the skills they require during the game, with the same types of movements. For example, when players are warming up shooting, it's a good idea to have them kicking a moving ball rather than a stationary one, because seldom in a game will they be kicking a non-moving ball. That means making sure that they get a few repetitions in all areas of the game, such as passing, receiving, and trapping, among others.

✔ **Rehearse your pre-match warm-ups:** During your training sessions, spend a few minutes going over with the team how they need to warm-up before their games. You don't want to waste valuable time organising players, introducing unfamiliar warm-up drills and bombarding your players with instructions when their attention is going to be on the game that is just minutes away.

✔ **Relaxation time:** Don't conduct your pre-match warm-ups right up until the start of the game. Ideally, you want to give the kids a couple minutes to get a drink of water and compose themselves before they step onto the pitch for the actual game. This little break can also be used as a final opportunity by you to remind them to have fun and do their best, before you send them out to compete.

The following is a sample of a pre-game warm-up that can be used:

✔ **Five minutes:** Callisthenics and light stretching. Break it down into a minute or so of jumping jacks to get the heart pumping, followed by stretches for the legs, trunk, neck, and arms. The older your players, the more in-depth the stretching should be. With younger kids just starting out in the sport, you just want to get them in a routine of stretching before activities so that as they continue on in the sport they have already begun developing healthy pre-game habits.

✔ **Five minutes:** Break the team into pairs and have them passing the ball back and forth to one another. Every few passes, have each player take a couple steps backward so they get work on passing and receiving at various distances. Stepping back also helps them get a feel for the ball and get their timing right. It also gives them a feel for what type of pitch conditions they are playing on that day. Make sure that the players use both feet in both their passing and receiving.

✔ **Five minutes:** Conclude the warm-up with a few quick drills that are game-like in nature. Running some 2-on-1 drills or 3-on-2 drills gets the kids acclimatised to having to make a pass or take a shot while contending with defensive pressure; and it gives your defensive players a chance to adjust to making tackles and pursuing the ball.

For more on warming up, see Chapter 18.

Kick Off!

The players have (hopefully) listened to your pre-game talk. They have gone through the warm-ups. They have taken their positions on the pitch for the start of the game. The ball is in play. While your players' skills are being put to the test on the pitch, your game management skills are also to be tested. All of a sudden, you've got to work the sideline motivating your players, communicating with them, and rotating them in and out of the game to ensure equal playing time.

Motivating during the game

Motivating kids is a never-ending part of being a successful youth football coach. Even though you may have delivered your best pre-game motivational speech, it can be rendered meaningless if you don't keep it going by positively motivating your players during the game.

During games, youngsters may become frustrated that skills that they had no problem performing at training just a couple days ago aren't going nearly as well now. You've got to convince your players that they are playing well and instil in them the confidence to keep plugging away out there.

Here are a few tips to keep in mind when it comes to motivating players during the game:

- ✔ **Don't suffocate:** Allow kids plenty of room to make some of their own decisions during the game. If you are constantly shouting instructions and telling them what to do every step of the way, you may hinder their growth and development in the sport. Yes, they are going to make mistakes, but that's all part of playing football and discovering the sport. Giving children the freedom to play and to make some of their own decisions fuels their growth and enhances their development.

- ✔ **Ease up on the yelling:** Your team is going to be excited on game day, and chances are, you will be as well. Keep your emotions in check and refrain from spending the entire game shouting instructions to every player who is on the ball. It can be disconcerting to players to hear their coach's voice booming every time they are involved in the action. Yes, you want to get a coaching point across at specific points in the game and the only way to deliver it is to shout it out to your players. Just be sure to convey the instruction in a positive manner. If you deliver instructions in a negative fashion or frustrated tone, they will not be readily accepted by the players and may be detrimental to their productivity.

- ✔ **Stand still:** A coach who runs up and down the sideline all game long – whether it's shouting instructions or simply being a supporter – can be a distraction to the players trying their best to focus on the game. If you find yourself getting an aerobic workout and covering as much ground during the game as some of your players, you'd be well advised to tone things down a bit.

- ✔ **Think about how you correct errors:** Children often react differently to receiving instruction and feedback in training than they do in a game. After all, being singled out during a game may be traumatic for some youngsters, who would prefer not to have all this attention heaped on them all of a sudden, in front of family, spectators, and the opposing team. So, choose your words carefully. If a player isn't following through on their shots like they typically do in training, offer some instruction in a positive manner. For example, 'Billy, remember to follow through with your kick at your target just like you did so well all during training this week.' By taking this approach, you've provided the player with some important feedback that can enhance their play during the game while giving them a boost of confidence by pointing out how well they have performed the skill in the past.

✔ **Encourage hustling:** You never want your players to be out-hustled, because that is one area of the game that isn't controlled by talent or athleticism. The least talented player on the pitch can make the biggest difference by beating a player to a loose ball. So, always encourage your players to give it their all when running after a ball and reward their chasing the ball down with applause and praise. Whether they got to the ball first or not doesn't matter. Getting that kind of effort from your players all game long is a real feather in your coaching cap.

Communicating tactics

In some sports, coaches have ample opportunities to signal what they want their team to do next on the pitch. As a football coach, you don't have that luxury. Football is a truly unique sport. One notable aspect is that because the play is pretty continuous, with very few stoppages, communicating on the run is crucial for success.

Encourage your players to talk to one another and communicate what is taking place on the pitch at all times. Their voices can be just as effective a tool as their feet and head, whether it is in attack or defence. Basic comments, such as 'I'm on you're right', 'I've got number five', or 'You've got a defender right behind you', can be extremely effective. Of course, be sure to monitor the communication techniques of your team and give them feedback, the same as you would when coaching them in any aspect of the game. There may be players who constantly yell that they are unmarked when they are not, which is counter-productive.

Conversely, when players are unmarked and are shouting for the ball, are their teammates able to get it to them? Or are they not aware of the communication and miss out on the opportunity? Let them know if the type of communication they have been giving was beneficial and appropriate for the game situation. Also, be on the lookout to see whether good advice that was communicated was used by teammates effectively. Communication among teammates is a basic skill that a lot of coaches tend to overlook. By encouraging communication among players, it's as though you have a few extra coaches on the pitch. Work on it at training, carry it over to the game, and you should see your team operating smoothly and as a cohesive unit.

Taking advantage of breaks in play

A break in play may occur for a number of reasons. It may be to retrieve a ball, to attend to an injury, or where, as in some forms of junior football such as junior futsal, a timeout during a half is allowed. These breaks can be used to accomplish a number of things. While your team gets a short breather, you can remind them of something you have spent a lot of time on in training, to make adjustments in strategy, or any number of other areas.

Be sure that you use such an opportunity to pump your squad up, not put them down. Enthusiastically applaud their efforts, point out the positive things that are happening on the pitch, and encourage them to keep giving it their best at all times. The players should restart play reenergised and feeling uplifted by your talk, not dejected and with a sense that they have disappointed you thus far.

If things aren't going the team's way, you can use your talk to boost sagging confidence and to keep their spirits up. Avoid talking about how well the other team is playing or what they are doing so right. Instead, keep the focus on your team. It's certainly okay to point out where your team is struggling, but be sure to provide a solution that the kids understand. Non-specific instructions such as 'work harder' or 'be more aggressive' probably aren't going to produce much change in the team's play.

With older or more advanced teams, you may want to remind them of a training-ground move that the team has become very good at executing in training. When kids are comfortable with such a move and can use it successfully during the game, it can swing the momentum and get them feeling good about themselves again and provide them with renewed confidence.

Substituting players

Most youth football leagues, particularly with kids of a younger age and in mini-soccer, typically allow coaches to make unlimited, roll-on roll-off substitutions during the course of games. The substitutions help to ensure that kids receive an equal amount of playing time and that no one is stranded on the bench for an uncomfortable amount of time. Often, you are allowed to interchange players as frequently as you like during any stoppages in play. Many beginner leagues may even allow you to change players during the actual course of the game. Being familiar with your league's rules (refer back to Chapter 2) is crucial for understanding when you can, and can't, bring in fresh players off of the bench.

The league policy dictates your substitution patterns and impact on kids' playing times, so this is one of those rules you really have to be familiar with. Generally speaking, most leagues allow you to substitute players after a goal has been scored, when the ball has gone out for a throw-in, if there is an injury break, or after a goal kick has been given for either team. There may be a total amount of playing time that any one player can be on the pitch for in the event of several games being played in one session. In more advanced leagues, where the rules of football are adhered to more closely, your opportunities to substitute players are greatly limited.

In most cases, substitutions can only be made with the referee's permission. Again, in beginner's football the rules regarding this are extremely flexible, so players can go back and forth from the pitch like an assembly line. In more competitive leagues, players stepping onto the pitch or leaving the pitch must do so at the halfway line, (refer to Chapter 3). A player must step off the pitch before his substitute can take to the pitch, though the referee won't often strictly enforce this rule in youth football leagues.

When you are substituting a player, it's a good idea to take them off after they have done something well, rather than when they have made a mistake or done something poorly. If a youngster makes a bad pass and is suddenly taken out of the game, they're going to become afraid of making a mistake in the future and losing playing time. Also, when you bring a player to the sidelines after they have done something well, it gives you the chance to give them a pat on the back or a high-five and recognise the nice move that they just made.

Making the Most of the Half-time Speech

Okay, the first half is over. During this time, you have probably seen goals scored, pretty passes, successful tackles, great saves, and, because this is youth football and the players are still improving and developing, a fair share of poorly executed passes, missed tackles, and other assorted miscues. If you are coaching beginner's football, you've probably even witnessed a player staring in the sky at an airplane while the ball rolled by him, or an opposing player dribbling past a defender who was waving to his Grandpa in the stands.

So, as your players come trotting off the pitch, how can you possibly relate all of your feedback concerning their play in the first half in a brief half-time speech? After all, you probably only have 10 minutes or so before the second half begins.

What are your responsibilities during half-time, and how can you make the most out of the little time you have? Obviously, your speech isn't one that can be rehearsed, like your pre-game talk. Every half-time is going to be drastically different all season long. You've got to adjust your message to fit the mood of the team and how they performed in the first half. What you say during your half-time team talk should be clear, concise, and uplifting. You don't have to verbally replay the entire half of the game for the team. After all, your players were out on the pitch and they know what happened. But you do want your time with your team to be productive, enlightening and beneficial.

Improvising is key. You can't break out the same half-time speech all season long. You can't cram everything you saw into the few minutes you have with the team. You've got to be selective and choose just a handful of points that you want to stress, or adjustments that you want to make.

Keep the following tips in mind as well when gathering your troops at half-time:

- **Rest and rehydrate:** The players have been running up and down the pitch. Give them a moment to sit down and drink some fluids before you begin talking to them. Giving them a chance to catch their breath makes them more receptive to your comments. If it is hot and you can find a shaded area off to the side of the pitch, that may provide an ideal place for your players to sit and get refreshed. Or if it is cold and wet, head back for the changing room if it is near enough. Sometimes getting away from the pitch for a few minutes does wonders for re-energising your squad for the second half.

- **Avoid rambling:** It's natural to want to share all sorts of information with your team at half-time. Rather than rambling on about a dozen different things, stick to just a handful of points that you want to get across before they return to the pitch. By limiting how much information you throw at the team, what you do say is more likely to not only sink in, but be used by your players in the second half. The last thing you want to do is send your troops back out on the pitch scratching their heads wondering what you were talking about.

- **Solve problems:** Comments such as 'we can't allow them to get in behind our defence' aren't going to be very productive. You need to offer solutions that the kids can grasp and put to use when they resume the game. A more appropriate approach would be to specifically tell the defenders to drop off a bit and play 5 or 10 yards back from where they have been playing, which youngsters can clearly understand.

- **Keep a poker face:** Never let the team know that you are frustrated or upset with their play. Being overly emotional detracts from your ability to coach and to interact with your players in the most effective manner possible. Regardless of whether your team is up by five goals, or trailing by five goals, you've got to maintain a positive attitude and demeanour. Kids feed off your emotions and your body language is a tell-all sign. Avoid slumping shoulders, bowed head, and a slow walk. Approach half-time with the same positive energy you brought to your pre-match talk and your team will respond accordingly.

✔ **Highlight the positives:** Remember, you want to stress great play by the entire team, not just a select few individuals. Point out the great way the defenders have worked together when they are pressured in their own half, for example. Or how the midfielders have fared well passing the ball through the opposition's defence to create good scoring opportunities. Hearing praise for the hard work they have put in during the first half should make them more enthusiastic to build on those efforts and duplicate those moves in the second half. While constructive criticism is critical to get the most out of your players, be sure to balance it out with plenty of positive reinforcement that will infuse them with added confidence.

✔ **Make adjustments:** One of the most challenging aspects of coaching football is that no two games are ever alike. Everything from the playing conditions to your opposing team's skill level and ability are always different. On top of that, your team will have games when everything you have worked on in training comes together perfectly, and other games when they can't seem to do anything right. Recognising the adjustments that need to be made, and being able to share them with your team during this brief time period, is one of the cornerstones of good coaching.

✔ **Focus on what you have worked on:** Sometimes coaches get so caught up in what the other team is doing that they lose sight of their own team's strengths and what they have worked on in training during the week. When your team has the ball, what skills have worked well for them in training or in previous games? Don't deviate and suddenly expect players to perform at a higher or different level. Pay close attention to how they performed and tell them to play their own game. Yes, it's a cliché, but it's one that can make a difference in how the kids perform. Play to your team's strengths. For example, if you're a great passing team, focus on ball control and connecting with teammates and don't worry so much about what the opposing team is doing. Reminding your team to play its own game generates a certain comfort level, while promoting confidence and a renewed sense of teamwork.

When coaching older or more experienced teams, you can use the half-time break for a number of other areas. Because you are under time constraints, you can't really get into in-depth strategies, but if your instructions are clear and to the point, you can impart some great advice that can impact on your team's second-half performance.

The following are some of the areas that you may want to touch on, depending, of course, on what has happened during the first half.

✔ **Get feedback from your players:** During the game, you have your vantage point on the sideline where you are taking in all the action. But with all of your responsibilities, you have simply no way to monitor every single thing that is taking place on the pitch. That's where your players can come in handy as you can use their different perspectives on the pitch for some great advice. By asking your team if they have any suggestions to employ in the second half, you are not only reinforcing your respect for them and their knowledge of the game, but you may well gain some valuable feedback that can benefit the team.

For example, your goalkeeper is in a great position to survey the whole pitch and maybe has picked up on how the opposing team has been able to manoeuvre the ball down the pitch. Or, perhaps one of your midfielders has noticed that the other team's defenders have a tendency to move up in certain areas of the pitch and that can be exploited with a long cross-field pass. Your players can be a wealth of knowledge, so don't discount the impact they can have when it comes to strategy and making those crucial half-time adjustments. Another added benefit of this approach is that once players know that you are seeking their advice, it makes them focus that much harder during the game and they'll be much more aware of different situations taking place on the pitch.

✔ **Be mindful of changing weather conditions:** Mother Nature can cause all sorts of disruptions and, in the process, wreak havoc with your strategy. If the weather changes during the course of your game, be ready to make the necessary adjustments in your team's style of play. For example, in windy conditions it can be advantageous when the wind is at your team's back to take a more aggressive approach because the opposing team is going to have greater difficulty moving the ball out of their half. (For more on the weather's impact, see Chapter 18.)

✔ **Keep moving:** Are your players constantly on the move or are they turning into spectators once the action moves away from them? Are they providing support for their teammates by sliding into open spaces when they don't have possession of the ball? Are they pushing forward when the team is on the attack as you want them to and how you have stressed they should in training? Are they moving back when their help is needed to defend? Quite often, younger players tend to stand around when the ball isn't near them because, with all the added distractions that accompany a game atmosphere, they sometimes forget their responsibilities. Standing around results in players who are flat-footed and are unable to react as quickly when the ball does return to their area of the pitch. Remind players that when they don't have possession of the ball, they must keep moving to ensure that they are always in the right position when they are called upon to make a play.

✔ **Make necessary adjustments:** Often your team may turn in a great half, only to come off the pitch a little frustrated because they don't have any goals to show for all their hard work. Use your observation skills here. Often simply making a minor tweak to the team's approach can actually make a major difference in their play. For example, perhaps your team has played a great first half in its ability to move the ball all over the pitch, control the pace of the game, and generate lots of scoring opportunities. Yet, they are showing signs of dejection because they haven't been able to notch up any goals. Maybe through your observations you notice that all your team's shots have been low on the ground. Mention to your team that they should try getting some shots in the air to test the goalie's skills in that area of the game.

✔ **Stick to the fundamentals:** Often, throwing out even the most basic reminders can make a big difference for your squad. Maybe the team is having trouble moving the ball up the pitch, not because of anything the opposing team is doing, but because they aren't looking up and scanning the pitch while they are dribbling. A quick, simple reminder not to look down at the ball the entire time they are dribbling can be the impetus to getting your attacking play back on track. With their heads up, they are able to make the right choice when it comes to delivering a pass to a teammate or taking a shot. Remember, you can never steer your team in the wrong direction by resorting to the fundamentals of the game.

✔ **Adjust to the ref:** Some referees are going to be strict with their interpretation of the rules and will whip out red and yellow cards here, there, and everywhere. Meanwhile, other referees may seem like they have forgotten they have a whistle dangling around their neck and allow lots of contact between players. Take note of how the game is being called and make any necessary adjustments in your team's approach. For example, if the referee is allowing a little more contact than your team is accustomed to, you may want to have your players take a slightly more aggressive approach when attempting to win the ball, for example.

✔ **Use the entire pitch:** With the pressure of the game and the added distractions around the pitch, players can suddenly become one-dimensional in their thinking. They may become enveloped with tunnel vision and disregard a lot of the pitch, except what is directly in front of them. It's tough to move the ball up the pitch with that type of limited view. Utilising the entire pitch is critical to the team's success. If your players are constantly trying to play through the centre of the pitch, that approach is easily defended by the opposing team. Stress to your team that they need to start sending some passes out wide along the touch-line to stretch out the defence and use the entire pitch. Such adjustments may be pretty helpful in creating some open space to generate more scoring chances for the kids. Perhaps all they have used are short passes. Suggest attempting some longer passes to different areas of the pitch to catch the opposition guard.

Winning and Losing Gracefully

No one wants to lose or enjoys losing. But when it comes to youth football, for every winner there has to be a loser. Many teams and players are even remembered more by how they behaved after a win or a loss. In the bigger picture, the ability to win and lose with grace and dignity transcend the football pitch.

Spend time talking to your team about playing fairly, abiding by the rules, and winning and losing with grace. Just as you devote time to coaching them in the proper way to deliver a header, talk to them about the appropriate way to congratulate a winning team and the right way to conduct themselves when they are celebrating a victory themselves. Ask them how they feel when they win and lose, how they want to be treated when they have lost, and how they should treat the opposing team when they have won. Opening the door to these types of discussions lays the foundation for some exemplary behaviour that will make you proud.

Winning gracefully

You've probably heard the saying 'It's not whether you win or lose, but how you play the game'. Those are certainly appropriate words to adhere to when it comes to youth football. There's no room in the game for showboating, rubbing goals in the other team's face or extravagant victory celebrations. Coaching children in how to win gracefully may be one of the most difficult chores you have as coach, considering all the poor examples of professional players that children constantly see on television.

First of all, players need to know that it's fine to celebrate goals. After all, the object of the game is to score more than the opposing team, and high-fiving teammates when something works well is certainly acceptable. You just want to instil in your players that they should refrain from excessive celebrations or exhibiting any kind of behaviour that may be perceived by the other team as crossing the line.

Sometimes mismatches are going to occur throughout the season. In youth football, they are simply unavoidable with such a wide range of abilities that are typically involved in leagues. If your team is dominating an opposing team that simply does not have the talent or skills to compete with you, it is a good idea to limit the scoring. Thrashing out of sight an obviously less talented opposition reflects poorly on you and your team, and serves no purpose in the development of your players. If you find yourself in a lopsided game, consider some of the following approaches, which can keep your team's interest level high, work on a broad range of skills and not humiliate the opposing team in the process.

✔ **Put the emphasis on passing rather than scoring:** Make your team complete a set number of passes in a row before taking a shot at goal. In this way they can work on another aspect of their game without piling on the goals on a lesser-skilled opponent.

✔ **Shift players around:** Move defenders up to midfielders and vice versa to challenge them by playing a different position. These changes help develop all-round players, allow them to work on different aspects of their game, and keep them fresh by providing new challenges.

✔ **Limit shots:** Allow your team to only take shots from outside the penalty area, which increases the difficulty of scoring. You can also make other subtle changes, such as any time a player takes a shot on goal it must be with their less dominant foot, or limit their shots on goal to headers.

Losing well

Losing isn't the worst thing to happen – but behaving like it is is. Crying, throwing equipment, sulking, blaming the outcome of the game on the officials, swearing, and refusing to shake hands with the opposing team are all examples of behaviour that simply can't be tolerated under any circumstances. (See Chapter 19, which addresses how to deal with some of these types of behaviour that may arise throughout the season.)

Regardless of the outcome of the game, have your players line up and shake hands with the opposing team. Yes, this can be difficult for players who have just given it their best effort and come up short. Ensure that your team has respect for other players and for the game of football itself. Make sure that they acknowledge a well-played game by the other team and keep things in perspective. Football is just a game, and next time they may be on the winning end. No matter how cocky the opposing team may have been, your team can rise above that, offer a handshake or high-five, and congratulate them by saying 'good game.' Be sincere. Sincerity in the face of adversity or a loss is a great attribute.

Making an Impact with a Post Match Talk

What you say to your team – and how you say it – following a game can have a tremendous impact on their enjoyment of the sport. A pat on the back, an encouraging word, and a genuine smile always go a long way in any dealings you have with your team. Don't allow the scoreline to determine your tone of voice or impact on your body language during your post-game talk. Don't use the number of goals your team scored as the determining factor in whether or not you are proud of them. Kids want to know that they are appreciated for the effort they gave, not for the outcome of the game.

Keep the focus on fun

The most obvious way to ensure that the focus is on fun is to ask the kids if they had fun playing following the game? Hopefully, you get a chorus of yes. If so, poll the team to see what they enjoyed most about the game. If you've got some kids who didn't answer quite as enthusiastically as you had hoped they would, find out immediately why they didn't have fun and make whatever adjustments are necessary to ensure that they have a smile on their face following next week's game. It may be something as simple as that they wanted to play in defence instead of being a midfielder, where they had to do a lot of extra running. Or maybe they got kicked in the shin or hit by the ball. Talk to your squad. Solicit feedback. Gauge feelings. Probe them for answers. Find out anything you can do to make sure that their experience continues to be fun, or returns to being fun immediately in the next game.

Accentuate the positive

It's easy to fall into the trap of allowing the scoreline at the end of the game to dictate what you say to your team afterwards. But that shouldn't be the case. Wins and losses don't define your team's effort, the improvements they are making in certain areas of the game, or whether they had fun playing or not. Too often, many coaches tend to focus too much on the negative, particularly following a loss. A miskick, a defensive lapse that resulted in the game-winning goal, or an easy chance missed, stand out like a sore thumb and it's an easy target to want to dwell on afterward when discussing the game with your team. Youngsters who have been around the game a few years know when they have missed a tackle or made a poor pass. They really don't need to be reminded of it afterwards or feel that they are being held responsible for the loss.

Your job, regardless of whether the team played its best game of the season or got thrashed, is to point out some of the good things that happened. Maybe there was some great communication among your midfielders that produced a great scoring chance. Maybe they made great improvements in the corner kicks they had been practising all week. By keeping the comments positive, your body language buoyant, and your tone of voice upbeat, you send them home feeling good about themselves and anxious to return to training in the coming days to continue working on their game.

Recognising good sportsmanship

Recognising rocket shots, pinpoint passes, and great defensive tackles are pretty easy, because those moments clearly stand out in your mind at the conclusion of the game. What's often a little trickier, but equally important, is recognising those displays of good sportsmanship that took place during the game. Pointing out these instances, and genuinely showing your admiration for them, reinforces to your team the importance of displaying good sportsmanship at all times.

So, be on the lookout for these examples and make mental notes when they occur during the course of play. It may be the way one of your players tells an opponent 'nice shot' after they have scored a goal, or how they congratulated an opposing player afterward for a nice defensive tackle they made. Even if you see a player on an opposing team demonstrate good sportsmanship, tell your team. A comment like, 'That was a nice move on number five's part to help Steve up after he gave away a foul for tripping on that move in the first half' sends a message to your squad that good sportsmanship is just as important as heading, trapping, and shooting. The more good sportsmanship is stressed, the more likely the entire team will adopt this wonderful quality and become a model team. Remember, how your team behaves on the pitch is a reflection of your coaching, so don't neglect touching on this area of the game in your post-game team talk.

See Chapter 19 for information on how to address unsportsmanlike behaviour in your team.

Dealing with defeat

Participating in youth football coaches the players on your team in many valuable life skills, but often it can be a painful process. As the coach, it's important to understand that regardless of how talented your team may be, or what a wonderful job you did preparing them for the game during the week, you're going to have games when the team fails to perform up to your expectations. In some games your team may turn in a splendid performance, but fail to come away with the victory because the other team simply plays better. You're going to have games when the ball takes a lucky bounce that results in the opposing team notching the game-winning goal. That's football.

No coach is immune to seeing their squad commit mistakes following a flawless week of training; or fail to convert scoring chances that were easy goals earlier in the season. Remember, rarely do teams go through seasons undefeated, so you are going to have setbacks. In fact, losses and how they are dealt with are great character builders for that game we all play every day called life. So, don't let the sting of a disappointing loss linger too long. Remember, what you say to your team – and how you say it – has a huge impact on their self-esteem and confidence and how they handle winning and losing during the remainder of the season.

If you are coaching older or more advanced kids, losing a league championship game or getting knocked out of a tournament are going to be disappointing events in these kids' lives. Here are some tips to help them bounce back.

- **Allow them to be disappointed:** Kids pour their heart and soul into sports, so it's only natural that they are going to take losing hard, especially if it was a cup match, a derby, or any other crucial fixture. Don't tell them that that the game wasn't important or that it was just a game. Those are hollow words that carry no weight with older children who have a love of football and a passion for competing and doing their best. Give them time to digest the setback and then help them move on.

- **Hand out the post-match snacks:** Don't fall into the trap of only rewarding your team when things go well. Sticking to the same routine, win, lose, or draw, helps reinforce what you've hopefully been preaching all along, that doing their best and being a good sport are what playing sport is really all about.

- **Help them benefit from the experience:** Every game can be used as a tool to help your team improve and grow in the sport. Take the time to discuss the game with them at the next training session when they should be most receptive to feedback. Ask them what they thought they did well, and what areas they struggled with. Then, work on those troublesome areas in training to help them become more confident and comfortable.

Chapter 8

Refining Your Coaching Strategies

. . . .

. . . .

The football team that you welcomed to your first training session of the season is going to be dramatically different than the one that you are working with as you reach the halfway point of your season. After several training sessions and games, your players are evolving right before your eyes, and the team is – hopefully – emerging as a cohesive unit.

How you adjust to the ever-changing dynamics of your team, from the exercises you choose to run to the training sessions you orchestrate, can make a major difference in whether the fun, discovery, and skill development continues on or grinds to a halt. Revising coaching strategies, adjusting training plans, setting goals, and reviewing each player's progress with their parents are all essential mid-season responsibilities. In this chapter, we take a look at how you can be sure to accommodate the ever-changing needs of your players to help ensure that the season continues to be a rewarding and memorable one.

Dealing with Shifting Team Dynamics

After watching your team – during training sessions and games– you start to have a pretty good sense of which players are catching on to skills and which ones are struggling a little bit and are lagging behind in certain areas of the game. Clearly, by the time you reach the halfway point in your season and the kids have had plenty of opportunities to get their team strips grass-stained, you should be much more aware of who the quick developer are and who requires extra one-on-one attention when introducing a new skill or concept.

Regardless, once the season reaches full swing, each of the kids on your team will have certainly improved in different aspects of the game. Some may be more proficient at passing, others will emerge as pretty decent defenders and some kids who at the start of the season didn't appear to have much in the way of basic co-ordination will have demonstrated that they can now run and kick the ball without losing their balance or stumbling, which is worth applauding as well.

Recognising improvements

Recognising every youngster's improvements, no matter how big or small they may be, is essential in the skill-building process. Keep in mind that what may seem minor and insignificant to you often looms large and impressive to young eyes. Making a big deal out of the smallest things, particularly at the youngest age levels, can help forge a lifetime love of football and keep kids actively involved in playing the sport for years to come.

During the season, players are naturally going to become more adept in certain areas of their game. Make sure that you closely monitor the progress of each child so that when they do reach new levels, you can deliver a high-five, a pat on the back, or enthusiastic praise. It may be something as subtle as using their weaker foot to deliver a pass during a three-on-two exercise, or it may be something as obvious as heading the ball into the goal during a training game. Your ability to recognise these improvements can be the difference in fuelling their desire to continue training and striving to add new skills to their repertoire, or disappointing them by making them feel that you didn't give their efforts your attention. Don't leave them wondering what's really in it for them to continue showing up at the pitch.

Don't rely on the scoreline after games as your gauge for whether your team is improving. Wins and losses aren't a good barometer for measuring the development of your team. Even if your team happens to concede a stack of goals during a game, taking a closer look may actually reveal that the team turned in one of its better defensive outings of the season. There may just have been a couple of unlikely bounces that led to a couple of goals, and perhaps your goalkeeper let a couple shots in that he would typically stop. If you take a closer look at the defensive area of the game that you worked on in training during the week – such as getting back into a good defensive shape more quickly when the team loses the ball – and the players excelled in that area, you've got to be sure to recognise that afterwards. Think about it. These kids listened to your instructions during the week, responded to your wishes and chased back in defence, which was a great improvement. If you use the scoreline as the determining factor in how well they played, they often won't get the recognition they deserve.

Revising your plan

As a youth football coach, nothing brings a smile to your face quicker than seeing your players improving, developing and progressing. After all, that means that the exercises you have been choosing to use are making a difference in the skill development of your players; the training plans that you have been putting together are producing the desired results; and the instruction and feedback that you have been dispensing is really sinking in with the youngsters. Even so, you can't be satisfied with these improvements. You've got to reach out and push the kids to excel and get even better during the remaining time you have them under your care. So now what do you do?

One of the most constructive problems you can ever have as a volunteer football coach is – as your youngsters acquire skills and improve – that you are forced to make alterations in how you approach training sessions and games. In order for youngsters to gain the most out of their participation with you, you have to continually challenge yourself to devise exercises that will bring out the best in your players and challenge them to continue their development in the sport. You can't simply rely on using the same core of exercises all season long because that will bring improvement and development to a halt, as well as bury all their fun in the process.

 Making changes to your training plans as you manoeuvre through the season isn't as difficult as you may think. You can take a basic exercise that you have been using the first few weeks of the season and make some minor adjustments to it that will increase the difficulty level and meet the needs of your developing players. For example, even the most basic exercise, like the two-on-one drill, can be easily revamped to incorporate a new challenge for your players. For instance, you can have the kids only use their weaker foot during the exercise to help promote that area of their game. It will also prove to be quite challenging for youngsters who have relied on using their strong foot for much of the season. Or, for more fully developed kids, get them to make the attempt on goal a header. This will force the passer to chip the pass into the air allowing their partner to make contact with their head. While it's always a good idea to incorporate several new exercises into your training sessions, you can also rely on tweaking exercises that you have used previously. Remember, new challenges and however you choose to go about providing them will add spice to your training sessions and help keep the kids' interest.

Undergoing a Mid-Season Review

Reviewing team progress at the midpoint of the season serves a number of valuable purposes. It can keep a season on track that has been moving along smoothly, as well as rescue one that is showing signs of drifting off course. Think of the mid-season review as the road map that will help you eliminate any wrong turns on the way to your desired destination.

When it comes to being involved in activities, adults are no different than the kids. Coaches want to hear how they're doing – especially when they're performing something really well. Think about when you start a job and you typically receive a review after a few months from your boss who gives you feedback on areas that you are excelling in, sheds light on areas that you may not have been aware of, and offers suggestions on those areas that they would like to see you make some additional strides in. Sharing this type of information with your players can keep them up to speed as the season moves along.

Pointing out progress and improvement

In order to maintain player motivation, make sure that you establish personal improvement goals that tie into trying to win games, but that are not strictly dependent on achieving those wins. Coaching your young players in the ability to compare their current performances with their performances from earlier in the season – rather than a performance evaluation based on which team won the game – will give them a true sense of their progress. Setting up individual goals that each child can realistically reach allows them to have much more control over their success, because winning games doesn't always correlate with which team played the best.

Setting goals

Goal setting is as popular a coaching tool as motivational halftime talks – and it can be one of the most effective means for getting the most out of your players when employed correctly. Choosing goals for each of your players to strive for builds confidence, promotes self-esteem and, over the course of a season, enhances performance. Goals also help keep kids focused and interested, as well as provide a real sense of accomplishment when they are able to reach those goals. Here's how you can incorporate goals into your team.

✔ **Encourage parental involvement.** Getting each child's parents actively involved in the goal-setting process will help to steer the kids down a successful path. Encourage the parents to be creative in working with their child. Goal setting should be a fun activity that allows the parent and child the chance to bond. For example, they can make colourful charts that can be put on the refrigerator or hung in the child's bedroom so that they can monitor their own progress in working toward whatever objectives you've come up with for them to aim for.

✔ **Create a balance.** When setting goals, you have to find the right balance and come up with goals that are neither too difficult for the youngster to achieve nor so easy that they are met right away and leave no further challenges.

✔ **Be realistic.** Only set goals for the kids that are going to work within the framework of the team setting. Setting a goal for a youngster of scoring ten times during the season is unrealistic for several reasons. First, these types of goals are largely out of the child's control and second, the youngster may become so consumed by reaching the ten-goal target that he begins taking shots that aren't beneficial to the team and ends up not passing the ball as often to his teammates in an effort to score.

✔ **Provide constant praise.** Even if the child fails to reach the primary goal you've set, make sure that you pile on the praise for effort and hard work. Positive reinforcement is vital for ensuring that kids will continue to strive to improve while participating in sport in the future.

✔ **Consider injuries.** If a youngster is returning from an injury take that into account before setting goals for that individual. Even though the youngster is quite talented, the goals may have to be lowered until the player has a few training sessions and games under her belt and is back up to normal speed. At this time, the goals can be revisited and adjusted to coincide with the health of the player. (For more on injuries, see Chapter 18.)

Setting team goals may seem like a good idea, but they can lead to all sorts of problems. For example, if one of your team goals is to win four of your last five games of the season, and the team drops two games in a row, suddenly the goal is unreachable, although you still have three games to play. Chances are the team may have played two of their best games of the season, yet because they lost, they're going to be disappointed in their performance. Team goals represent the proverbially double-edged sword. When the team is winning and meeting goals, confidence is soaring and everyone is pleased with the outcome; but when games don't end in victories the team becomes blanketed in disappointment and self-doubt.

Making plans for players

In order for goal setting to be most effective, you need a good idea of the skills and abilities of your players. After half a season of training sessions and games under your guidance, you should be ready to sit down with each player and map out a plan for the remainder of the season. If you are coaching a team of 6-year-olds in a mini-soccer league, then simply selecting a basic goal for the entire team to work towards may be sufficient – such as making accurate passes rather than simply running with the ball. But, with older and more advanced players, you've got to choose specific goals for them to strive for that are going to be vastly different than those of their teammates'.

When creating goals, keep the following pointers in mind:

✔ **Use short-term goals.** Remember, the younger the child the shorter the attention span, so working with a series of short-term goals will lead to greater improvements and increased confidence in a quicker period of time.

✔ **Have backup goals.** When choosing goals for the players to work toward, have several levels. By doing so, if a child doesn't reach the top goal, but manages to reach the second out of the list of five, he will still gain a real sense of accomplishment. Having just one goal to strive for turns it into an all or nothing proposition that risks leaving the youngster disappointed in their performance, which should never be the case.

✔ **Get player feedback.** It's always a good idea to have a short discussion with each of your players to gain some insight on which areas of their game they would like to improve on. If you are choosing the goals for each one of the players without giving them any say in the matter, the process is not going to be nearly as effective. For example, a youngster may have her heart set on finding out how to deliver a header, but if you've chosen trapping the ball with her chest as the goal you want her to achieve, you're probably not going to get quite as enthusiastic an effort from her. Letting players have a say in the matter and helping them select realistic goals that they have an interest in achieving will help drive their development.

Regardless of the outcome of the game take the time to applaud and acknowledge players who are reaching their individual goals. For example, if one of the goals for a youngster on your team was to become comfortable taking shots with their weaker foot, and during the course of the game the situation called for them to use that foot and they got in a good shot, he needs to be recognised for that.

Failing to acknowledge this type of progress, which can be easy to overlook if your team happened to get beaten 8–0 that day, will send the message that goal setting and working to achieve and improve performances really isn't all that important to you after all.

Chatting with Parents

Pre-season parent meetings (refer to Chapter 4) open the lines of communication before the first football is ever kicked. Once you have laid that foundation, ensure that you don't lose contact with the parents when the season begins and everyone becomes consumed by juggling their hectic schedules. Parents can be a wonderful source of information to tap into as your season moves along.

For example, one of the best ways to gauge whether the youngsters are enjoying the season is to solicit feedback from their parents. After all, parents can share with you whether their son or daughter is excited about games and is wearing their team shirt around the house two hours before the game, or if they basically have to be coaxed to the car when the time comes to leave for the pitch.

 Setting aside some time to talk to the parents about how their child is enjoying the season demonstrates how much you truly care. It will also be comforting to parents, many of who may be involved with their child in an organised sport for the first time. Most importantly, talking to a parent will give you some valuable insight into what their child is thinking and feeling about playing football for you.

 As your season approaches the halfway point, let parents know that you would like to set aside a few moments in the upcoming week to speak to them regarding their child and their thoughts on how the season has gone so far. A good time to make such an announcement is following a game when most of the parents are most likely to be on hand. Find out when would be a convenient time to call them during the week for a brief conversation or, if convenient, perhaps setting aside some time after training to chat in person will work best for both you and the parents.

Sometimes what you will hear from the parents isn't going to be encouraging, and as a coach you have to be prepared to deal with that. The situation is really no different when you ask your players to bounce back from a loss and put forth their best effort at the next training session and game. The same applies to you. If something isn't working quite as well as you had hoped with a youngster and they are rapidly losing interest in playing football, you've got to explore all the options at your disposal.

 It's never too late to rescue a child's season.

When things aren't going the way kids hoped . . .

Say that after speaking with the parents, you discover that Junior isn't as happy as you had hoped. The solution may be something as simple as pencilling the youngster in at a different position. Hopefully you've been rotating all the kids around so they've had a chance to play a variety of positions and maybe the problem is simply that at the halfway point of the season a couple of kids haven't had the opportunity to play a position they've had their eye on all season. That's easily correctable. Other things aren't quite as easy fixes.

Sometimes a youngster may have had a bad game, or is embarrassed by something that occurred during the course of a game. If a kicked ball struck them in the face or they tripped over the ball while on a breakaway, those types of memories tend to sting and reside in a child's consciousness badly enough so that they actually impact the youngster's enjoyment of the game. Anytime you recognise that a child may have been embarrassed by something that happened on the pitch, exercise your best judgement as to whether speaking with the child is warranted or not to help ease any feelings of humiliation.

Sometimes, for the child's sake, you shouldn't say anything. The less attention you direct toward the event, the less likely the child may be to worry about it. If you do feel the need to soothe the child's bruised feelings, try sharing something humiliating that happened to you during the course of your youth sports career. When children get a sense that everyone endures humorous moments and that they are a part of participating in sports such as football, that will free them up to put the event in the past and move forward.

Maybe the youngster was hoping she would be placed on a team with some of her friends, but it worked out that she didn't know any of the other kids and has struggled to forge any friendships. If that's the case, you may consider incorporating more types of team-bonding exercises into your training sessions, which allow the kids to get to know one another better. Not only will that help the child in question, but if the players on your team know one another better and have tight bonds with each other, this can pay big dividends in the quality of their play.

Often youngsters get enrolled in a sport like football that they didn't realise involved so much contact. A few games of getting kicked in the shins, or taking the occasional tumble when they're tripped by an opposing player, and suddenly the game isn't quite as much fun as they thought it would be. Unfortunately, if that's the primary culprit for their anti-football feelings, you can't do very much about it. All positions on the pitch include the chance of a youngster's chances of being in contact with opposing players.

While you never want to encourage a child to quit a sport, in such cases, it may be best to speak with the parents, share your concerns that you don't want to make the child any more miserable than they already are, and perhaps suggest some other sports that you think would best suit their child if you feel comfortable making those types of recommendations.

Part III
Beginning and Intermediate Football

'Remind me to have a word with young
Darren about hogging the ball.'

In this part . . .

A coach who doesn't have the ability to communicate fundamental techniques and provide good training drills to share with his team is about as effective as a repairman who owns no tools. In the following chapters, we serve up an array of attacking and defensive techniques, skills, and drills that promote learning and leave the kids begging for more.

Chapter 9

Mastering the Fundamentals

. . . .

In This Chapter:

▶ Coaching beginners

▶ Getting basic football skills across

▶ Fixing potential problems

. . . .

*O*ne of the most important characteristics of being a good football coach is being able to get kids to understand.

Even if you consider yourself pretty knowledgeable in the sport, played it yourself growing up, or perhaps enjoyed a high level of success playing competitively, none of this is going to do you – or your players – any good if you can't pass along information that helps them to acquire and develop skills.

Being good at getting kids to understand translates into good coaching, and that means good times for the youngsters under your supervision.

Being a top-quality football coach means being able to present information correctly and clearly while providing useful and positive feedback. It means acknowledging and applauding skills performed properly and recognising when improper techniques are being used, as well as being able to correct them. It also means employing a coaching style that promotes discovery, rewards effort, stresses safety, and focuses on fun.

This chapter starts from square one, with the basic football skills that every player needs to acquire and work on. These skills can start out simply and progress to more advanced stages. Here, we go over the basic first steps to demonstrating the elementary football skills including shooting, ball control, passing and receiving, heading, goalkeeping, and attacking and defending. This chapter discusses these skills largely in the context of teaching the youngest of budding football stars, but the fundamentals are applicable to players of any age.

Introducing First-Timers to Football

When children are starting to read, you don't give them Charles Dickens. You don't even mention nouns, verbs, and adjectives at this point. You start them out with basic sounds and words, slowly work up to simple sentences and build from there. If you think about it, that approach should be applied to coaching football.

Let's face it, football is a complex sport that requires a broad range of skills, and your job is to help your players develop the full range of skills. But that doesn't mean you have to churn out an army of miniature super talents destined to earn professional football contracts. When it comes to children who have never played the sport before, you must make sure that you stick to the basics, regardless of their age.

Remember, your training is their first introduction to football, and overwhelming them with long-winded instructions, complex drills and intricate set plays isn't the route to helping them foster an interest or love of the sport.

Be realistic and start with the basics. You are only going to be with them a couple hours a week. Typically, with younger children, you have one training session and one game each week. So, if you can provide them with a strong foundation of a few basic skills – and put a smile on their face while doing so – then you deserve a pat on the back for a job well done. And when you see the kids returning to play in the league next season or, better yet, they request to play on your team again, then you know you truly made a difference in their life.

Football has a unique language all of its own, so don't be silly and use lingo and terminology that is just going to confuse the kids. Even seemingly simple terms like *shooting* and *ball control* can be pretty perplexing to a child who hasn't even found out yet that they can't touch the ball with their hands.

Only use phrases or terms that you have taken the time to clearly explain and that you can confidently say that all the kids on the team have a firm grasp of. Clear instructions using terms that everyone understands make your training sessions more effective and enjoyable.

Shooting

Kids love scoring tries in rugby or getting someone out in cricket, so when it comes to football, their primary interest is going to be – you guessed it – scoring goals. For a young football player, nothing matches the thrill of kicking a ball into the net and feeling that sense of excitement. Well, except for those youngsters that get more pleasure from chasing butterflies in the middle of games!

Children just starting off in the sport need to be introduced to the basic element of correctly kicking a football at a target. Giving them a feel for aimed kicking allows them to achieve success and, in the process, build their confidence. And there's no better target than an empty net.

Start them off with no goalies, no defenders, no pressure: Just line them up and have them kick the stationary ball into the empty net. As children improve and gain confidence in performing this skill, you can make slight alterations to increase the difficulty and provide challenges that enhance their development.

The next logical step is adding motion to the drill. You can accomplish this in several ways:

- ✔ Roll the ball to players and have them kick it toward the goal to help them get used to dealing with a moving ball
- ✔ Have them run toward a stationary ball and kick it.

Once youngsters gain proficiency in these areas of the game, bump up the challenge even further by adding a defender or goalie to the drill (for more information on adding these extra hurdles, see Chapter 13).

Explaining the instep kick

Children have a natural tendency to kick the football with their toes, but that isn't the most effective area of the foot to use. Getting youngsters to use the inside of their foot and their instep (the area on top of the foot where the shoelaces are located) is much more beneficial. It is easier to kick the ball more accurately and longer distances using those areas of the foot instead of the toes. The inside of the foot and instep can also be used for delivering passes, which is discussed later in this chapter. Check out Figure 9-1 for correct and incorrect contact points when performing the instep kick.

Figure 9-1:
Show your players the right way to kick a football.

Right   Wrong

Before demonstrating to children the art of the instep kick, make sure that you let them know where their instep is located. Most youngsters can quickly point out where their sole and inside and outside of the foot are, but the instep may be completely new to them.

To get them to understand the instep kick, have the player:

1. **Pick out a target.**

   Children need to look up from the ball to pick out their target. The target should be something large, such as the goal. Or, it can be a teammate stationed a short distance away.

2. **Look back at the ball.**

   As with most ball sports, the general rule when making contact with the ball is to keep your eye on the ball. After locating their target, beginners need to then look back at the ball when they are ready to deliver the kick. If they're not looking at the ball, they're probably not going to be able to make an accurate kick.

3. **Plant the non-kicking foot alongside the ball.**

   One of the most important factors in determining the success of a football kick is the placement of the supportive, or non-kicking foot. Greater ball velocity can be generated when youngsters approach kicking the ball at an angle (as you can see in Figure 9-2a) because of the increased hip rotation; in other words, the ball goes faster and harder when you plant your foot alongside the ball and kick (see Figure 9-2b). Children who plant their foot directly behind the ball are more likely to kick with their toes.

4. **Make contact with the instep – not the toes.**

   Kicking the ball with the toes reduces the accuracy of the shot. By approaching the ball at an angle and kicking with their instep, their shots have just as much speed, and go where they aimed.

5. **Kick the middle of the ball.**

   Kicks that miss the centre of the ball rise or roll along the ground. As children progress, they can be taught how to work the ball in various ways, but mastering connecting with the centre of the ball (see Figure 9-2c) is vital before venturing on to other kicking skills.

6. **Follow through.**

   Many youngsters have a habit of stopping their foot as soon as it makes contact with the ball, which results in a big loss of power. Train them to kick through the ball to achieve maximum force on each shot (see Figure 9-2d).

a   b

c   d

Figure 9-2:
A child lines up, takes his shot, and follows through on his instep kick.

If the instep pass goes awry, the problem may be

- ✔ **Lack of speed:** Often youngsters don't get all the power on their shots that they are capable of because they don't follow through. This leaves a lot of untapped power in reserve. Get your kids to follow through with their leg all the way through the kick and finish pointing at the target and they will see a big increase in ball speed.

- ✔ **Kicking the ball into the ground:** Youngsters, in their excitement to score a goal, understandably forget some of the basic kicking fundamentals from time to time. When that happens, they often won't make direct contact with the ball. If their planted foot is too far away from the ball when they go through the kicking motion, they are only going to contact the top half of the ball, which results in a shot that dribbles along the ground. Adjust their spacing so that their plant foot is nearer the ball and they should notice a big difference in both the power and accuracy of their shots.

Ball Dribbling

Ball control, ball control, ball control – the key to success in football. The more often your team has possession of the ball, the greater likelihood that good things are going to happen. Maintaining possession of the ball is the bearer of good news: It means fewer scoring opportunities for the opposing team and additional attacking chances for your team, and that's the name of the game.

Ball dribbling consists of moving – and maintaining possession – of the ball. A player needs it to move the ball down the pitch to create scoring opportunities, as well as to keep the ball away from the opposing team while backed up in the shadows of your own goal.

Dribbling is one of those skills that can be a little tricky to impart to children who typically are going to be more interested in kicking the ball as hard as they can. To get them started:

1. Have them walk while bumping the ball forward with their foot, keeping it in close proximity to them as they go.

2. Once they become comfortable doing this, encourage them to walk as quickly as they can while controlling the ball.

3. Eventually, they can progress up to jogging and then running at full speed with the ball.

4. Ultimately, your goal is to have your players become comfortable enough that they can move with the ball without having to constantly look down to see where it's at.

Tips to keep in mind:

✔ The player's head should be up as much as possible in order to scan the pitch for unmarked teammates, as well as to protect the ball from approaching defenders (see Figure 9-3).

✔ In order to maximise the chances of maintaining possession of the ball, the closer an opposing player is, the closer the attacking player should keep the ball to their body.

✔ Players should never run faster than the ball can be controlled.

You probably have players who are great at dribbling the ball in training, but during a game they turn into a completely different player. The nervousness of playing in front of family and friends or having unfamiliar kids charging at them trying to get the ball are common culprits in this area.

Figure 9-3:
Dribble with
the head up,
scanning
the pitch,
not looking
down at
the ball.

Right   Wrong

The most common problem is that kids have a tendency to stare down at the ball. Yes, this is one of those rare instances where the most basic of sports instructions – keeping your eye on the ball – isn't always such a great idea. During your training sessions, have kids work on controlling the ball without glancing down at it. They can walk alongside you and carry on a conversation without looking at the ball; or get parents involved in the training session and have them walk next to their child and see if the youngster can look at them the entire time they are working their way down the pitch with the ball.

Passing

Passing the ball is often about as much fun as homework and early bedtimes for a lot of children. After all, the attention – and cheers – are usually piled on the player who scored rather than the one who delivered the pass that resulted in the goal. So, getting kids to understand that setting up goals is just as important as scoring them will take a concentrated effort on your part. Your effort is well worth it though, when you see your team working as a cohesive unit. Impress upon your squad the importance of passing to the team's overall success – be sure to continually acknowledge good passes during training sessions and games – and your players should begin to embrace this aspect of the game.

The inside-of-the-foot pass is the most commonly used technique for delivering a ball to a teammate, particularly for beginners. Players use a long follow through as they push the ball toward their target (see Figure 9-4). As players progress in their football careers, they will use their instep to make longer passes (see Figure 9-5), as well as the outside of their foot for shorter passes.

Figure 9-4:
A short inside-of-the-foot pass.

Figure 9-5:
For longer passes the youngster kicks the ball with her instep.

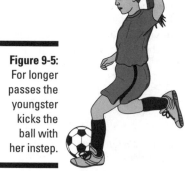

In order to deliver a pass:

- ✔ The ball should be directly between the player and their intended target.

- ✔ The player's non-kicking, or 'plant' foot (a right-hander's plant foot would be their left foot) should be approximately 3–6 inches from the ball and pointing toward the target.

- ✔ The planted leg should be slightly bent.

- ✔ The kicking leg should also be slightly bent and the player should make a short backswing.

- ✔ Contact is made in the middle of the ball with the inside of the foot at the arch and the leg should follow through toward the target.

Becoming an accurate passer of the ball takes time and lots of practice. So early on in kids' development they are going to experience their share of frustration when their passes don't hit the intended target.

- ✔ **The ball is missing to the left or right of the target:** Youngsters often stop their kick as soon as they make contact with the ball, which cripples the accuracy of their pass. Have the child concentrate on following through at their target and their passes will start finding their mark with much more regularity. If you want a useful explanation a child can easily relate to, tell them that their belly button should be pointing toward their target.

- ✔ **They have trouble keeping the ball on the ground:** If a player's plant foot is too close to the ball, the tendency is for the ball to pop up in the air instead of staying on the ground. Have the player move their plant foot back a few inches, which provides greater control and accuracy.

Trapping

Just about every part of the body can be used when it comes to *trapping*, except the hands, of course. The essence of trapping is gaining control of the ball – whether it's bouncing, rolling, or airborne – and keeping it near the body by using the feet, the thighs, or the chest.

The art of trapping involves cushioning the football as it makes contact with the player's body. An effective approach for introducing children to the concept is to have them visualise a water balloon or egg coming at them that they must keep from breaking.

The ball bouncing off the body and out of control is the most common problem associated with trapping for youngsters. When using their foot to trap, the ball is going to ricochet off their leg if the leg is held out stiffly. The leg should be bent and relaxed and pulled back toward the body as soon as there is contact. The same goes for the thigh. The longer a player can keep the ball in contact with their thigh, the more control they are going to have.

When using the foot to trap an incoming ball, a player must:

1. Extend their leg and foot out before the ball arrives.

2. As the ball makes contact with their foot, they need to pull their leg back trying to keeping in contact with the ball to help soften or cushion the ball and keep it in their possession (see Figure 9-6).

3. While all parts of the foot can be used for trapping, keep the focus on the inside of the foot for younger players because the inside of the foot is the easiest to pick up. As players gain skills and experience, they discover how to trap with the inside and outside of their foot, as well as their ankle and thigh.

Figure 9-6:
Trapping a
ball with
your foot is
an important
skill.

The thigh is an extremely effective area of the body to use for trapping because of the large size of the contact area. Players using their thighs must

1. Be positioned in front of the incoming ball

2. Stand on one foot

3. Raise their other knee and thigh to meet the ball keeping the thigh as close as possible to parallel with the ground (see Figure 9-7).

4. As the ball makes contact with the thigh, help cushion the contact by lowering their knee until the ball drops down to their feet.

Figure 9-7:
The right
and wrong
way to trap
the ball with
the thigh.

Right   Wrong

The chest is typically the most difficult area of the body to train youngsters to trap with simply because it brings their hands into the picture, which often results in handball being called. To successfully trap the ball with their chest players must:

1. Be in front of, and square to, the approaching ball

2. When meeting the ball, have their chest puffed out

3. Quickly pull back the chest as the ball contacts it to cushion the impact and allow the ball to fall to their feet. See Figure 9-8 for the correct way to trap the ball with the chest.

Figure 9-8:
Trapping the ball with the chest is tricky, because kids may be tempted to use their hands.

Right   Wrong

The biggest problem associated with trapping with the chest is that youngsters can easily become off balance, thus the ball strikes their chest and bounces out of their control. Make sure that they hold out their arms to the side, which improves their balance and enable them to suck in their chest at contact to ensure greater control.

Receiving

Naturally, goal scorers must be good at kicking. They must also be exceptional at receiving passes and have a great first touch. Otherwise, their goal-scoring opportunities are going to be greatly diminished. Not only is the ability to control the ball when receiving it integral to producing scoring opportunities, but ball control is also vital to escape defensive pressure when your team is backed up in front of its own goal.

On the receiving end

1. The pass receiver's foot should be about 4 inches off the ground, or about halfway up the ball, when it gets to them.

2. The pass should be controlled with the side of the foot, more toward the ankle. If the ball takes an unexpected bounce, the leg helps control the pass because the ball is being played closer to the ankle.

3. The foot should be relaxed, which helps to control the pass, particularly passes that are coming at the player quickly.

Table 9-1 shows you how to correct common receiving errors.

Table 9-1	Common Receiving Errors
Error	*Solution*
The ball bounces over the player's foot.	Check the height of the player's receiving foot. If the foot is not a few inches off the ground, the ball tends to bounce right over the youngster's foot. Also, if he is receiving the ball with the front of his foot instead of in the centre, with the arch, that can contribute to control problems as well.
The ball bounces off the player's foot and can't be controlled.	The foot is too firm on contact. If the pass is coming quickly, the player needs to relax their foot at impact with the ball and pull it slightly back to soften the contact, similar to cushioning the impact discussed earlier with trapping.
The player isn't getting to the pass.	The player isn't reacting to the ball quickly enough. As soon as the pass is delivered, the youngster must begin running in order to beat the defender to the ball.

Heading

On the list of skills you need to train your team in this season, heading ranks at the bottom as far as importance goes. That's simply because children at the youngest age levels basically aren't going to be able to get the ball airborne, so the opportunity to head a ball isn't going to come into play. You should certainly introduce them to the skill so they are aware that the head can be used though, and as they gain experience and advance within the sport, heading can gradually become more a part of the game for them.

Be sure that you use your head when introducing heading to your players, because you must ensure that proper technique is followed at all times when coaching this skill. The safety of your players should always be a top priority. So be aware of the type of ball that is used in your league. If the league you are coaching in requires the kids to play with a regulation football rather than one whose size and weight is modified for younger children, you do not want to use that when introducing children to heading. A heavy ball can injure a child's still developing head and neck.

The best way to introduce children to heading is to use a softer plastic ball or beach ball. It is great fun for the kids, but more importantly, they get the proper technique down before they ever attempt heading with a real football (see Figure 9-9 for the correct technique). In order to execute a header:

1. The player must keep their eye on the incoming ball at all times.

2. Their feet should be shoulder width apart and their knees flexed.

3. As the ball makes contact with their head, they stiffen their neck and chest muscles while driving the ball toward the target.

4. They should use the forehead to connect with ball for powerful headers and good direction.

5. They must attack the ball and not just passively allow it to hit their head.

Figure 9-9:
Heading a ball can be scary; make sure your players do it the right way.

Right   Wrong

To correct heading errors:

✔ **The child's head isn't making solid contact with the ball.** Younger and inexperienced children often have a habit of closing their eyes right before contact with the ball. Work with them on keeping their eyes glued to the ball.

> ✔ **The ball isn't finding its intended target.** If the child's neck muscles aren't tight at impact, the ball is simply going to bounce off their head. Tight neck muscles, and following through by pointing the head at the target, get those headers going in the right direction.

Goalkeeping

Goalies are the only players allowed to use their hands to touch the ball on the field of play (see Chapter 5). Thus, their position requires a wide range of skills that are vastly different from anything else that you are coaching the rest of the team in.

First and foremost, when stopping the ball, goalies must know how to tightly secure the ball and pull it closely into their body (see Figure 9-10). After a shot has been stopped, your team doesn't want to give up another scoring opportunity simply because the goalie failed to protect the ball in his grasp.

Figure 9-10: Securing a loose ball on the ground.

Young goalies have small hands, and although the ball the league is using is hopefully the appropriate size for the age range you are coaching (refer to Chapter 3), it can still be awkward for youngsters to gain total control over. This is particularly true when opposing players are bearing down on them and they have a huge goal area that their team is counting on them to protect.

For youngsters getting their first taste of this complex position, the best approach for handling shots is make sure that they place the tips of their thumbs together with their palms toward the ball and their fingers pointing upward (see Figure 9-11).

When there's a loose ball, tell children to cuddle the ball the same way they would protect a puppy in a rainstorm. By surrounding the ball with their body, they safely secure it while also reducing the risk of suffering injuries to their fingers or hands by the studs of opponents looking to score a goal. (See Figure 9-12 for the right and wrong ways to gather the ball.)

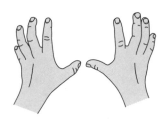

Figure 9-11:
The ready position and proper hand position for handling shots.

a

b

Right

Figure 9-12:
A goalkeeper should bend his arms and gather the ball gently, while keeping his knees together.

Right

Wrong

When saving a shot in the air, encourage the goalie to jump up with one knee pulled up in front of her. The jump not only protects the goalie from opponents charging toward the net but it also discourages them from even trying to do so. (Check out Figure 9-13 to see how a goalkeeper should deal with a ball in the air.)

Right

Figure 9-13: These goalies demonstrate right and wrong ways to deal with a ball in the air.

Right   Wrong

When a midfielder makes a mistake during a game, the mistake usually results in his team losing possession of the ball. When a goalie makes a blunder the result is a lot more obvious: A goal for the opposing team. While goalkeeping is simply one facet of the game, is the position is accompanied by a lot of pressure. Coaching in the sound fundamentals can go a long way toward reducing that burden on your young goalie.

- **Keeping their eye on the ball:** There can be a lot of traffic in front of goal and it's easy for goalkeepers to get caught up in the excitement of watching all the other commotion that is going on. Work with your goalie to focus on following the path of the ball at all times and being in the proper position to make a play on the shot.

- **Staying focused:** It can be extremely difficult for a youngster to stay focused on the game, particularly if his team is dominating and he is spending the majority of the game at the other end of the pitch. Consequently, when he is finally called upon to make a save, his concentration is not at its peak. Lack of concentration is the perpetrator of many goalkeeping mistakes.

Work with your goalies to ensure that they follow the ball all game long. Encourage them to watch the ball closely when the action is at the other end of the pitch, and to focus on how they would position themselves to make saves based on where their own team is attacking with the ball. Even though they are not being called upon to make saves at that particular moment, they can still improve their own play by visualising proper positioning based upon where the shots are coming from.

Defending

For children, finding out how to play in defence certainly not as appealing to them as shooting, or as interesting as some of the other skills that we have covered in this chapter. Nonetheless, playing in defence is a significant aspect of the game, especially considering that roughly half of every game your team is involved in will require them to play in defence.

Playing in defence is all about reading and reacting. As the youngsters on your squad have little, if any, playing experience, this means introducing them to an entirely new concept. Initially, you can start a child off basically playing one-on-one against another youngster who has a ball, with one player dribbling the ball and the other trying to dispossess them.

In football, in order for the defensive player to be successful, they must keep themselves between the opponent and the goal. When there's an opening and the defensive player attempts to win the ball, that is called tackling. Tackling involves the defender winning the ball from the opposition player without committing a penalty. Effective tackling relies on timing as the defensive player's foot pokes the ball away from the attacking player and takes control of it.

Here are a few common defensive mistakes:

- ✔ **Players running by them with the ball:** This is usually the result of a defensive player not keeping their eye on the ball. Attacking players who use stepovers and other tricks can get a defender leaning in the wrong direction and then dribble past them with the ball. Defensive players who focus on the ball and not the other players are more likely to be in the proper position to win the ball or force the other player to attempt a pass.

- ✔ **Lack of focus:** A child's mind tends to wander when their team loses control of the ball and they find themselves suddenly stuck in defensive mode. Simple reminders and encouragement that they need to win the ball back in order to get shots on goal may help refocus their attention and enthusiasm for playing defence.

Determining What to Do If a Kid Just Doesn't Get It

You may well be the best coach in your league. Your training sessions are more fun for the kids than a trip to the local toy store. Your players are developing and progressing – well, except for a couple of youngsters who just aren't quite getting it.

They haven't grasped the fundamentals of kicking a football yet. For weeks, their timing has been off on their passes. They keep repeating the same basic mistakes that the rest of the team haven't made since the start of the season. So what do you do?

Your attitude here is where the real challenge of coaching football comes in. All kids don't progress at the same rate. Some are going to pick up what you say in minutes and follow your instructions perfectly. Others require a couple of training sessions before everything sinks in and they are performing skills exactly like you intended. And then there are those kids who struggle mightily every step of the way.

Making a difference

Anyone can call himself a coach, but only those that are able to really make a difference in the life of every child under their care can call themselves a good coach. Ask yourself a few questions about how you're coaching the kids that are struggling and see what adjustments you can make in your methods to steer them back on the right track.

- ✔ **Are you spending too much time talking?** Nearly all children have short attention spans to varying degrees. If what you say during the course of your training sessions, or how you say it, doesn't interest them, the simple fact is that their minds are going to wander. Distractions abound in an outdoor sport like football. Parents nearby, a noisy car down the road or a big weed in the pitch are just some of the things that may lure a child's attention away from what you are trying to convey to them and derail their progress.

  Keep your instructions basic and simple and repeat them several times. Children only develop and improve by performing the skill, not by listening to you talk about the skill. Increase the number of repetitions your strugglers are getting during training and see if that generates significant improvements.

- ✔ **Are they happy with the position they are playing?** Maybe the child had her heart set on being the goalie, and when she was told she was going to be a midfielder her interest in training, and playing, quickly fizzled out. Make sure that you give all the kids a chance to play all the positions. Yes, it can be difficult to pull this rotation off considering you may have more than a dozen youngsters on your team. But giving them a complete introduction to the sport in this way keeps their interest and energy levels high. So, talk with the child that is struggling. Maybe the chance to wear the goalkeeper's gloves and to protect the team's goal can jumpstart her enthusiasm.

- ✔ **Is the child simply mismatched with football and another sport that coincides with their interest and abilities may be more suitable?** Some children simply aren't attracted to contact sports like football. Maybe they are tired of being kicked in the shins or aren't getting any enjoyment out of all the running that is required during the course of a game. If the child's parents seek your advice about whether he should continue with football, be honest and helpful. Suggest specific sports that have the potential to provide their child with the opportunity to enjoy a fun and rewarding athletic experience.

Recognising physical problems

A child's development can be hampered because of issues that are simply out of your control. Yet, if you spot the warning signs, you may be able to make a difference.

✔ **Attention deficit hyperactivity disorder:** A child's lack of focus may be the result of attention deficit hyperactivity disorder (ADHD). According to experts, the most common characteristics of a child with ADHD are distractibility and poor sustained attention to tasks; impaired impulse control and delay of gratification; and excessive activity and physical restlessness. If you think someone on your team may be displaying signs of ADHD, talk to the player's parents about your concerns.

✔ **Vision problems:** A child's struggles with properly kicking a football or his inability to deliver an accurate pass to a teammate may be due to a vision problem that can be easily corrected. If you sense this may be the problem, mention it to the child's parents. Perhaps a trip to the optician is all that is needed to pull everything into focus for the child and turn their season around.

One of the most important reasons to hold a pre-season parents meeting is so you can find out about any children on your team who may have special needs that you need to be aware of. If a child has a hearing problem and you don't know about it, the child will be having enormous difficulty trying to keep up with what is being said. Or, if a child has a physical limitation or past injury that is going to hamper how they perform a certain skill, you need to be conscious of that as well. The same goes for everything from asthma to diabetes, all of which can impact on a child's performance.

Coaching with dignity

When offering feedback, don't make a spectacle out of a child who is struggling. Children, especially as they get older, know how their skills match up to the rest of the team. The last thing they need is for the coach to make their deficiencies stand out even more during training by being singled out for extra work. If a child just hasn't been able to master delivering passes, the last thing you want to do is work one-on-one with that youngster on that skill while the rest of the team performs another drill at the other end of the pitch. While it may seem like you are helping by giving the child extra attention and practice, attention in this case going to embarrass the child and make her feel even worse about her lack of development in an area of the game.

Instead, find a much better way to go about it. For example, devise a drill in which you have a designated passer whose job is to get a two-on-one started. By taking this approach, the youngster is getting a high number of repetitions in an area of the game that she needs help on; she's working with her team rather than being isolated from them; and your training time isn't being compromised by one player's struggles because everyone is actively involved in the drill.

Whatever the situation, never allow the tone of your voice to reveal frustration or disappointment. The same goes for your body language, too. Be calm, patient, and understanding as you work with the youngsters. Don't neglect them or give up hope on them just because they haven't been able to contribute as much during games as most of your other players. Stick by these kids; encourage them and applaud their efforts every step of the way. They need you. Who knows, years from now when they are still actively involved in the sport, they may look back and realise that you are the reason they are still strapping on shinguards every season.

Chapter 10

Fundamental Drills
for a New Team

• •

In This Chapter

▶ Getting warmed up

▶ Practising drills for attack and defence

• •

*H*elping youngsters acquire and develop the many skills needed to play football is going to take place during your training sessions. It won't occur on the day of the game when they may be more interested in waving at their dad over at the sidelines with his camcorder than they are in kicking the ball that is rolling towards them. With all the excitement that surrounds match day there may be simply too many distractions for a young child to completely focus on the game and what you are saying.

The best instruction and the most skill development takes place during your mid-week training sessions. These are the sessions where you can share your knowledge of the game, pass along pointers, and enhance the kids' abilities in all aspects of the game through the fun-filled drills you choose to employ. Clear directions and well organised and monitored drills will ensure progress and be the springboard to long-term enjoyment of the sport. Of course, before you begin conducting your training session drills, you should spend a few minutes getting them warmed up so their young bodies are prepared for the exercises to follow.

Warming Up Right

It is never too early to establish good warm-up and warm-down habits with youngsters. This is particularly true in a sport like football where so many different muscles are used. Stretching the muscles enhances a youngster's agility and flexibility, provide them with an improved range of motion, and reduce their chances of being injured. Setting aside a period of time to get the heart rate up and the muscles loosened up before training clears the way for a productive session.

For younger kids, your warm-ups don't need to be elaborate. Simply have the kids perform a series of jumps to get their heart pumping and toe touches to stretch out ready for action. You can also incorporate a football into their warm-ups. Have each player place their ball in front of them and alternate putting their right foot on top of the ball, and then their left foot, to get their heart pumping.

With older children, ensure that they properly loosen up, because they need to rely upon all their muscles during the course of the training session. Stretching the hamstrings, the quadriceps, the calves, the neck and upper back, the lower back and the area around the waist are all important, so make sure that your warm-up covers all those areas.

The following are basic drills to loosen up each area of the body:

- **Hamstrings:** Players sit in a hurdle position on the ground with one leg straight out and the other bent behind them. Slowly, they lean forward and reach for their toes. They should hold the stretch for a few counts and then release. Make sure that they aren't lunging for their toes. They also shouldn't feel any pain, just a slight stretch on their muscles.

- **Quadriceps:** In the same position used above for the hamstring stretch, players lean slightly back to stretch the quadriceps on the leg that is bent.

- **Waist/lower back:** Sideways bends. Players stand with their feet beyond shoulder width apart and gently arc their right arm over their head and point to the left while their left arm rests against their left knee. Have the team perform a few repetitions in each direction.

- **Calves:** Players stand and lift themselves up on their tiptoes as high as they can and hold for a couple of seconds before returning their feet flat on the ground.

- **Neck:** Players stand and slowly turn their heads all the way to the left and then all the way to the right. They then tuck their chins to their chests to help stretch out the back of the neck.

- **Upper back:** Players stand and stretch both arms behind their back while puffing their chests out. They hold for a few seconds and then release.

Here are a few other warm-up tips to keep in mind:

- **Be aware of the conditions.** If the weather is considerably hotter or more humid than normal, don't wear out your team during warm-ups so that they have less energy to perform during games or training sessions. You just want to get their heart rate up a little bit without taxing them too much physically.

✔ **Don't allow the warm-ups to turn into competitions within the team.** If you decide to use football specific drills in the warm-up period, such as jogging while dribbling a football ball, make sure that it doesn't evolve into competition. You want to avoid teammates competing against each other and probably expending more energy than you would like, which may detract from their play once the game or training session begins. Keep any of these types of drills team oriented in nature and remember, you want to get the kids loosened up during this period, not running at full speed.

✔ **When conducting stretches with younger children, explain which muscles they are stretching and why stretching them is important.** For example, when doing a hamstring stretch, point out what exactly the hamstring is, where it is located, and why stretching it properly enables them to run faster and kick the ball harder.

✔ **Don't allow any mucking about during these exercises.** Keep the kids' attention focused on the specific stretch they are performing.

✔ **Emphasise slow movements.** With younger children, just a couple of repetitions of each stretch are adequate. This will also help ingrain in them at an early age the importance of always stretching before performing an activity.

✔ **Don't allow bouncing.** Don't let the children bounce into stretches. Stretching should be a gradual movement into the stretch, then holding the position when they feel the stretch and then release. Bouncing and other sharp movements are more likely to cause harm than be beneficial.

✔ **Join in.** As the coach you will be running around coaching and instructing during the course of the training session, so why don't you and your assistants join the kids for the stretches. This further instils the idea of the warm up's importance to the youngsters, and helps you to avoid being helped off of the pitch with a strained or pulled muscle. If you are conducting a training game or any drills that also involve the parents, get them out on the pitch to warm-up with their child, too (refer to Chapter 6).

✔ **Be consistent.** Always start your training session with a warm-up. Repetition is important and if youngsters know that stretching comes in to every training session, they will start to understand that the stretching is an important part of the game.

At the conclusion of your training sessions have a short warm-down period. A warm-down is a gradual slowing down of activity, followed by light stretching. Youngsters should get into the habit of going through the warming down process every time they participate in a training session or game. The warm-down doesn't have to be quite as focused as the warm-up session, as the purpose is to wind down from the activity rather than build up to one.

Drills for Attacking Play

The talent level of your players dictates which drills you use during your training sessions. If you have a group of exceptional players who have been playing football for several years and are pretty efficient in most areas of the game, you may want to jump to Chapter 17, which provides a series of advanced drills you can use. Or, you can pick and choose from the drills that are presented in this chapter.

Remember, you can also take one of the following drills even if it seems too basic for your squad and make any adjustments regarding its difficulty level to best match the needs of your players.

The beauty of your training sessions is that you can select any drill and fine-tune it to specifically meet your team's needs. For example, if your team is struggling in attack, you can conduct a two-on-one drill that may not only help them develop their skills but build their confidence level as they enjoy success moving the ball down the pitch. The long-range goal of your training sessions is to get the players comfortable and confident in their execution during small-scale games and drills so that they can transfer those skills to the playing pitch on the day of the game.

Passing and receiving

Impress upon your squad the importance of passing to the team's overall success – be sure to continually acknowledge good passes during training sessions and games – and your players will begin to embrace this aspect of the game.

Passing fancy

Purpose: Players acquire the skill of to making accurate passes with a moving ball because this drill doesn't allow time to gain control of a ball by stopping it before kicking it. With the emphasis on speed and accuracy, players have to be quick on their feet and constantly kick a moving ball.

How it works: Mark off a grid with cones about 15 metres long and 15 metres wide. In the centre of the grid, place several cones, to serve as obstacles. Position three players on each side of the centre line, and give each of them a football. On your command, the players begin kicking the ball to the other side of the grid. Play quick one- or two-minute games. The object is for each team to try to get all six balls onto the other half of the pitch. With the cones placed at different points along the centre line (use fewer cones for inexperienced or less-skilled players), players are forced to not only make quick passes, but accurate ones. See Figure 10-1 for how it comes together.

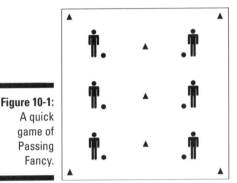

Figure 10-1:
A quick game of Passing Fancy.

Coaching pointers: Because this drill forces children to rush their passes, which will be called upon to do many times during games, they may tend to get a little sloppy on the techniques you have worked on. So keep a close eye on the positioning of their feet and how they are delivering the passes. Encourage short side-foot passes in this drill and make sure that the kids are making contact in the middle of the ball with the inside of their foot at the arch and that they are following through toward the target.

Passing and receiving frenzy

Purpose: To help youngsters find out how to make accurate touch passes with their instep to a nearby teammate.

How it works: Position three players in a line, with about five metres in-between each of them. The player in the middle starts with a football. Position another player – with a football – opposite the threesome, about 10 metres away. On your whistle, the players begin passing the balls back and forth between them. The single player is forced to make quick and accurate passes because the balls come at him pretty rapidly. Continue for a minute and then rotate so that each child in the group gets a few turns being the single player. Check out Figure 10-2 to see how this drill should work.

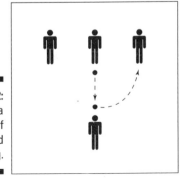

Figure 10-2:
Practising a frenzy of passing and receiving.

Coaching pointers: Keep a close eye on the accuracy of the single player's passes. If balls are missing their mark, make the necessary corrections in the kids' technique to get their passes back on track. The child may be using their toes to kick the ball instead of their instep, which drastically decreases their accuracy.

Shooting

Kids love scoring goals. For a young player, nothing matches the thrill of getting a shot on target, and shooting drills are always popular.

Hit the coach

Purpose: When introducing beginners to the sport, this exercise serves as a great way to kick off training, loosen the kids up, and get them comfortable with you.

How it works: Give each of the kids a football. The idea is for them to kick the ball at you, while you do your best to avoid being touched by any of the balls headed your way. This drill gets the kids running around, laughing and having fun right away, which is what you want; to start off your training session on a high note. Plus, it actually doubles as not just a team ice-breaker, but a skill-building drill as well as the kids are working at kicking the ball at a target they are aiming at.

Coaching pointers: Refrain from instruction and just let the kids have fun. This is simply one of those drills where you want the kids at the youngest age levels to begin getting comfortable being around one another and getting a feel for kicking a ball at a target.

Give and go

Purpose: This is a simple drill you can run that covers passing, receiving, shooting and goalkeeping. See Figure 10-3 for the set-up.

How it works: The goalkeeper (GK) takes her position in front of the net. Approximately 15 metres away, station an attacking player, another 5 metres beyond that the designated shooter for the drill, and 10 metres to the right of him another attacking player, who begins with the ball. This player starts the drill by delivering a pass to the designated shooter (1), who gains control of the ball and delivers a pass to her other teammate (2) and then runs at roughly a 45 degree angle (3), where she receives a return pass (4) and takes a shot at goal (5). The difficulty of the drill can be increased for older kids by adding a defender into the mix. Or, you can make the initial pass to the designated shooter purposely more difficult by bouncing her so that she has to use her chest or thighs to trap the ball; or by sending the pass out of range so she really has to work at chasing it down and gaining control of it.

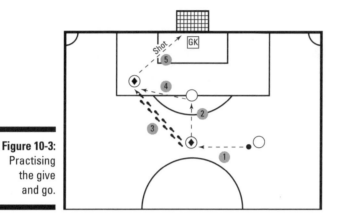

Figure 10-3:
Practising
the give
and go.

Coaching pointers: Shooters are going to be anxious to get to the point where they can deliver a shot on goal, so watch closely to see that they're using the right techniques to control the pass, give the return pass, and take a quality shot on goal. If they didn't have much force behind their shot, they probably didn't follow through when they kicked the ball. Or, if the shot dribbled along the ground their plant foot was positioned improperly, which usually results in a youngster only making contact with the top half of the ball.

Ball dribbling

The ability to keep control of the ball in a variety of situations is an important skill for every young player to have. Here are some drills that you can use to help them build these skills.

Elimination

Purpose: Elimination helps youngsters figure out how to dribble the ball with their heads up, to protect the ball from oncoming players, and to steal the ball from other players.

How it works: Mark off a playing area with cones and place a group of players in the area, each with a ball (see Figure 10-4). The object is for the players to maintain control of their ball while attempting to knock other players' balls out of the playing area. When a player's ball is knocked out of the area, they are eliminated from the game. Knock-out type games are not highly recommended because often times the lesser-skilled players are eliminated first, and are left standing on the sideline, losing out on more valuable training time. With a drill like this, be sure to have another side drill going so as soon as a player is knocked out of your main drill, they move over to the next drill.

Figure 10-4: Each player tries to knock each other player's ball out of the playing grid.

Coaching pointers: You've got a lot going on during this drill, but make sure that players are using legal techniques when attempting to knock another player's ball away.

Keep ball

Purpose: This drill has a little bit of everything. It provides an ideal way for players to work on their touch passes, their receiving, their manoeuvring the ball with both feet, shielding, tackling, and pressuring.

How it works: Select four attackers and two defenders and mark off a playing area with cones. Begin the drill by giving footballs to two of the designated attackers (See Figure 10-5). The object is for the attackers to keep possession of the balls. Award the attacking team a point every time they successfully make three passes in a row, and give the defending team a point every time they win the ball. Have enough of these games going on simultaneously so that no one is left standing around watching.

Coaching pointers: Stress proper passing and receiving technique, and make sure that the defenders don't foul as they try to win balls. Remind players that the closer a defender is, the closer they must keep the ball to keep possession.

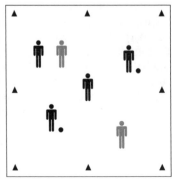

Figure 10-5: The attacking players try to keep both balls away from the defensive players.

Heading

With younger children, one of the best ways to introduce them to the art of heading is to use a light plastic football or a beach ball.

Quick reaction

Purpose: This drill is a pretty basic approach to get them used to directing the ball where they are aiming. (For more on heading, see Chapter 9.)

How it works: Break the kids into threes (see Figure 10-6). Each threesome should stand in a line with the two end players, each with a ball, facing each other. One of the players on the end tosses the ball to the player in the middle, who heads it back to them and then quickly turns to receive another lob from the player on their other side, which they head back to them. Repeat until the player in the middle gets used to spinning around and heading the ball.

Figure 10-6: The player in the middle must have quick reactions.

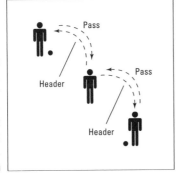

Pass

Header

Pass

Header

Coaching pointers: Heading is often one of the most difficult skills to impart to children, and they really have to be accurate with their technique when performing this one. Remind your players to keep their eyes open throughout the drill because youngsters just discovering this skill often have a habit of closing their eyes right before contact, which dramatically reduces the chances of delivering a successful header. Make sure that you have spent several training sessions with your team on this skill working with a beach ball and that they have the proper technique down before introducing a regulation football into the mix.

Circle headers

Purpose: Circle headers give youngsters a feel for using headers to deliver passes as well as to take shots on goal.

How it works: Position a goalie (GK) in front of the goal and a player a few metres in front of one of the goal posts (see Figure 10-7). Have the designated header for this particular drill begin about 15 metres away, with you or an assistant coach (C) about 7 to 8 metres away with a ball in your hand. Begin the drill with you lobbing a ball to the player, who heads it back to you and then sprints toward the net, where they receive another lob pass and attempt to head it past the goalkeeper. For more experienced players, the lobs can be chip passes delivered by players.

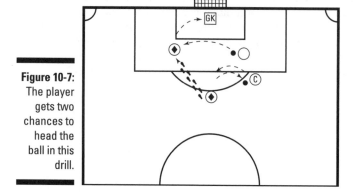

Figure 10-7:
The player gets two chances to head the ball in this drill.

Coaching pointers: If players aren't able to head the ball back accurately at the beginning of the drill, or get much force behind their headers on goal, be sure to provide them with a quick refresher on their technique. More than likely, the youngster's neck muscles aren't tight at impact and they probably aren't attacking the ball or following through with their header. Reinforce the point that their head should be pointing at their intended target.

Defensive Drills

While playing defence may not seem as glamorous to youngsters just starting in the game, in order to be well-rounded players half your training sessions and drills should cover this aspect of the game. If your defensive drills are creative, challenging, and really grab the kids' interest, you just never know. All of a sudden you may have kids begging to play defensive positions on game day to help their team protect the goal.

While even several of the attacking drills mentioned earlier in this chapter have defensive benefits, as well, the following exercises really emphasise the defensive side of the game. You can use them, make your own modifications, or perhaps seeing one may give you an idea for a whole new drill you want to try out.

Tackling

Nothing disrupts the flow of an attack quicker than defenders who are skilful when it comes to taking the ball away. Sound tackling techniques are a necessity for any team at any level.

Race to the cone

Purpose: This drill gives defensive players a lot of tackling practice in a short period of time with attacking players rapidly moving all around them. They also get good practice on how to take the right angle to win the ball from a player.

How it works: Position several cones at random spots around the playing pitch, and give each child a football. Select a couple of players to serve as defenders, and be sure to rotate players often so everyone gets a chance to be both a forward and a defender (see Figure 10-8). The object of the game is for players to dribble their balls from cone to cone without losing possession. The cones represent safe spots, where players can't have their ball taken. Only allow players to remain at the safe spots for a few seconds to keep the game moving – they should be constantly moving with the ball.

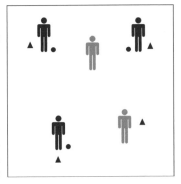

Figure 10-8:
Rotate players so that they all get a chance to attack and defend.

Coaching pointers: While this drill also promotes dribbling skills, be on the lookout for defensive players using proper tackling techniques. This is where the foundation of good defence can be built so that your players don't receiving unnecessary fouls during games for being too rough.

Ball touch

Purpose: Ball touch helps youngsters practise competing for a loose ball and making the switch from attack to defence.

How it works: Begin with a player on each side of you. Roll a ball out and on your command the two players race to see who can gain control of it (see Figure 10-9). Once the player has the ball in their possession, they must see how long they can protect it before the other player is able to take it off them. Continue the drill for anywhere from 30 seconds to a minute as players continue to switch from attack to defence based on whether they have possession of the ball.

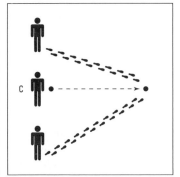

Figure 10-9:
Ball Touch helps players switch from attack to defence and back again.

Coaching pointers: This drill can cause some contact among players going for the loose ball, particularly among older and more experienced players who may be more competitive. So keep a close watch to ensure that fouls aren't being committed as players vie for the ball.

Defending

The better your team becomes at defending, the happier your goalkeeper is going to be. Besides giving him less work, the more proficient the team becomes in this area of the game, the more likely the team is to spend more time at its opponent's end of the pitch.

One-on-one

Purpose: Being able to successfully stop a player from running with the ball down the pitch is one of the benchmarks of great defensive play. This drill focuses on defensive footwork and also incorporates attacking skills, as well.

How it works: Set up two cones 25 metres apart. Start the drill with one player at the cone with a ball and the defender about five metres away (see Figure 10-10). The object is for the forward to work the ball down the pitch to the other cone. If the defender knocks the ball loose, you can work the drill a couple of different ways. First, when possession of the ball changes, you can have the players switch roles, and the player who stole the ball then tries to move it down the pitch towards the opposite cone. Second, when the defensive player pokes the ball away, the attacking player retrieves it and continues once again to work toward reaching the cone with the ball.

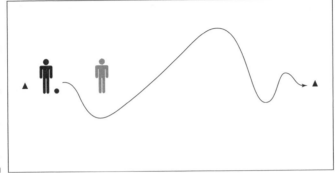

Figure 10-10: A child gets a lot of practice with the 1-on-1 exercise.

Coaching pointers: Encourage the attacking player to work the ball with both feet to keep the defender off balance and to shield the ball when the defensive player closes in on them. Also, watch the defender's movements to ensure that fouls aren't being committed in their efforts to win the ball.

Two-on-one

Purpose: The purpose here is to train defenders in how to control a two-on-one. This drill also provides attacking players with the chance to work on their passing, dribbling, and attacking skills.

How it works: Place two cones a couple of metres apart. Designate two players for attack and one player for defence. The attacking players must dribble the ball through the cone without losing possession of it (see Figure 10-11). This isn't a shooting drill, so emphasise that players must maintain control of the ball while attempting to get through the cones. Allow players to manoeuvre with the ball past the cone, but they can only go through the cone in one direction.

Figure 10-11: The defensive player has his work cut out for him in the 2-on-1.

Coaching pointers: This really tests your defensive player's footwork and reactions because they are required to cover a lot of ground all by themselves. Remind them not to be fooled by stepovers, body swerves, and other feints and dummies, but to keep their eye on the player's chest, body shape, and the ball, to help reduce the chances of being caught leaning to one side and creating an opening that the attacking players can use to their advantage.

Goalkeeping

The position of goalkeeper is a tough one, with shots coming in from all directions. Proper footwork, hand to eye coordination, and quick reflexes are all valuable assets for any young goalkeeper.

Read and react

Purpose: This drill works on several aspects of goalkeeping. It helps youngsters begin to read an opposing player's body language and whether this opponent is setting up to unload a shot or deliver a pass to a teammate. It also tests their footwork as the drill requires quick movements from side to side in order to stop the back-to-back shots that are coming their way. This drill also provides benefits to the attackers, who will work on their passing, receiving, and shooting skills.

How it works: The goalkeeper (GK) assumes his usual position in front of goal. Position two players out in front of the goal about 15 metres from the goal and about 10 metres away from each other (see Figure 10-12). For younger or less experienced players, you should move them in a little closer. Also, put two attackers about five metres away from each goal post, and give them each a football. On your whistle, the players with the balls deliver passes to the players out in front (1). After receiving the passes and controlling the ball, one player delivers a shot on goal (2). The other youngster returns a pass back to the player who just sent him a pass (3), and this player fires a short-range shot on goal (4). The first few times through the drill, you can let the goalie know which player is initially delivering the shot and which one is making a pass. For more experienced players, or those who have become comfortable with the drill after going through it a few times, you can pick which player you want to shoot and which one you want to pass without letting the goalie know. This really works on their reaction skills and reading the footwork of players to determine if they are shooting or passing.

Coaching pointers: While this is a drill for goalies to work on reading the situation, reacting and moving from post to post, don't neglect watching the techniques used by the attacking players, too. You want to see accurate passes, proper technique receiving passes, and a correct follow through when delivering a shot on goal.

Figure 10-12:
Several shots on goal in a row test the goalie's ability in Read and React.

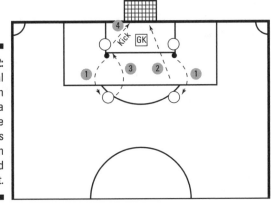

Goalie's delight

Purpose: This drill helps goalies become proficient at stopping a flurry of shots when they are facing pressure during games. It also helps to develop shooting skills in attacking players.

How it works: The goalie takes his normal position in front of the goal. Position two players about 15 metres away and give each player five balls in a row (see Figure 10-13). The drill begins with one player taking a shot on goal (1). As soon as the kick is delivered, the second player sends a shot on goal (2), and the players just keep alternating shots as quickly as they can (3, 4). This forces the goalie to make several difficult saves in succession from a variety of angles.

Figure 10-13:
Goalie's Delight gives the goalie ten chances in a row to make saves.

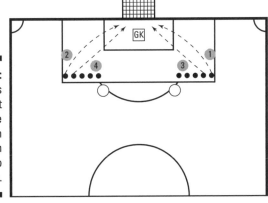

Coaching pointers: Watch the goalie's hands to ensure that they are properly positioned on their saves. This means the tips of their thumbs must be together with their palms toward the ball and their fingers pointing upward.

Breakaway

Purpose: Breakaway helps goalkeepers practise moving side to side and getting in position to stop shots. The attacking players gain practice on both their passing and shooting skills.

How it works: The goalkeeper takes her position in the goal. Two players start about 20 metres away from the goal. The players move in on the goal, passing the ball back and forth to each other until someone decides to take a shot. To increase the difficulty, add a defender to the mix. Or, make players deliver shots with their weaker foot.

Coaching pointers: In order to effectively defend breakaways, goalies must be able to quickly move from side to side. That means footwork is crucial to their success and should be monitored closely during this exercise. Also, make sure that, when they stop a low shot on the ground, they protect the ball with their entire body. This eliminates opponents from getting their foot on the ball for a follow-up shot, and reduces the chances of the goalie's hands or fingers being injured if an opponent tries kicking at the ball.

Chapter 11

Coaching Basic Attacking

*W*hat do kids love most about playing football? Sure, some may go for the colourful team shirt and the cool shinguards, and others may simply enjoy chasing the ball up and down the pitch. But for a lot of kids, what they love the best is the chance to score goals and feel the exhilaration that accompanies booting the ball into the net. When it comes to attack, kids typically hunger to discover this part of the game, and offering to coach them in attacking techniques is like waving bags of sweets in front of their faces. The eyes widen, the ears perk up and smiles form. This aspect of football is really interesting and exciting, and kids' enthusiasm for upgrading this area of their game typically grows.

As a football coach, this is where your job becomes more fascinating – and also more fun. Once your players have a couple years of football experience behind them and have a pretty good understanding of the basics of the game, you get the chance to look at different forms of attacking and challenge them to reach new heights in their play. You can coach kids in a variety of different attacks, as well as an array of new passes to introduce that should enable them to create additional scoring opportunities. Your team will be anxious to acquire these new attacking skills so let's get started.

Planning Different Types of Attacks

When your team gains that coveted possession of the football, they are ready to proceed with the attack. But what type of attacking approach is best suited to your squad? Well, that depends on a number of factors, including the experience and ability levels of your players. You have several styles of attack to choose from:

✔ **Counterattacking:** This approach tends to be a bit risky simply because it relies on players moving the ball with long diagonal or through passes, or requires a player to push the ball through midfield by dribbling. A counterattack can capitalise on an opponent who isn't properly prepared to defend because successful long passes can chew up big chunks of the pitch and quickly get the team into prime scoring position. A counterattack is particularly effective against out-and-out attacking sides. One of the major disadvantages of a counterattack is that one long pass can be intercepted by the opposition, so as quickly as your team gained possession of the ball, just as quickly it can give it away and find itself right back to defending again.

✔ **Frontal attack:** This type of attack unfolds much more slowly than a counterattack. A frontal attack also brings more players into the picture because the essence of this style of play is that it encourages safe, short passes that are used to manoeuvre the ball down the pitch. This is a reliable ball control approach that can be great for young players because it keeps everyone actively involved in the game. The biggest disadvantage associated with this approach is that by making so many passes, even relatively safe ones, the player has a greater chance losing the ball.

✔ **Overlapping:** This is one of the more advanced attacking approaches in youth football that puts a real premium on accurate passing and receiving, the type of attack that should only be used with experienced players who can handle the requirements of this style of play. Still, even with younger or less experienced players, you can introduce the concept so that they are at least somewhat familiar with it as they continue on with their football career. (For more information on overlapping, see the sidebar.)

Finding your own space: Overlapping explained

The basic point of overlapping is that the player with the ball receives help from a teammate who overlaps him, rushing up the side of the pitch at top speed to receive the pass, which immediately creates new attacking possibilities for the team. Typically, overlapping is used to get by the opponents on the wings. The overlapping player can come from the player's right and shoot down the sideline (see Figure 11.1a), or he can come from the player's left and loop around (see Figure 11.1b). Here are a few other tips to keep in mind regarding overlapping:

✔ **Make the defender commit:** In these situations, the defender has a real dilemma because he doesn't know if the person with the ball will distribute the ball to an onrushing teammate or keep it themselves and dribble up the pitch. If the defender chooses to tackle the attacker, that opens the door for the overlap.

✔ **Play the ball ahead of the player:** Because the overlapping player is running at full speed, the pass must be played well out in front of him. Passes that require the overlapping player to slow down make the overlap less effective.

✔ **Practise passing:** Because overlapping requires efficient passing skills, this attacking technique should be introduced once the team has a pretty good handle on the basics of passing. Coaching youngsters in passing a ball to a spot, instead of directly to a player, will take lots of practice to get right as kids figure out how to adjust their ball placement to the speed of their teammates.

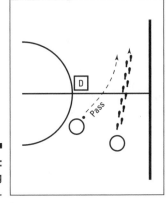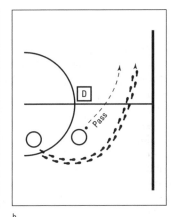

Figure 11-1:
Overlapping
pass options.

a   b

The following are a couple of other basic attacking tips to keep in mind
this season:

✔ **Constant movement:** An attacking team whose players are constantly
on the move – whether they have the ball or not – is much more difficult
to defend against than a team that stands around watching the player
with the ball dribbling around looking to create something. Continually
encouraging your players to keep moving and working to get free and
unmarked so they can receive passes will make a big difference in the
effectiveness of your attack. If no one is available for a pass, the dribbler's responsibility is to send a square pass back to a teammate to keep
possession and begin the attack again, or dribble to a different area of
the pitch and create space, where she can deliver a pass towards goal.
Forwards who are constantly moving put enormous pressure on a
defence, and the more they are forced to move and react the greater
the chance is that they will be pulled out of their defensive formation
in a way that results in an advantage for your team and possibly a great
scoring opportunity as well.

✔ **Spread out:** The more space that exists between your players, the
greater the chances of producing a successful attack. Players who are
able to keep plenty of space between themselves and their teammates –
and avoid the dreaded bunching up syndrome that is especially
common among young football players – have more dribbling room to
operate and more opportunities for executing passes that efficiently
move the ball down the pitch. Teammates who bunch up bring more

defenders into the picture, thus providing them with more chances – and easier chances – to win the ball.

✔ **Keep the ball moving:** When your team is on the attack, you want your players doing everything they can to make things as difficult as possible for the defence. That means keeping the ball moving. One of the biggest mistakes beginners make is that the player receiving a pass stops to gather himself and get the ball under control. A stationary target is easy pickings for defensive players – and they are going to pounce all over it. So, make sure that you work with your team on two-touch passing and three-touch passing to keep the ball moving on quickly, and also when receiving passes and trapping balls to make sure that the ball isn't stationary for long. If you allow the opposition to simply run right at your player, they are going to win a lot of balls and ruin a lot of your team's attacks in the process.

✔ **Involve everyone:** The best way to develop football players who want to be strapping on shinguards for years to come is to focus on a more possession-oriented attack that keeps all players actively involved in the game. Relying on just a handful of players to knock the ball down the pitch and hopefully occasionally get onto the long passes isn't going to be a whole lot of fun for the rest of the players involved and it can hinder their development and drain some of their enthusiasm for playing the game.

Understanding Positional Play

As players gain more experience, they should start to recognise in what areas of the pitch they can be more aggressive with their passes and what areas pose more danger. Certain areas of the pitch dictate that players rein in their aggressiveness so that it doesn't hurt the team. Even with the youngest of players, talk about what areas of the pitch require certain types of play, in order to give them a sense of what they should and should not be doing. Dividing the pitch in half is a little too simplistic for players with some experience playing the sport, but breaking the playing area up into thirds gives youngsters a pretty good gauge of how their play should be handled. Depending on the nature of the particular game and the type of team they are playing, your kids are likely to find themselves in all three areas of the pitch at various junctures throughout the game. How they respond while there makes a difference to how your team fares in moving the ball and creating scoring opportunities, as well as how successful the team is in limiting the opposing team's attack.

✔ **Attacking third of the pitch:** This is the area at your opponent's end of the pitch where your team can be at its most aggressive on the attack. Down here in the shadows of your opponent's goal, losing the ball isn't nearly as costly as it would be elsewhere on the pitch and mistakes aren't as magnified. Think about it. An errant pass down here isn't going to result in a scoring opportunity for the other team. While you hate to give up possession of the ball at any time, if your team is going to do so, you would much rather it occurs down here where the opposition still has the entire length of the pitch to negotiate, rather than in front of your own goal, or even in midfield, where they are one pass away from putting themselves into position to generate a great scoring opportunity.

✔ **Middle of the pitch:** With games involving kids with a couple years of football already behind them, often the play in this area of the pitch makes all the difference when it comes to which team generates more scoring opportunities. Basically, the team that is best able to control this area of the pitch is probably going to win the majority of the time. If you have players who have a pretty good grasp of their responsibilities, you can take a more aggressive approach when your team is in control of the ball in this area of the pitch. As long as the entire team is aware that they need to be alert and on their toes, you can encourage aggressive passing. If the other team gains possession, your team has to be able to react quickly and cover for one another, especially if the opponent is a counterattacking team.

✔ **Defensive third of the pitch:** This is that area of the pitch where your players can have you biting your nails and reaching for the antacids if what you have been drumming into them about pitch positioning hasn't sunk in quite yet. This is the end of the pitch where your team can find itself under the most pressure. A poorly executed pass or an ill-timed manoeuvre can create immediate problems for the team, particularly your goalie, who is suddenly staring at a booming shot from the opponent from close range. You want your team to be fully aware that at this end of the pitch you want players to send clearing passes toward the touchline, not down the middle of the pitch. An opposing player who picks off a pass in the middle of the pitch is in a great position to get off a shot on goal or create and pass to a teammate for a scoring opportunity. Clearing passes that are kept to the outside pose far less risk. If they go to the opposition, it still puts far less pressure on your team because the touchline serves as an additional defender. Defenders who are pinned in along the line are more limited in which direction they can proceed. Dribbling one-on-one should also be more limited in this third of the pitch, as well, because the opposition has nothing to lose by being ultra aggressive here. Sticking to safe passes that move the ball out of danger is the best plan.

Kicking the Attacking Skills Up a Notch

Before you can introduce any attacking philosophies, you must ensure that your players have at least a sense of some of the other skills that are needed for their age, experience, and level of ability. Having the knowledge to perform different types of passes that make running your attack more efficient is one of the keys to generating successful attacks. Players with the basic skills of dribbling, passing, shooting, and receiving are ready to progress to the next level – and you can help them get there.

Shielding

In order to be an effective dribbler of the football, players must be efficient when it comes to shielding. The shielding technique in football simply means that the attacking player keeps her body between the defender and the ball. Players who can fathom this art of controlling the ball by relying on their body to shield the opponent are going to be effective attackers because they have less chance of surrendering possession of the ball. The ability to maintain control of the ball while encountering defensive pressure, and being able to manoeuvre in tight quarters, is a great skill to have in the arsenal. It is a big asset to the team because the player can distribute the ball to an open teammate and help their team generate good scoring opportunities that never would have materialised without the ability to shield. A few points to keep in mind when coaching shielding:

✔ **Stay sideways:** The proper position for shielding is for the player to turn sideways (see Figure 11-2). This technique puts more space between the ball and the defender. It also opens up the attacking player's pitch of vision and enables him to pass to a teammate.

✔ **Don't turn back:** While it may be natural for players, especially younger and more inexperienced ones, to want to turn their backs on a defender to protect the ball, this simply gives the defensive player unnecessary advantages. Besides making it easier for the defender to poke the ball away, when the attacking player has his back turned he can't see his teammates down the pitch, which brings the attack to a standstill. It also restricts his ability to beat the defender one-on-one.

A great exercise to help young players become familiar with the concept of shielding is to pair players up and give each twosome a ball. The object of the exercise is for the designated attacking player to keep the defender from touching the ball – while not touching it themselves. By doing this, the players gradually realise that by keeping their bodies sideways they make it difficult for the defender to gain possession of the ball.

Figure 11-2:
Shielding
involves
keeping
your body
between the
ball and the
opponent.

Square pass

Passes that are played square (out to the side or behind) a player are
referred to as possession passes. While making possession passes isn't as
glamorous to kids as threading a diagonal pass through a maze of defenders –
and they may be about as much fun as being told to eat a vegetable they're
not fond of – they can be instrumental in how successful your team's attack
is. Players with the discipline to refrain from making a risky pass that only
has a small chance of working and who are willing to send a square pass to
a teammate are going to be real assets to the team. Getting your players to
understand that a teammate behind the play may actually be in a more
advantageous spot and have a better angle to keep the attack progressing
takes lots of practice. The square pass is one of those skills that should be
introduced to players who have playing football for a couple of seasons.

Using exercises where the attacking team is outnumbered can help your
kids find out the value of a square pass. While coaches often devote a large
amount of time to practising three-on-twos and two-on-ones, you should also
sprinkle your training sessions with drills such as two-on-threes and three-on-
fours, where attacks are forced to utilise possession passes until they open up
an opportunity to strike and can take a shot on goal. While your team will
have advantages in numbers on occasions throughout the game, they are just
as likely to encounter situations where they are a man short. So practise both
of these scenarios to best prepare your team for all situations.

Through pass

Anytime your player has the ball, you want their head to be up and their eyes
scanning the pitch for an open teammate or a gap in the defence that can be
exploited by dribbling or passing. If she has an available teammate up the pitch,

you want her to make the pass – often referred to as a through pass – because it has penetrated through the defence and your attack is moving forward.

Chipped pass

A chipped pass is one that is lofted with backspin and can be used all over the pitch. Players use it to get the ball over a defender. Here are the steps to follow in getting the message across:

- ✔ **Inside:** The ball is struck with the inside of the foot and contact with the ball is made below the centre of it (see Figure 11-3a).

- ✔ **Snap it:** The player snaps the knee while coming forward at the ball.

- ✔ **Lock it:** The player keeps his ankle in a locked (firm) position at contact (see Figure 11-3b), which helps to ensure that backspin is delivered on the ball and that the ball travels in the air (see Figure 11-3c).

Figure 11-3:
This player uses a chipped pass to get the ball over the defender.

a   b   c

Crossfield pass

A crossfield pass is, as the name suggests, simply any pass that goes from one side of the pitch to the other. This pass is used for several reasons. Often it used to switch play from an area of the pitch that is crowded with players to an area where the team's players are relatively unmarked. It can also be used against teams that defend high up the pitch and that leave a lot of space in behind their fullbacks. Putting a crossfield ball behind the opposition full-back puts their team under pressure as they have to turn around to get back to the ball. Finally, when your team is under pressure in its own half, rather than just booting the ball up the pitch, a crossfield ball towards the opponents corner flag can both relieve and, sometimes, retain possession.

Outside of foot pass

Many times throughout the course of a game, when going against a defender, the only opportunity to advance the ball to a teammate is by using an outside of foot pass. This pass can be a little tricky to explain simply because delivering one does not come naturally for kids and requires an awkward motion to complete. Here are the steps to help your youngsters use the outside of foot pass effectively.

- ✔ **Lock it:** When delivering a pass with the outside of the foot, the ankle must be locked.

- ✔ **Point it:** The child's passing foot (see Figure 11-4) should be pointed down and slightly inward.

- ✔ **Turn away:** In order for the youngster to have ample room for his passing foot, his non-passing foot should be turned just slightly away from the ball.

- ✔ **Strike it:** When the player follows through with the pass, he makes contact in the centre of the ball with his little toe.

Figure 11-4:
Using the proper techniques for the outside-of-foot pass can be awkward.

The one-two

This is one of the most basic passing combinations in football. Also referred to as the give-and-go, the one-two is a good tactic for a pair of attackers to take advantage of a single defender in the area and create chaos with the defence. Here's how it works: The player with the ball beats the defender (see

Figure 11-5) by using a teammate to bounce the ball behind the defender – much like bouncing the ball against a wall. One of the best opportunities for utilising the one-two is when the attacking player is able to force the defender to close her down. When this happens, the player with the ball delivers a pass to the second attacker, who executes a one-touch pass to the open area behind the defender, and then runs forward to join the attack. Other points to keep in mind when demonstrating the one-two to kids:

- ✔ **Sidefoot it:** The sidefoot pass, because of its accuracy, is the best method to deliver the ball to the wall player.

- ✔ **Targets:** Defenders that are slow-footed, who have a tendency to mark players with the ball closely, or who keep their eyes glued on the ball and aren't paying real close attention to what is going on throughout the rest of the pitch are susceptible to the one-two pass.

- ✔ **Practice:** The pass only works when both attacking players recognise the opportunity. While practice exercises help with the timing of the one-touch passes into open space, this type of pass is best perfected during games as players begin to recognise when situations call for this type of pass. There must also be sufficient space behind the defender to pull off this type of pass, otherwise it probably results in losing possession.

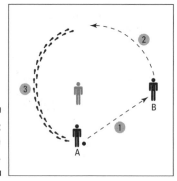

Figure 11-5:
A simple
one-two.

Bend it like Beckham

When your players have developed sound fundamentals on kicking the ball straight and pretty accurately, you can introduce them to the banana kick, whose name may get a chuckle or two from younger players. It can also be referred to as a swerve kick. This type of kick can be a great attacking weapon when players are able to curve the ball around defenders to get the ball to their teammates. Here are a few helpful tips to use when working on the banana kick.

✔ **Approach from the side:** The ball bends, or curves, when a youngster delivers the kick by coming across the ball (see Figure 11-6) instead of straight on.

✔ **Go low to get it high:** In order for the ball to curve, someone has to put it in the air. Players must make contact with the ball at its bottom half.

✔ **Inside of foot:** As the youngster approaches the ball, she strikes it with the inside of her shoe and above her big toe and drives across the ball.

Figure 11-6:
The banana
kick is an
advanced
attacking
technique.

You can also swerve the ball the other way, away from the body. For a right-footed player, this means dragging the kicking foot across the face of the ball so that the outside of the foot in the area of the three outside toes connect towards the underneath and inside of the ball. The ball then curves away from the player. This is a very difficult skill to execute, especially on a moving ball, and children must be careful not to kick the ground, rather than the ball, and in doing so twist their ankles.

Driving

A player uses this method when they have lots of open space and are running at full speed and don't want the ball to slow them down. Driving is a bit like making a pass to yourself because the player pushes the ball several yards ahead of himself and then, when running toward the ball, is able to make decisions about what to do next with it. How far the player pushes the ball ahead depends on how much space they have to work with and how close the nearest defender is that they are running towards.

Chapter 12

Coaching Basic Defending

*W*atching your team delivering precision passes up and down the pitch, creating good scoring chances, and firing in all those goals during a game is great fun. But what about when your team doesn't have the ball? How do they respond when the ball is deep in their own half and they are under attack from the opposing team? What do they do when they lose the ball in midfield? What defensive style should you be coaching them in?

In football, just like any other team sport, playing defence is a major element of the game. Remember that, during games, roughly half of your team's time is spent defending, so players knowing and understanding the techniques involved in defending are going to derive more enjoyment and success from the game. Sure, it may not be as glamorous as discovering attacking skills, but slowly your players should begin to savour the ability to derail and disrupt an opponent's attack. Defending attacks on a consistent basis is also the mark of a well-coached team that understands how to play a complete game of football.

Exploring Different Types of Defence

You can use a variety of attacking approaches (see Chapter 11), and the same goes for implementing the team's defence. You need to base the methods you choose for your team on several factors, most notably how much experience they have playing the game.

The most commonly used defensive style of play taught at the youngest age levels is *man-to-man marking,* which is exactly what it sounds like – a player is responsible for marking a specific player on the opposing team. As kids gain more experience, you can introduce them to *zone defence,* which tends to be a bit more difficult to understand because players are responsible for an area of the pitch rather than a particular individual. Of course, you can even get really creative with your defence and incorporate aspects of both styles into your approach. The following sections take a closer look at these styles of play.

Man-to-man defence

Man-to-man is the most basic style of defence to start beginners with because they find it fairly easy to understand that they are responsible for following Number 12, wherever he may go on the pitch. If you have any players who have played other team sports, such as basketball for example, they may have been exposed to the man-to-man concept and therefore have a head start on some of your more inexperienced youngsters. With this defensive approach, your players cover the opposing player regardless of where he is on the pitch, and when your team has possession of the ball, they join in the attack.

One of the advantages of going with a man-to-man defence is that it is easy to tell who is accountable for each of the opposing players. For example, if an opposing player is continually dribbling down the pitch, you're going to clearly see who she is beating with her tricks and you can adjust who is responsible for marking that player, which usually remedies the problem. (See the section on marking later in this chapter.)

Thinking about defensive support

During a game, your youngsters will lose track of the player they are marking, or the opposing player is faster and beats the defender down the pitch with the ball. Introduce the idea of *defensive support* at this point. While explaining defensive support to youngsters, work with them to pay attention to what is going on all over the pitch. Train them to recognise that when a forward beats one of their teammates, it is the responsibility of the nearest defender to lend support and put pressure on the attacking player who has broken free.

Of course, defensive support can be a pretty difficult endeavour with youngsters who are just starting out and can be easily distracted. After all, some kids are going to be more interested in what kind of ice cream is being sold at the ice cream van than what is taking place with one of their nearby teammates. But as players progress in the sport and gain experience playing games, they start to become familiar with those situations that require them to move from their position on the pitch and help provide defensive support to one of their teammates.

Modifying basic man-to-man defence

With man-to-man defence, you can make various modifications to fit the needs and abilities of your players. For example, you can choose to make it an aggressive defence that also brings more risk into the picture, or you can opt to go with an approach that involves a lot less risk but also allows the opposing team to control much of the action.

✔ **Pressing:** Pressing is where the team applies an aggressive defensive approach in football to try to regain possession of the ball as quickly as possible whenever their team loses possession. It often combines man-to man marking with zonal defence. The signature of pressing is that the dribbler is always immediately closed down by one and sometimes even two players in an effort to force errors, stall the attack and restrict the opponent's ability to get the ball moving up the pitch. Meanwhile, while the person on the ball is being pressured, the other defenders press forward to help cut down the number of options available for the player to pass to teammates. It can be a real fun style of play for kids who enjoy going after the ball.

When operating this type of defence, one of the most important things you have to instil in the kids is the mindset that as soon as their team loses the ball, their sole focus is to regain possession as quickly as possible before the other team even has a chance to set up and compose its attack.

The biggest weakness associated with this pressing is that it leaves the team highly vulnerable to a counterattack because you have all your players pressing forward. It is also very tiring over the course of a game and can make teams that employ these tactics vulnerable later on.

✔ **Dropping off**: At the other end of the spectrum from a pressing game is dropping off. With dropping off, any time the team is dispossessed players quickly move back into defensive shape to prevent any type of deep penetration by the attacking team. It's a great style of defence for protecting a lead because the attacking team is going to have to play good inventive attacking football to break the defence down.

One of the drawbacks of dropping off is that the attacking team have a chance to dictate play and have plenty of time to set up its attacks, and to probe the defence for weaknesses before attacking; and because its players won't be under any defensive pressure they can pick their passes.

Of course, you have plenty of room to make modifications with this approach. For example, you can have one player taking an aggressive approach and providing immediate pressure on the opposition player with the ball, which provides a few extra very valuable seconds for the rest of the team to get back and set up in its proper defensive formation. Or you can choose to have a couple of players provide the defensive pressure as soon as your team loses the ball, and the other players are responsible for retreating back toward their goal. Remember, the defensive tactics can be altered to fit your team's strengths.

If you are facing a team that has a player who is highly talented and makes all the play for the opposition, you may want to consider marking that player out of the game. Designate one of your most tenacious players to tracking this favoured player around the pitch, whatever is happening elsewhere, and preventing him from receiving the ball; or if he does get the ball, from doing anything constructive with it. Any player assigned to such a task needs to be very determined, able to concentrate, and to enjoy being given a very specific role.

Zonal defence

When youngsters have been involved in football for a couple of years and have a basic understanding of the principles of good defence, you can begin coaching them in the zonal defence system. Basically, zonal defence makes players responsible for a specific area of the pitch. Figure 12-1 is an example of what area of the pitch each player is responsible for in this 3-5-2 formation. (See Chapter 14, which goes into greater detail on the advantages and disadvantages of different formations.)

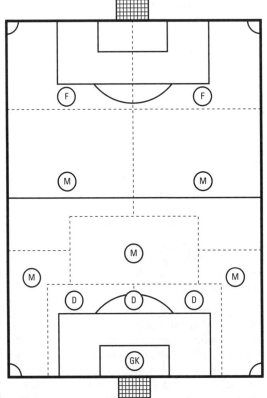

Figure 12-1:
You can see which areas of the pitch the players are responsible for.

In the zonal defence approach, anytime an attacking player enters a defensive player's zone, she is immediately marked. When the attacking player moves out of that defensive player's zone, some coaches instruct the defender to continue marking her, even though doing so means the player is leaving her zone to stick with the other player and the ball. Other coaches prefer that, when an attacking player moves out of a specific zone, the responsibility for marking her transfers to the defensive player of that respective zone. Decide which technique works best with your squad.

Regardless of what type of defence you choose for your team to play, the following are basic defensive principles that any team, at any age or level of experience, should adhere to.

- ✔ **Protect the scoring area.** The area in front of goal is the prized piece of territory. Keeping the opposing team out of this area drastically reduces the number of good scoring chances they get against your team.

- ✔ **Help out.** The essence of team defence is lending support when needed. This means recognising that when an attacker dribbles past a teammate, it is important to move over to help defend against that player, and prevent a clear shot on goal.

- ✔ **Beat the ball.** The more players you have between your goal and the opposing team when it has the ball, the more likely your squad is to be able to make a successful defensive stand. Whenever your team loses the ball, the more players you have able to rush back and put themselves between the ball and their own goal, the greater chance that you can derail the attack.

- ✔ **Clear out.** Make sure your defenders – and really any player who gains possession of the ball in front of the goal – know that they must clear it out quickly. These kicks should never be played across the front of your own goal, where an interception can quickly lead to a scoring chance for the opposition. Rather, they should be played to the nearest touchline to help ensure that the opposing defenders can't get their foot on the ball , and if they do, they will have limited options available to them.

- ✔ **Get close.** Any time your defensive player finds himself outnumbered, such as a two-on-one situation, he should try to position himself in such a way that prevents both the pass and the shot. The most important thing is to get close enough to the player on the ball to prevent the shot. You never want to give the player with the ball an easy and direct route to the goal. At the least, by covering the dribbler, you force him to make a pass, which produces a greater chance of a miscue and losing possession of the ball.

- ✔ **Stand up.** Defensive players who jump in for the ball rather than sticking to sound tackling fundamentals make it drastically easier for attacking players to manoeuvre the ball towards the goal. When a player commits to the tackle and lunges for the ball, they take themselves right out of the game and allow the attacking player the opportunity to continue dribbling, or to take advantage of the space to get a clear shot on goal or deliver an unobstructed pass to a teammate. Encourage players to stay on their feet and hold the attacker up by presenting an impassable obstacle instead of jumping into the tackle and watching the attacker sail past. Whenever you spot a player lunging during an exercise in training, immediately correct the mistake and demonstrate what type of body position or tackle would have been best to use in that particular situation.

✔ **Maintain proper depth.** Playing sound defence requires maintaining proper depth at all times. Your defenders should not be lined up flat across the pitch. All it takes for the attacking team to beat this type of alignment is one good through pass, which is a lot easier to make when defenders are in a straight line. Instead, have one of your defenders in the defensive line nearest the ball, and the rest should angle back towards the goal, in a staggered line, making it harder to play a ball through the defence for the opposing forwards to run onto. Also, on goal kicks the central defenders may drop off deeper into their own half as the kick is taken, in order to anticipate the ball going over the heads of the defensive line.

✔ **Approach at an angle.** Your defensive players should always approach an attacking player from an angle, rather than directly at them. Taking an angle forces the attacking player to send a pass backward or to a specific area of the pitch, because the angle has eliminated a lot of the passing options.

✔ **Force the attacker to use the wrong foot.** Tell your defenders to pay attention to which foot the attacking player favours. Then the defender should try to keep the attacking player on their wrong foot by closing down the attacker from the side they favour. Often, preventing a right-footed player from getting the ball on that foot will be enough to prevent them from getting a good shot in.

✔ **Practise defence.** Remember, your team will spend approximately half of every game defending, so don't neglect your defensive play during your training sessions. Also, while the team is performing any type of exercise, it can be easy to get caught up watching the attacker and her mechanics passing or shooting. Don't forget to devote an equal amount of attention to the defender. Pay attention to whether she used the appropriate type of tackling method, which is covered later in this chapter.

When a youngster makes a great move in defence, maybe anticipating the attacker's run, or putting in a goal-saving tackle, make sure that you recognise the effort with a verbal comment during the game or a high-five when the team comes to the touchlines for a breather. Kids will understand the importance of defence, and give you a strong effort in that area of the game, if they sense that you put equal importance on that area of the game. If the enthusiasm you exhibit for a goal your team scores matches your enthusiasm when your squad stops a great scoring opportunity from the opposing team, then your team is on its way to being a well-rounded squad.

Improving Defensive Skills

In much the same way that players on the attack must have a wide range of skills and moves to choose from in their arsenal in order to enhance their chances of being successful, the same goes for youngsters in defence. A child that is resourceful and has an assortment of defensive techniques that he can use keeps the attacking player off balance, disrupts the attacking team's attack and increases the likelihood of his team regaining possession of the ball. You need to have a smorgasbord of individual defensive techniques available to you, which you can pass on to your team.

When conducting exercises to practise all the different tackling techniques covered in this chapter, be sure that you put the kids in a wide range of situations that force them to use both their left and right legs. For example, if you only practise the sliding tackle coming from the right side, and in a game one of your players needs to perform it coming from the left side, you can't expect him to pull it off.

Marking

The foundation of all good defensive play begins with marking, which simply means that the defending player is in-between the attacking player and her own goal, or between the attacking player and the ball. Marking an attacker prevents her from dribbling or passing the ball, or slows down her progress while the defence is under attack. Here are a few points to keep in mind when coaching marking skills:

- ✔ **Get close**. The closer a defender sticks to the attacking player, the more difficult it is for that player to manoeuvre the ball, deliver a pass, or get off a shot. If the defender gets too tight to their man, however, then she will be easier to dribble past. So it is a question of finding that optimum distance to close down the attacker without offering an opportunity to slip the ball past.

- ✔ **Be aware**. Youngsters are only in good defensive position if they are between the player they are marking and their own goal – and they have sight of where the ball is. Whenever a player loses sight of where the ball is, their ability to defend is weakened.

- ✔ **Notice tendencies.** With older and more experienced players, stress the importance of paying attention to tendencies. Does the player always break the same way when they dribble? Do they come inside or move out towards the touchline? Making a slight adjustment in the angle of approach to an attacker can make a big difference in how effectively that player is marked. By preventing attackers from making their favourite moves, defenders can force attackers away from goal and increase the chance of dispossessing them. Does the player look down a lot when dribbling? If so, he is susceptible to losing the ball and the looking down is probably a sign that he is not totally comfortable with dribbling, which means that by putting tight defensive pressure on him your player has a pretty good chance of forcing a mistake, resulting in possession for your team.

Block tackle

The best time for defensive players to resort to a block tackle is when an opposing player is dribbling the ball directly at them (see Figure 12-2a). In order to execute a successful block tackle, the defender moves directly toward the player and uses her entire body to tackle the opponent. The defensive player blocks the ball by applying steady and even pressure to it with the inside of her leg (see Figure 12-2b). She should also tense all the muscles in her leg, which also helps to protect the knees.

Figure 12-2: The defender uses the block tackle against the player coming straight at him.

a

b

When explaining the block tackle, keep the following tips in mind:

- ✔ **Staggered:** As the defensive player moves toward the attacking player, one foot should be slightly ahead of the other and he should be focused on the player's chest.

- ✔ **Crouched:** The defender should be slightly crouched, which enables him to be properly positioned to react to the dribbler moving to his left or right.

- ✔ **Attack the ball:** When the defender is ready to attempt the tackle, he must go after the ball, not the player. He should use the inside surface of his foot and keep it firm as he drives it into the ball and blocks it so that the attacking player is unable to continue moving forward. Make sure that your defender knows to keep their weight over the ball and move forward through the tackle. If they lean back without their weight over the ball, they risk injury to the knee.

Shoulder charge

While football may be a game played primarily with the feet, players who understand how to use their entire body to their advantage while in defence are going to enjoy increased levels of success. The use of the *shoulder charge* can be slightly controversial, but if correctly executed is an excellent defensive technique to use when a defender finds herself running alongside an attacking player as she is chasing after the ball (see Figure 12-3).

Figure 12-3: Successful shoulder charges rely on using the whole body.

a   b

A lot of contact happens between players during games and, generally speaking, players are usually allowed to make contact with an opponent's shoulder, if they keep their elbows close to the body, and if the ball is in close proximity. Of course, this all depends on the referee's interpretation of the rule and the attitude towards shoulder barging adopted by the league. It is easy to overdo the contact in a shoulder barge and give away a foul, as players in the professional football leagues discover week in, week out.

Here's what to keep in mind when executing a successful shoulder barge.

✔ **Leverage:** The key to making a shoulder barge is being able to use the entire body to gain a better position to make a play on the ball. The player who is able to get their shoulder in front of the opposing player's shoulder, without giving away a foul for pushing, is at a distinct advantage.

✔ **The feet:** When the players arrive at the ball, the player who has the advantage in shoulder position uses the foot that is farthest away from the defender to play the ball (see Figure 12-3b). Using the inside foot makes it easier for the opponent to take the ball away. Using the outside leg, and the outside portion of the foot, makes it extremely difficult for the opposing player to have any chance at the ball.

Side tackle

A *side tackle* is used when a defender finds himself running alongside an attacking player that is dribbling the ball and is looking to get a shot on goal in or deliver a pass to a teammate. Executing a side tackle requires the defender to be right next to the attacking player. When the attacking player is about to pass or kick the ball (see Figure 12-4a), the defensive player reaches his leg in, extends his foot, and knocks the ball away by using the toes of the foot nearest the defender (see Figure 12-4b).

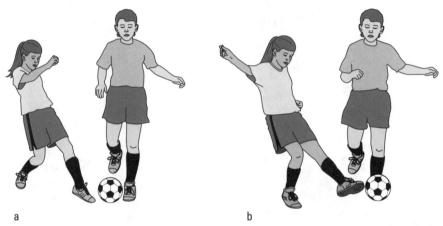

Figure 12-4: This player attempts to knock the ball away from her opponent with a side tackle.

a   b

Remind players that they must be right next to the attacking player to make a side tackle. If a defender isn't close to the player running with the ball when attempting this move and he extends his leg out, he will fail to make any contact at all or, alternatively, be late and catch the player but not the ball, giving away a foul in a dangerous area. Once the ball is poked away, if no other players are in the vicinity it comes down to who can react more quickly to get to the ball. Players that carry out the side tackle shouldn't be satisfied with simply knocking the ball away from the opponent; encourage them to continue to jockey and hustle to gain possession of the ball for their team.

Sliding tackle

The *sliding tackle* is used by defenders who are outside of block, or side tackle range. Because it is easy to give a foul away with a slide tackle, it is often a last ditch attempt to prevent a scoring opportunity. In many youth football leagues slide tackling is not permitted because of the injury risk involved for both the attacking and defensive player. Being well-versed in all of your league's rules is critical (see Chapter 2), and you obviously don't want to devote training time to a technique that is not allowed.

In the more advanced levels of youth football the sliding tackle is a part of the game and it's one of those skills that is extremely important to coach correctly to minimise the injury risk for your players. Where the sliding tackle is allowed your team should use it sparingly and call on it when no other defensive options are available. That's because if a sliding tackle isn't successful, it puts the defensive team at a real disadvantage because the defender who attempted the tackle is on the ground and be in a difficult position to recover and help out against the opponent's attack. So, the sliding tackle is not just one of the more difficult tackles to impart to young players, it is also one of the more riskier ones to make during a game.

While starting youngsters on this technique, stress the importance of making contact with the ball first, otherwise a foul is the likely result.

Here's how to make a sliding tackle.

- **The approach:** When the defender has been beaten, or is trying to catch up with an attacking player dribbling down the pitch, he has to approach from the side (see Figure 12-5a). Note that the tackle from behind is illegal, so correct positioning is crucial. He has to be close to the player, otherwise once he begins the sliding motion the attacking player may have dribbled out of range.

- **Sliding leg:** As the defender nears the player he drops his lower body and begins the sliding motion with the leg closest to the player (see Figure 12-5b).

- **Top leg:** As the defender's leg makes contact with the ground he bends and tucks it underneath him while extending the top leg straight out (see Figure 12-5c).

- **Knock away:** With the top leg the defender knocks the ball away from the attacking player with as much force as he can generate so that the opponent is unable to play the ball while he is still lying on the ground (see Figure 12-5d).

The sliding tackle involves a lot of physical contact, perhaps the closest and most aggressive physical contact that is likely to occur in the game outside of heading the ball following a corner or free-kick or goal kick. Often it is not only the ball that gets played, but during the follow through the player with the ball. For this reason, young players need to be aware of the challenges involved in making this tackle, as well as avoiding making a sliding tackle recklessly. On a muddy pitch, however, the sliding tackle can be both effective and fun.

Because the sliding tackle is one of the more difficult tackling techniques to master for youngsters, start out by having a stationary ball. Have the kids run up alongside the ball, perform the slide, and make contact with the ball. It's going to take lots of practice and plenty of repetitions to figure out when to gauge to begin the slide against a moving player. So, focus on proper sliding technique with just a ball and, once they start progressing in that area, you can incorporate a moving attacking player into the exercise.

Figure 12-5:
The sliding tackle is an advanced defensive technique.

a

b

c

d

Hook tackle

The *hook tackle* is similar to the sliding tackle in that the defensive player drops to the ground to carry it out. It also carries the same risks. The biggest difference between the two is that hook tackles are done when the attacking player is dribbling right at the defender. The following are the steps to carry out a successful hook tackle.

✔ **Wait for commitment:** Once the attacking player commits to going left or right, the defender can begin to make the tackle (see Figure 12-6a).

✔ **Get low:** For example, as the attacking player moves to his right (see Figure 12-6b) the defender drops his body low to the ground and uses his right hand for balance. A common mistake many youngsters make when practising this technique is that they fail to get low to the ground right away. When they don't get low, they are often off balance and wind up lunging for the ball rather than making a hooking motion with their leg.

✔ **Top leg hooks ball:** While bending the bottom leg the player's body contacts with the ground and he swings his top leg in a hooking motion to steal the ball (see Figure 12-6c). Make sure youngsters know to focus on making contact with the ball with the tops of their shoelaces. As your players become more experienced with this technique some may actually be able to hook the ball and immediately gain control of it themselves.

a

b

c

Figure 12-6:
A player uses a hook tackle to win the ball.

Part IV
Advanced Football Strategies

'Well, as the team's new coach, my first recommendation is to use a smaller size ball.'

In this part . . .

Football is more than kids running up and down the field, chasing the ball, and waving at grandma in the stands. In this part, we offer up some additional insights to help take your team's attacking and defensive play to the next level.

Chapter 13

Taking It Up a Notch: Drills

*Y*ou've reached that point in the season where your team is starting to get a fairly good grasp of the basics of passing and receiving. Your goalie has become pretty proficient at making the routine saves. When your team is under pressure deep in its own half, it enjoys its share of successes in halting the attack. You've even had a couple players make a header in a game. Your team is developing and making progress and that should bring a smile to your face. In order to ensure that the discovery and skill development doesn't come to a grinding halt, it is time for you to take your training drills up a notch.

So now what? You've got to match your team's increasing skill level with drills that continue to challenge, motivate, and excite them. Relying on a drill you used during the first week of training with a team that has been together for quite a while now isn't going to carry with it the same type of benefits as it did earlier. The drills in this chapter can help re-energise your team enthusiasm and continue pushing your players down that path of and skill acquisition and development.

Attacking Drills

The ability to create good scoring chances, particularly whenever your team outnumbers the defence, is the mark of a well-coached team that understands how to operate efficiently when these types of situations arise throughout the course of a game. While your team isn't always going to score a goal in such situations, the more times they are able to generate good scoring opportunities, the more it will pay dividends for them over the duration of the season.

Attacking

The ability to create quality scoring chances, particularly when your team has the advantage of outnumbering your opponent's defence, is the mark of a well-coached team.

Drill: Two-on-one

✔ **Purpose:** This drill helps youngsters find out how to exploit a two-on-one advantage to the full and generate a scoring opportunity.

✔ **How it works:** Position an attacking player on each side of the goalie, who begins the drill holding a ball (see Figure 13-1). Also position a defender about 10 yards in front of the goalie. The two attacking players move away from the goal and the goalie delivers a pass to one of them. Then, the attacking pair spins around and works to beat the lone defender and get a good shot on goal.

✔ **Coaching pointers:** Observe the goalie to ensure that she uses the proper technique while delivering the pass. Also, monitor the attacking pair to see whether they take a shot too early in the drill or whether they make good-quality passes to fully capitalise on their numerical advantage.

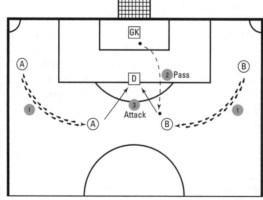

Figure 13-1: The 2-on-1 starts with the goalie holding the ball.

Drill: Three-on-two

✔ **Purpose:** This drill encourages youngsters to take advantage when they have an extra player in their attack. It also allows players to work on their throw ins, as well as their passing, receiving, and shooting skills. By being outnumbered, it also forces the defenders to be quick on their feet in reading the game.

✔ **How it works:** Set up an attacking player on the sideline to throw the ball in (see Figure 13-2). Position two more attacking players in the drill area, along with two defenders and a goalie. Once the player throws the ball in, he should look to create space to stretch the two defenders out. The player who received the ball can press forward and take a shot on goal, or pass to one of his teammates flanking him, depending on what the defenders do.

✔ **Coaching pointers:** Initially, make sure that the child made a legal throw-in and dragged his foot while releasing the ball (see Chapter 16, where this is discussed in more detail). Focus on the attacking player who receives the throw-in to make sure that he dribbles with his head up and delivers a pass if a teammate is unmarked, or gets a shot in if that turns out to be the best scoring opportunity.

Figure 13-2:
The attackers have a good chance of scoring with the 3-on-2 drill.

Passing

You may have a number of players who are proficient at putting the ball into the net, and that's a great asset. But if few teammates can get them the ball when and where they need it, the number of scoring chances your team generates is going to sink. These drills hone those all-important passing skills.

Drill: Fancy foot

✔ **Purpose:** *Fancy foot* drills develop a kid's weaker foot so that she becomes comfortable passing and receiving with either foot.

✔ **How it works:** Set up a basic two-on-one drill with the object being for two attacking players to try and work the ball down the pitch against a lone defender. The twist is that the attacking players can only pass the ball, as well as receive it, with their less dominant foot.

✔ **Coaching pointers:** It can be frustrating for kids to become at ease using their weaker foot as during games they are naturally going to use their stronger foot. So be patient, provide lots of encouragement, and help them to understand that when both their feet are equally good they become that much more of an attacking threat, or that much stronger a defender.

Drill: Diagonal passing

- **Purpose:** This drill works on the accuracy of a player's short and long passes, their ability to get the ball airborne when the situation requires, and their ability to receive and get under control different types of passes.

- **How it works:** Diagonal passing can be run simultaneously with the entire team broken down into groups of four (see Figure 13-3). Position two players about 10 yards apart and position two more players about 20 yards away. Each player starts with a ball. The drill begins with the two players nearest each other exchanging passes. One player must send a side-foot pass along the ground while the other player delivers a chipped pass to get the ball in the air so that the balls don't collide. After receiving the passes, the players deliver long crossfield passes to the player across from them. Again, one player delivers a pass along the ground while the other sends one into the air. Rotate the types of passes the players are using so that everyone gets practice doing both.

- **Coaching pointers:** Make sure that the kids are following through toward their intended targets. Knowing that they have to react quickly to receive an incoming ball, they may have a tendency to cut their follow through short in preparation for receiving a pass.

Figure 13-3:
Diagonal
passing
works on
several
skills at
once.

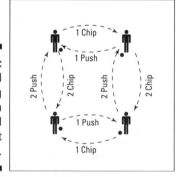

Shooting

Choose a variety of shooting drills that challenge your players to work on their accuracy, distance, and technique. In match situations, kids have to shoot from different angles and distances; using the drills in this section gets them prepared to take shots during matches.

Drill: Bending balls

- ✔ **Purpose:** *Bending balls* works on a youngster's shooting skills with both feet and perfecting shots at challenging angles with a defender in the way.

- ✔ **How it works:** Position two attacking players about 30 yards away from the goal, with one player the designated shooter and the other the passer. Also, have a defender out about ten yards in front to serve as an obstacle that the shooter has to work the ball around. The drill begins with the passer delivering the ball to the shooter, who shoots while the ball is rolling (see Figure 13-4a). With the defender between her and the goal, she has to chip the ball over the player's head, or if she's more advanced, work on putting sidespin to bend the ball around the player. Next, (see Figure 13-4b) she receives a diagonal pass that forces her to go to her left and take a shot with the other foot while the defender slides over to cut down the shooting angle. Third, (see Figure 13-4c) the shooter has to cut back to her right to receive another pass and get off a shot at a sharp angle with the defender again standing in the way.

- ✔ **Coaching pointers:** Watch to see whether the passer puts the ball in the most advantageous position, whether the attacker takes the right angle for the shot and whether the defender and goalie work together to eliminate the player from getting a quality shot off.

Drill: Zig-zag

- ✔ **Purpose:** This drill helps kids work on their shooting technique and accuracy from a variety of distances and angles.

- ✔ **How it works:** Begin with the shooter about 30 yards away from the goal (see Figure 13-5). Position a passer (A) about ten yards away from him with a ball, as well as another player (B) by the side of the goal with two balls. The drill begins with the passer giving him a slow moving ball that the shooter strikes while running straight ahead. The passer at the side of the goal follows with a diagonal pass and then another pass at a sharp angle.

- ✔ **Coaching pointers:** On the initial kick, make sure that the player gets full force behind the shot and follows through at the goal. Watch the positioning of his planted foot on the other shots because technique can get sloppy sometimes on sharply angled kicks that he may not be used to taking.

Ball handling

Good ball handling plays a prominent role in a team's success at both the attacking and defensive ends of the field. Players who can dribble out of trouble while pinned back near their own goal save their goalie from being forced to make more saves than he has to. Also, players who don't lose the ball while on the attack apply additional pressure on the opponent, which can translate into extra scoring chances.

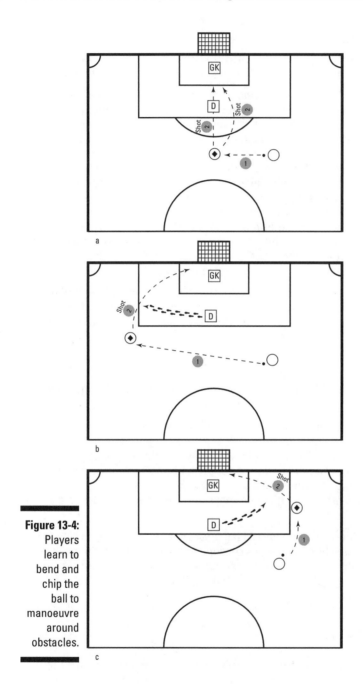

Figure 13-4:
Players
learn to
bend and
chip the
ball to
manoeuvre
around
obstacles.

Figure 13-5:
A player
takes
several
shots in
succession
with the zig-
zag drill.

Drill: Musical football

- ✔ **Purpose:** *Musical football* helps youngsters get to grips with handling the
ball in tight spaces while being pressured by a defender.

- ✔ **How it works:** Mark off a playing area of about 15 yards by 15 yards.
Place three balls in the centre of the playing area and have five players
positioned around the outside of the area. On your command, the players run in and battle for possession of the ball. Run the drill for a minute
or two. The object is to see who can maintain possession of the ball
when the time runs out. Kids of all ages have fun with this drill, and if
you begin counting down out loud with ten seconds left, you really get
the competitive juices flowing with the kids as they try to make a last-
second tackle or try to cling to possession of their ball.

- ✔ **Coaching pointers:** With several players in a tight area, keep a close eye
that fouls aren't being committed by players trying to win balls, or by
those trying to protect them illegally.

Drill: Gridlock

- ✔ **Purpose:** *Gridlock* works on ball skills in both a one-on-one setting, as
well as those difficult one-on-two scenarios.

- ✔ **How it works:** An attacking player starts in the midfield with the ball.
For about 20 yards, they dribble along the pitch against a defender. If
they reach the 20-yard marker that you have designated with a cone,
they continue trying to move on for another 20 yards, but this time
against two defenders. If, while going one-on-one, they lose possession
of the ball, they start over from the spot the ball was taken and continue
on until they reach the marker.

✔ **Coaching pointers:** Be sure to match up players of similar abilities for this drill. You don't want the player with the weakest dribbling ability going up against your best defender and not being able to get to the marker.

Heading

Well-rounded footballers are able to use all parts of their body to move the ball where they want. Using the ol' noggin can be a great weapon for scoring goals, as well as clearing the ball out of danger. The following are some drills to get your kids thinking and using their heads.

Drill: Line 'em up

✔ **Purpose:** This drill helps players zero in on an incoming ball and realise how to make quick adjustments and head a pass to an unmarked teammate.

✔ **How it works:** Position a player about ten yards in front of you. Toss a ball up in the air to them and, as they are getting into position to make a header, take a few steps to the left or right. The player must adjust according to your movements and head the ball back to you.

✔ **Coaching pointers:** Make sure that the child keeps a close eye on the ball and relies on their peripheral vision to locate which direction you have moved in. Otherwise, they won't be able to make solid contact with the ball and their headers will be off target.

Drill: Cross and head

✔ **Purpose:** *Cross and head* works on heading, delivering accurate crossing passes and helping goalies figure out how to defend against headers.

✔ **How it works:** Position one player to the side of the goal, and the designated header about 10 yards away from the goalie (see Figure 13-8). The drill begins with the player at the side delivering a cross to be headed at the goal. The goalie, who makes the save or retrieves the ball, then throws the ball to the passer, who delivers the ball in the air to be headed again. The goalie then passes along the goal line, and the player delivers another cross to be headed.

✔ **Coaching pointers:** If the crosses aren't on target, watch where the youngster's foot is making contact with the ball. On headers, you must make sure that you remind the player to follow through with their head at the target to get the maximum force behind their shots.

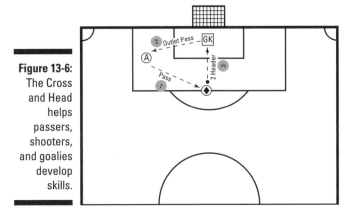

Figure 13-6:
The Cross
and Head
helps
passers,
shooters,
and goalies
develop
skills.

Defensive Drills

In much the same way that attacking players work on different ways to control the ball and negotiate their way down the pitch, the same goes for defenders when it comes to mastering the skills required of their position. You must help them to acquire different techniques to win possession of the ball and find ways to prevent the opposition from capitalising on a scoring opportunity when they have a numerical advantage in attack. Your team can use any of a number of methods available (see Chapter 12). Now, let's take a look at drills to improve some of those skills.

Tackling

Nothing disrupts the flow of an attack quicker than defenders who are skilful when it comes to taking the ball away. Sound tackling techniques are a necessity for any team at any level.

Drill: Chase and catch

✔ **Purpose:** The *chase and catch* drill helps players to discover that they need to use their entire body, and specifically their shoulders, to take possession of the ball from an opposing player.

✔ **How it works:** Position two players about ten yards apart with a player in-between them with the ball. The youngster with the ball uses a side-foot pass to send the ball towards goal. The two players flanking her run and try to gain possession of the ball. The player who gains control of the ball continues on and tries to score a goal while the other player takes a defensive role and tries to poke the ball away and prevent a shot on goal.

  ✔ **Coaching pointers:** Make sure that the kids keep their elbows tucked close to their body, because often they have a tendency to use them to muscle the opponent off the ball, and they will concede a foul and therefore possession.

Drill: Pressure

  ✔ **Purpose:** The pressure drill shows kids how to receive a throw-in and gather the ball under control and maintain possession of it while they are facing heavy pressure from a defender.

  ✔ **How it works:** Pair your players up and give a youngster in each pair a ball. The drill begins with the pairs facing each other with about ten yards between them. At your command the kids with the ball deliver a throw-in to their partner. After delivering the throw-in, they immediately charge towards their partner and try to win the ball. Run the drill for five or ten seconds. Or, keep it going until possession of the ball is lost. Keep rotating who delivers the throw-in to so that players get practice in both scenarios.

  ✔ **Coaching pointers:** Make sure that the child receiving the ball is watching it as they receive. Kids sometimes have the tendency to look at the player charging at them, which disrupts their ability to control the ball.

Defending

The better your team becomes at defending, the happier your goalie is going to be. Besides giving him less work, the more proficient the team becomes in this area of the game, the more likely the team is to spend more time in its opponent's end of the field.

Drill: Taking on two-on-ones

  ✔ **Purpose:** This drill gives defenders work in a number of areas, including battling for balls one-on-one and disrupting two-on-ones from close range.

  ✔ **How it works:** Position two attacking players near the penalty arc with a defender at the top of the six-yard box, with a goalie in the goal (see Figure 13-7.) From off to the side of the goal, send a high ball between the three players. The defender is forced to make a quick decision on whether the ball is in range for him to go for it, or whether the risk is too high and he may end up out of position with his goalie in a precarious situation. The drill continues until a goal is scored, the goalie makes a save or the defender clears the ball out of the area.

  ✔ **Coaching pointers:** On balls that you deliberately kick long, make sure that the defender isn't going after them. Tell him to only go after balls that he has a realistic chance of reaching so that he doesn't put his team at an unnecessary disadvantage.

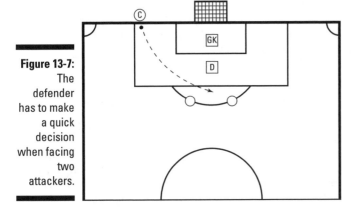

Figure 13-7:
The defender has to make a quick decision when facing two attackers.

Drill: Tackling three-on-twos

✔ **Purpose:** This drill rewards strong defensive play in a game-like setting and forces the attacking team to make quick decisions under the pressure of the clock.

✔ **How it works:** Play a series of 30-second games in which the attacking team tries to score a goal in this three-on-two set up. Award the attacking team two points if they score a goal, and one point if they get a shot on goal. Award the defending team two points if they are able to prevent any shot from reaching the goal.

✔ **Coaching pointers:** Make sure that the defenders aren't over-committing, which creates an even bigger advantage for the attacking team. Also, make sure that the attacking team is aggressively trying to get a shot in, as they have little time to work with.

Goalkeeping

Manning the goalie position is no easy task for youngsters, who are challenged to make stops on kicks coming at them from all sorts of angles and distances. The ability to make saves, both on the ground and in the air, takes plenty of practice.

Drill: Diving one-handers

✔ **Purpose:** _Diving one-handers_ gets goalies comfortable – and confident – with making one-handed saves.

✔ **How it works:** Position two players, both with balls, about 15 yards away from the goal and at an angle. The first player takes a shot and the goalie must dive and attempt to block the shot with one hand. Then, getting up quickly and beginning at the other post, she's got to dive in the opposite direction to make a save from the other kick.

✔ **Coaching pointers:** Make sure that the goalie is at full stretch in order to make it as difficult as possible for the striker. When the goalie does make a save and is lying on the ground see whether she cradles the ball like a puppy and protects it with her body.

Drill: Mystery saves

✔ **Purpose:** This drill improves the reaction skills of your goalie.

✔ **How it works:** Position two players with balls in front of the goal about 10 yards away from each other. You stand out of the goalie's view and signal which player is to actually take the shot on goal. On your whistle, both players approach their balls at the same time, but only one player delivers a shot on goal. The uncertainty forces the goalie to really concentrate on each ball and quickly react to the incoming shot.

✔ **Coaching pointers:** Make sure that the goalie follows the shot all the way in to his hands and doesn't allow the ball to bounce away for a dangerous rebound.

Putting It All Together: Sample Training Session

Now that you're armed with a new set of drills that you can incorporate into your training sessions, you need to put them together. A well-structured session that features new drills for the players to perform keeps their attention levels high and continues their progression in the sport. You can use the following one-hour sample training plan with your players, utilising the drills covered in this chapter.

✔ **Five minutes:** Stretching and callisthenics

✔ **Ten minutes:** Split the squad in half. At one end of the pitch, the players perform the passing fancy drill. At the other end of the pitch, have them work at the chase and catch drill. After five minutes, blow the whistle and have them reverse the drills they are performing. The reversal gives the entire team the chance to work on both their passing skills as well as their tackling skills.

✔ **Fifteen minutes:** Break the team up into three groups. In the centre of the pitch, run the diagonal passing drill; at one end of the pitch work the zig-zag shooting drill, and at the other end of the pitch the diving one-handers exercise for goalies. At each five-minute interval, have the players rotate so that they go through each of the three drills during this 15-minute segment.

✔ **Five minutes:** Keep the team in their same three groups, and run three games of the musical football drill. This drill is a fun, yet highly competitive game that puts a smile on the kids' faces right in the middle of the training session.

✔ **Ten minutes:** You have devoted the first half of the training session to working on a lot of individual skills, so now is a good time to get the kids working together on those situations that arise during the game. Now is a good time to incorporate the tackling three-on-twos drill at one end of the pitch, and the mystery saves for goalies drill at the other end of the pitch. As players go through the three-on-two drill, interchange them with the players involved at the other end of the pitch to give everyone a chance to do everything.

✔ **Ten minutes:** At one end of the pitch, use the taking two-on-ones drill, and at the other end of the pitch have players work on their corner kicks in both corners of the pitch. (If you are in search of good corner-kick drills to use with your kids, jump to Chapter 16.) After five minutes, be sure to rotate the kids.

✔ **Five minutes:** Conclude the training session with a fun practice game that has proven popular over the season. A quick game of the kids against the coaches and parents (see Chapter 6), is always a winner with the youngsters, and a great way to send everyone home happy and looking forward to returning for the next training session.

Chapter 14

Upgrading Attacking Tactics and Skills

hoosing a formation for your team to play is sort of like trying to decide on dessert after a meal at a fancy restaurant. You have so many options, and they all look good. You can introduce a variety of formations to your team after they've mastered the basics of the game. (Refer to Chapter 3, for more on the basics.) Some formations cater to an attacking style of play, while others lean toward a more defensive approach.

In this chapter, we delve into some unusual formations biased towards attacking. While these formations may not be very practical in match situations, they are very useful in training for working on building attacks and improving forward play. These formations are designed to produce a high number of scoring chances when your players are able to maintain possession of the ball dribbling and make accurate passes to their teammates. (See Chapter 15, which takes a look at formations more suited to a match situation.) We also take a closer look at upgrading your players' skills in the areas of delivering crosses and heading those crosses, as well as using a wide range of tricks to get past defenders and create shots on goals.

Upgrading the Attack

A *formation* is the basic format that assigns players to specific areas of the pitch – in different formations, players have different responsibilities in their positions. Formations can be attacking, defensive, or fairly neutral, depending on positioning of the players, how you tell them to play in those positions, and what you are trying to accomplish.

Whatever system you choose to use with your players, make sure that every player does his best to fulfil his responsibilities in order for the system to operate as smoothly as possible. Because you have a number of different systems at your disposal, you should definitely introduce your team to several of them. You may come across one that really fits the team's personality and its players really well, but you'll never know if you don't experiment a little.

All formations do not work for all teams. You and your coaching staff need to pick the system that takes full advantage of your team's talents. Some formations are going to work, and some aren't going to be nearly as successful. Go ahead and introduce your team to a wide range of formations and experiment with them to see what they enjoy playing more, what works best for them, and then go from there.

When announcing the name of a formation, the first number represents the number of defenders, the second the number of players positioned in the midfield area, and the last number is the number of players at the front of the attack. The goalie is not mentioned.

Two-three-five formation

The two-three-five is a heavily attacking formation designed to generate lots of scoring chances and keep the ball in the opponent's half of the pitch, because the bulk of the players are forward type players. Your team has five attackers – the left and right forwards, an inside left and right, and the centre forward (see Figure 14-1). The following list outlines the players' tasks in this set up.

- **Defenders:** The players manning these positions play behind the midfielders. They tend to switch between two roles (or one player may stick to each role). During the game, one defender positions a little behind the other and assumes a sweeping role, where the main job, as the position title suggests, is to sweep all balls out of the goal area. Because these players are the last line of defence before the goalie, and the majority of the team is positioned away from the goal, the better defenders are at handling attacking pressure from the opposing team, the more success the team is likely to enjoy employing this system of play

- **Midfielders:** The centre midfielder orchestrates the attack once the team has possession of the ball. Her duties include gathering the ball from her defensive teammates and moving it up the pitch with an accurate pass to the forwards or other midfielders. The left and right midfielders move the ball up to the forwards, and when the ball is in the opponent's half of the pitch they move forward, well past the centre line. They are also responsible for making sure that the opposing team's wingers don't push the ball past them down into the corner kick areas when the opposing team has the ball.

✔ **Forwards:** The focus of the forwards is to work the ball along the touch-lines and toward the corner flags and to deliver crosses to the centre to teammates in the goal area. The inside forwards distribute the ball to the forwards and the centre forward. The primary responsibility of the centre forward, or *striker* as she is often called, is to get the ball in the back of the net. In the more competitive levels of youth football, the player in this position must be an excellent dribbler and have an accurate shot for the two-three-five system to truly be successful.

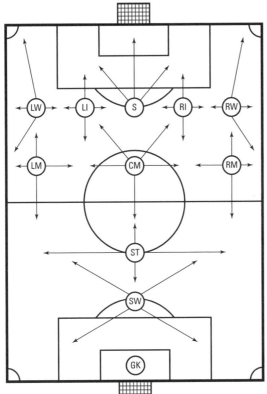

Figure 14-1:
These players are in the 2-3-5 formation.

The two-three-five relies on having some very good defenders holding the fort while the rest of the team presses forward. Without this line of defence, the team is likely to leak a lot of goals.

Four-two-four formation

The four-two-four is the most balanced type of formation you can use, because you have an equal number of players on both attack and defence (see Figure 14-2) with four attackers and four defenders, as well as two midfielders. Here's how it works.

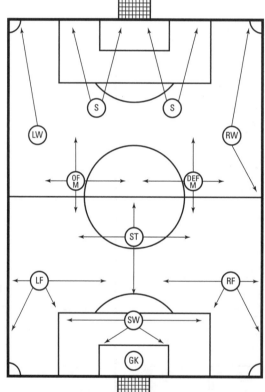

Figure 14-2: The 4-2-4 formation is a balanced attacking formation.

✔ **Defenders:** The defence is comprised of the right and left fullbacks, and the two centre backs. The left fullback's job is to monitor any players that line up opposite them on the pitch or come into their area of the pitch, and help prevent them from manoeuvring into the penalty area and getting a dangerous shot on goal or creating a scoring chance for a teammate. The right fullback does the same against the left side off the opposition's attack. When the defence is under an enormous amount of pressure, the midfielders also retreat back to provide support as well.

✔ **Midfielders:** The two players handling these positions have defined roles as the attacking or the defensive midfielder. As their name suggests, the attacking midfielder plays more with the attack than the defence, and vice versa. Regardless of which role they are playing, make sure that they know to return to their position on the pitch as soon as they have finished supporting the attack providing defensive cover.

✔ **Forwards:** Using this style of attack, the left and right wingers look to move the ball down the touchline toward the corner kick areas, or work a pass into the middle of the pitch if any openings present themselves. One of the two strikers has a dual role in the four-two-four formation because he attacks when his team has possession of the ball, and falls back to assist in midfield when the team is defending

Three-three-four formation

The three-three-four system places greater emphasis on attack than the four-two-four, because it has four attackers, along with three midfielders and three defenders (see Figure 14-3).

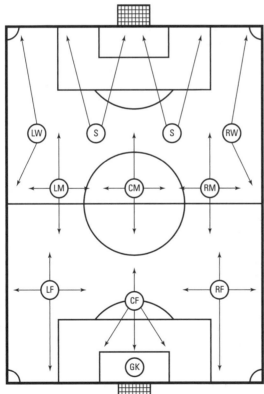

Figure 14-3:
This diagram shows the 3-3-4 formation.

✔ **Defenders:** The three players handling these responsibilities – the right and left fullback and the centre fullback – are positioned in the penalty area and rarely stray from their positions within the box as they provide support for the goalie.

✔ **Midfielders:** The system is similar to the four-two-four system we just covered. If you are using a four-two-four alignment and simply move one player from defence up to midfield, now you've got a three-three-four. With this system, the right midfielder takes a more attack-minded approach, while the left midfielder's role is more defensive.

Most formations are fluid and the higher the level of football the more likely it is that teams move from one formation to another. This is particularly the case as they attack, probe for weaknesses in the opposing team and then exploit the weaknesses. So a formation such as four-four-two (see Chapter 15) can switch to four-two-four as the right and left midfielders push on, or to four-three-three if one of the centre midfielders moves into attack.

✔ **Forwards:** The front four consists of the right and left wingers, along with the two strikers.

Three-five-two formation

The three-five-two system (see Figure 14-4) evolved from the four-four-two system (see Chapter 15 for more on this), which emphasises controlling the play in the middle of the pitch. It provides a bit more attacking punch than the relatively defensive four-four-two, while still attempting to control the midfield area.

Because of the tight, five-player formation in the midfield area, this is an excellent formation to use if you want to play on the counter attack. Also remember that the opposition will more often than not line up in four-four-two formation. Two attackers against three defenders can often turn into two-on-two over the course of a game – which is why not so many teams play three at the back once you get to a higher level.

✔ **Defenders:** The left and right fullbacks patrol the area in front of the penalty box, as well as the centre of the pitch and the touchline nearest to them. The lone central defender is responsible for moving laterally and getting the ball out of the penalty box area.

✔ **Midfielders:** By clogging up the centre of the pitch with your attacking players, the opposing team faces greater difficulty gaining control of the midfield area. As a result, they are not able to work the ball through midfield and are restricted to lumping the ball over the top of the midfield to their forwards. They are also susceptible to a counterattack as the team is likely to win possession in the midfield a lot. The key to the success of using the three-five-two formation is to ensure that the five midfielders are working together and constantly communicating.

✔ **Forwards:** The forwards have to carry the attack and act as a target for forward passes in this formation. They also have to chase down the opposition defenders and prevent them from passing the ball out of defence. Hopefully with five players behind in midfield, the forwards should get plenty of midfield support.

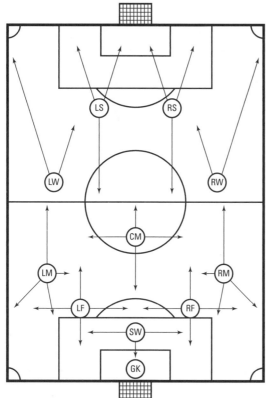

Figure 14-4:
The three-five-two formation puts five players in midfield.

Three-four-three formation

The three-four-three is a rather popular formation (see Figure 14-5) at the younger age levels because it provides balance at both the attacking and defensive ends of the pitch.

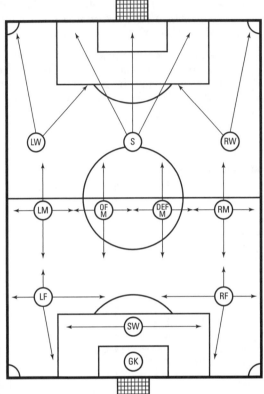

Figure 14-5:
The three-
four-three
formation is
balanced at
both ends of
the field.

✔ **Defenders:** The left and right fullbacks are responsible for controlling
the area in front of the penalty box, as well as the touchline nearest to
them. The lone central defender is positioned in the penalty box area
and is responsible for moving laterally and getting the ball out of the
penalty box area.

✔ **Midfielders:** If you happen to have several youngsters on the squad
who are pretty quick on their feet, this formation can be used to your
advantage because they can be aggressive in the tackle and quickly
join the attack in the opponent's half.

✔ **Forwards:** The left- and right-wingers are responsible for moving the
ball down the touchline and sending crosses to the striker. With three
forwards, the bulk of the scoring responsibilities fall on the striker's
shoulders rather than expecting a lot of midfield runs into the opponent's penalty box. Your forwards must stop the defenders on the other
side from passing the ball out of defence.

Introducing New Attacking Skills

As your team gains experience moving the ball up the pitch and attacking during games, it is going to encounter a variety of defensive styles and techniques. Having the ability to use different attacking approaches to help generate scoring opportunities for the team is a real asset. The position of the defenders during that particular moment in the game dictates, to a large extent, what type of attacking approach works best. In this section, we take a peek at three areas that can bolster your team's attacking prowess and clear the way for more goal-scoring opportunities:

- ✔ Crosses
- ✔ Heading crosses
- ✔ Feints and dummies

Delivering crosses

A football team that is able to continually make good crosses ensures that more of its trips into enemy territory are rewarded with decent scoring opportunities. Your team has a number of crossing options to choose from. For example, a player with the ball on the right touchline (see Figure 14-6) has the option of delivering the ball to the following areas: the area around the near post; the central area, which is the region between the posts; the far post, which is the area in front of the far post and extending beyond; and the edge of the box, which is that area of the pitch that comprises the penalty spot and reaches to the edge of the penalty box.

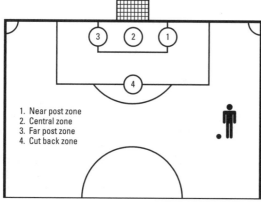

Figure 14-6:
A player who can deliver a successful cross has a lot of options.

1. Near post zone
2. Central zone
3. Far post zone
4. Cut back zone

There are no set rules when it comes to determining which type of cross is the most appropriate to deliver. Each game situation poses a number of different challenges for the players. Whenever a crossing opportunity presents itself, the player has to take into account the situation as it unfolds while she is dribbling the ball and examine how the defence is positioned. From there, she has to determine which is the best option for getting the ball to her teammate in the desired area. She may have to chip the ball over a defender to her attacking teammate positioned on the far post, or she may spot a teammate out of the corner of her eye behind the play who she can cut the ball back to her for a shot on goal.

One of the most common mistakes young players make when delivering a cross is failing to recognise the defender positioned at the near post. If balls aren't delivered with enough pace on them, the defender can easily step out and intercept them. Also, if they aren't lofted high enough in the air when attempting to send them to the far post, the defender can head them out of danger rather easily. (See Chapter 17, which takes a look at some crossing drills that you can incorporate into your training sessions to help ensure that your team is making the most of their opportunities at this end of the pitch.)

When a ball is crossed, the attacking team can rarely get to the ball without a defender to contend with. So, constantly encourage your players to go after the ball when receiving a cross. They can't afford to wait on the ball because that allows defenders the opportunity to converge on the ball and squash the team's goal scoring opportunity.

Heading crosses

A youngster's head can be an equally potent scoring weapon as his foot when your team is on the attack. Players with the header in their bag of attacking skills are going to pose quite a threat to opposing teams. When a youngster is jumping up to head a cross from a teammate, keep the following tips in mind:

- ✔ **Eyes open:** Many youngsters have a tendency to close their eyes as their head is about to make contact with the ball, which wreaks havoc with the accuracy of their headers.
- ✔ **Protect the body:** Attempting a header in the penalty area is difficult for a number of reasons, most notably dealing with all the other players in the vicinity. While players are jumping into the air to deliver the header, they often, quite naturally, lift their arms up.. Tell your players that they must be careful not to elbow the defenders while they are jumping and that, if possible, when heading throw-ins for example, to try to keep their arms by their sides as they jump. Remind players that they can't be pushing or grabbing at opponents because they will concede a foul, but that they can use their hands as a barrier for additional protection.

✔ **Attack the ball:** When a cross is headed toward a youngster, he needs to respond aggressively in order to take full advantage of the pass. Responding aggressively means attacking the ball with the forehead. Sometimes youngsters fall into the trap of allowing the ball to hit them on the top of the head instead of taking the initiative to go after it and deliver a solid blow with the top of their forehead.

When working with youngsters on heading exercises that involve delivering headers on goal, be sure to help them coach them to direct those headers both up into the air, as well as towards the ground. Often a more difficult shot for a goalkeeper to stop is one that is directed at the ground near the goal line.

Sometimes the cross isn't up in the air, but closer to ground level, which requires the player to leave his feet and execute a dive header. This is an extremely difficult header to make and should only be taught with older and experienced players because it involves diving and landing with the full force of the body on the ground. To execute a proper diving header, the player launches herself toward the incoming ball (see Figure 14-7). As the player makes contact with the top of her forehead, she lays her arms out with her palms facing down to help cushion the body as it hits the ground. The referee may give a foul if she thinks that the forward's diving header is dangerous to the forward and places her at too much risk of being kicked in the head by defenders. (Refer back to Chapter 9 for more on heading.)

Feints

Once your players have got to grips with dribbling, spotting teammates in space and delivering the ball to them fairly accurately, it's time to help them work *feints,* also known as *dummies,* into their arsenal of attacking skills. Feints are when the ball handler pretends to do something in an effort to get the opponent to believe that he is doing one thing when he is actually doing something completely opposite. For example, he may shape up to dribble to the left when he is actually going to attack to the right.

During games, your players are sometimes going to encounter situations on the attack when they are going to be unable to fend off a defender who is stuck to them tighter than their own shadow. And to make matters worse, there won't be any teammates available to rescue them. So now what? Well, these are the situations where your players benefit by being able to resort to any number of dummies that are available to help get the defender off balance, create a little space to work with and gain a one- or two-step advantage on the attack. Such an advantage is often all it takes to initiate a goal-scoring opportunity.

Figure 14-7:
You should
teach diving
headers
only to
experienced
players.

The ability to deceive an opponent is a valuable skill to have, particularly because it can be used in all areas of the pitch. Near the opponent's goal, when your player is squeezed in tight along the touchlines by a defender, a good trick can get that defender leaning off balance for just a split second, which may be just enough time to get a quality shot in or find an unmarked teammate with an excellent scoring opportunity. Feints can also be used in other areas of the pitch. Perhaps when you win possession, your team needs a little extra time to get properly positioned for its attack. A feint can be used to buy a couple of extra seconds of dribbling time.

Having players who can use feints to their team's advantage is a real luxury, particularly as the risk is low and the payoff is high. Using them doesn't jeopardise your team's possession of the ball by risking a pass or dribbling into a bunch of defenders. A feint is simply a one-on-one move that allows an attacking player to escape trouble. The following list covers tricks connected with shooting, kicking with the heel, turning, passing, and body swerves.

✔ **Shooting:** A player being closely marked in the vicinity of the opponent's goal can rely on a dummy to get a shot off if no good passing options exist at the moment. The player plants her left foot and bends her right foot back just like she would while delivering a shot (see Figure 14-8a). As she does this, the defender is likely to stick out her left foot (see Figure 14-8b). The attacking player stops the swinging motion of her right foot and uses the inside of the foot (see Figure 14-8c) to move the ball to the defender's right. This split second where the defender is leaning off balance to her left gives the attacking player a chance to get a shot off.

Figure 14-8:
The steps of a shooting feint.

Ideally, the player should now deliver the kick with her left foot, which is the furthest away from the defender. Chapter 9 covers the importance of working with your players to become comfortable using both feet for dribbling, passing, and shooting, and this is certainly one of those situations where being comfortable shooting with either foot comes in handy. Because the feint usually only creates a small window of opportunity – often just a second or so, the defender may still be nearby and you don't want your player to waste a good trick by using the right leg to kick the ball. By doing so, that leg is still rather close to the defender and may allow her to lunge at the ball, poke it away and win the ball.

✔ **Kicking with the heel (the heel feint):** Players being challenged while running down the pitch find the heel feint a valuable resource to help shake off the defender. When a player dribbling the ball has a defender running side by side, or even a half step behind him (see Figure 14-9a), he actually steps over the ball with his right foot, which brings the ball to a stop (see Figure 14-9b). The heel feint should be used with the foot furthest away from the defender. So, when the defender is on the attacking player's left-hand side, he relies on his right foot for the heel feint. As the player steps over the ball, the defender, who has been running at top speed to stay even with the player, typically isn't prepared to stop as quickly as the attacking player did and shoots past.

The attacking player, with this momentary advantage, has a couple of options at his disposal. He can use the extra seconds to survey the pitch and deliver a pass to a teammate, or he can change direction and continue dribbling the ball forward. A variation is to put the foot on top of the ball instead of stepping right over it. All feints take lots of practice, but the heel feint requires more practice than most because it can be quite challenging to keep a rolling ball under control using just the heel.

Figure 14-9:
The heel feint works when the defender is behind or next to the dribbler.

a

b

✔ **Turning:** Trick turns can be used in defence and attack to gain a seconds advantage, which allows the player with the ball to change direction and find enough space to pass, shoot or cross the ball, or continue their run. When an opponent is on a player's back, the turning feint can be used to shed the player. As the player is dribbling with his back to the defender, she leans her body slightly to the left (see Figure 14-10a) and brings her right foot toward the ball, giving the indication that she is headed to the left. As the defender begins moving in that direction, the player swings her foot over the ball (see Figure 14-10b) and, with the outside of her right foot, moves the ball to her right (see Figure 14-10c). This type of manoeuvre usually creates at least a step or two of extra space.

✔ **Passing:** The passing feint – similar to the shooting feint – is especially useful when a defender is headed at an attacking player straight on. In this situation, the attacking player spins his body to the right as though he is going to deliver a pass in that direction (see Figure 14-11a). As he brings his foot down toward the ball (see Figure 14-11b), he sweeps it around to the side and moves the ball to his left (see Figure 14-12c), while the player has probably lunged to block the pass. From this position, he now creates several options for himself, including continuing moving the ball forward with his left foot.

✔ **Body swerving:** The body swerve is using any part of the body in an exaggerated motion, in the opposite direction a player intends on moving. For example, as the player runs forward, she can firstly drop her right shoulder which makes it appear that she is about to run to the right. Secondly, she can then push off in the other direction using her right foot. At pace, body swerving is a devastatingly effective move that can get a player past several defenders, as Manchester United's Ryan Giggs has proved over many seasons.

Figure 14-10: This player feints to his left and moves the ball to his right.

a   b   c

Figure 14-11:
The attacker spins as though she's about to deliver a pass to her right.

a   b   c

As your players gain more experience, they can come up with their own moves to throw off defenders. Encourage players to be creative when working on these moves until they find those that they are comfortable using and that tend to work well for them during games.

While the preceding feints are the basic ones that can really benefit your team, when they have mastered these and are comfortable using them in game situations, encourage them to work on their own. You maybe surprised at some of the moves the kids come up with that actually prove to be quite effective during games. As youngsters discover how to incorporate their own special touches into their skills, their enjoyment level for the sport – and playing for you – will skyrocket.

Chapter 15

Advanced Defending and Formations

*A*s your season rolls along, you may begin to notice that many of the youngsters in your league are adding all sorts of attacking skills to their arsenal. You observe them becoming more dominant with their dribbling, more efficient with their passing, and more accurate with their shooting. While this improvement is hopefully occurring on your own team as well as others in your league, it also presents new and exciting challenges for you and your squad at the defensive end of the pitch. The ability to improve your team's defensive skills translates into them enjoying the sport even more than they already do. The kids also derive additional satisfaction by consistently being able to spoil the opposition's attacks.

As you begin upgrading your defensive efforts, you can introduce team formations that best match your team's playing skills and abilities; and, just as importantly, you can begin to coach your players in how best to defend against the different formations that other teams use against you. You can start explaining techniques, such as moving out of your 18-yard area and the offside trap, which are key components of a strong defence. You can also share with your team the basics of clearing the ball away from goal, which they need to understand if your team hopes not to surrender an avalanche of goals during the season.

Experimenting with Defensive Formations

Choosing a system of play to use with your team is really not a whole lot different than shopping for a new car. You have many styles and options to choose from and usually, after looking around and taking test drives, you settle on the one that best fits your needs and turns out to be the most comfortable. The same goes for determining the best formation for your team. With so many different systems of play out there, including several attacking approaches (see Chapter 14), the only way you'll discover what is the most comfortable fit for your team is to try the approaches out during training or in friendlies with other teams.

While you won't necessarily want to spend the entire season forcing the kids to play a particular formation, understanding the merits of each approach can prove valuable at different points in the season. Whether your team finds itself going against a high-scoring team that needs to be slowed down, or whether you are simply trying to protect a one-goal lead in the closing minutes of a game, choosing the right defensive formation can be enormously valuable for all involved, just as when you are chasing the game you may need to be more adventurous, and change your attacking formations.

Four-three-three formation

The four-three-three is one of the more popular formations used in youth football because it happens to be one of the easiest for teams to fathom and operate in. This system of play works well for teams without a lot of tactical experience playing the game, which is why the four-three-three formation is often used with younger, less experienced players. The system's (see Figure 15-1) back line features a left and right fullback, and two centre backs, one marking and one covering, or both marking; the midfield consists of right, left, and centre midfielders, and the front line comprises a right, left, and centre forward:

✔ **Defenders:** The four-three-three features a highly balanced set up, particularly along the back line with the four defenders. The primary responsibilities of the left and right fullback are to defend their area of the pitch and clear the ball whenever an opposing player brings it into their territory. While the players manning these positions can sometimes join the attack, they must exercise extreme caution so that they aren't caught by a team's counter-attack. Their top priority, though, remains clearing the ball out of danger.

Ideally, the players you choose to handle the centre back responsibilities must be fast, confident, steady under pressure and have a firm grasp of the style of play you are employing. A centre back may spend more time dropping off, controlling the area in front of goal and co-ordinating the defensive unit. So, when an opposing player is racing down the left side of the pitch, he's got to move over in that direction to serve as an extra layer of defensive support in the event that the opposing player gets past the left fullback.

Besides serving as the defensive anchor while the opposing team is on the attack, the centre backs need to have the skills to make clearing kicks when the ball gets in close to the goal, or to use headers to knock the ball out of danger if the situation calls for it. They are also responsible for working, in conjunction with you, to organise the defence for corners and free kicks. One of the centre backs may end up doing more marking than anything else. His basic responsibility is to immediately clear balls out of his area before the opposing team can strike. Any mistakes made by this centre back often result in a good scoring chance for the opposing team, particularly if the other centre back has been forced to provide assistance to one of the two fullbacks.

✔ **Midfielders:** The left and right midfielders do a large amount of running because they step up when the team is on the attack, and must race back when defending to lend support to the fullbacks along the flanks. The centre midfielder has a wide range of responsibilities. Most notably, she vies for loose balls in the middle of the pitch all game long. The more successful she is at out-duelling opposing players for the ball, the more attacking chances she generates for the team.

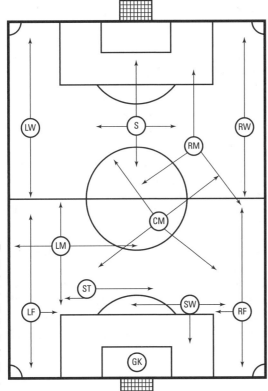

Figure 15-1:
The popular four-three-three formation should be easy for your team to employ.

✔ **Forwards:** The centre forward probably takes the bulk of the team's shots on goal, so players with the ability to take accurate shots from a variety of distances and angles are best suited for this position. The outside forwards are the playmakers of the unit and have the job of continually looking to move the ball down the wings and to create scoring opportunities for themselves or the centre forward.

Four-four-two formation

The four-four-two formation is the most common formation in professional football in the UK and also in junior football 11-a-side games. The four-four-two is more defensive than the four-three-three (see preceding section) because you have one more player in the midfield area (see Figure 15-2), as well as four players in the back filling the left and right fullback positions, plus the centre backs.

This system works pretty well with most kids as you can explain the jobs of the players in the various positions fairly easily. It also spreads the physical workload evenly among the players, unlike systems such as four-five-one, or other systems that use a lone striker and attacking and defending full/wing backs. Even if your team isn't creating a lot of scoring opportunities, maintaining possession of the ball is often easier with the four-four-two system, limiting the number of attacking chances that the other team enjoys. The deployment of players is as follows:

✔ **Defenders:** In this set up, the defenders form a *flat back four*, roughly in a line in front of the goal, much the same as with the four-three-three, with the centre backs in the centre, and the two fullbacks off to each side.

With a flat back four, you need to remember a number of things. The formation may be called a flat back four, but the only time the defenders want to be in a flat line across the pitch is when they are pushing up, playing the offside trap (see the section 'Offside trap', later in the chapter). Most of the time, one defender is pressing the ball and the rest are at an angle and not in a flat line. With speedy opposition, it is essential that your back four defenders deny their speedy forwards space to run into. You may want to play with one of the centre backs dropping off into the space behind the defence or, more likely, defending closer to your goal and the 18-yard line. If you do this, all those through balls for the quick forwards to run onto just run through to the keeper, or out for a goal kick.

✔ **Midfielders:** The four midfielders in this formation spread across the pitch, depending on where the ball is. The left and right midfielders do large amounts of running, as they join the attack along the flanks, as well as being expected to provide strong defensive support when the opponent has possession of the ball. In the centre, one midfielder may play a holding role in front of the back four, protecting the defence, breaking up the opponent's passing play through the midfield and distributing the ball quickly once won. Having a holding midfielder allows the other centre midfielder to get forward more often.

✔ **Forwards:** These players' scoring opportunities depend on several things. They need to be supported by the midfield in attack. They also need to be able to link up well together. Many managers like the little and large combination: a tall strong forward to win the ball in the air and act as a target for long forward passes, and a speedy skilful forward to feed off of the headers and knock-ons from the tall strong forward.

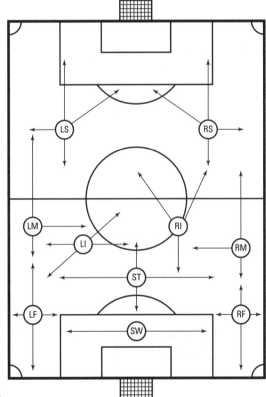

Figure 15-2:
The defenders, midfielders, and forwards get into position for the four-four-two.

Four-five-one formation

The four-five-one system of play (see Figure 15-3) works well when you have a lot of good passers of the ball and plenty of energy in the team. The plus points are that it can give your side control of the midfield, where you usually outnumber the opposition. The downside is that the formation relies on the midfield getting forward to support the lone striker. These players soon get tired and if roll-on substitutions are allowed, you need to deploy them here. If you come up against a team playing this formation, you can match it, equalising the midfield advantage, or bypass the opposition midfield by playing the ball over the top of the midfield as well as down the flanks. The four-five-one system is useful against stronger opponents; five players clogging the midfield area and four defenders along the back line makes it pretty difficult for opposing teams to make a lot of progress down the pitch. The team lines up like this:

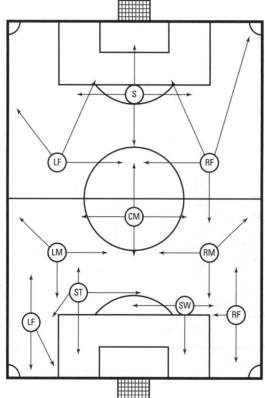

Figure 15-3:
The four-five-one formation is useful for an energetic, passing team.

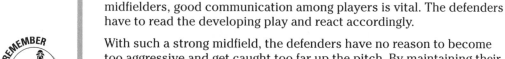

✔ **Defenders:** With a left and right fullback, two centre backs, and five midfielders, good communication among players is vital. The defenders have to read the developing play and react accordingly.

With such a strong midfield, the defenders have no reason to become too aggressive and get caught too far up the pitch. By maintaining their proper positioning, they can make it extremely difficult for the opposing team to penetrate.

✔ **Midfielders:** Because in this formation you have so many players working in the middle of the pitch, make sure that your team knows that proper spacing must be kept between the players. The defensive system is disrupted if two or three players end up patrolling the same area of the pitch, leaving wide spaces for the opposing side to run into and pass through, and weakening the defensive midfield area. Communication is absolutely essential here. Often two central midfielders mark and one acts as a playmaker providing a creative force in midfield and getting forward to support the attack. With older players, the marking and free midfielders can rotate during the game.

✔ **Forwards:** Any forward who plays as a lone striker needs to be strong and fit, and in particular strong on the ball, good at holding the ball up, and keeping possession until midfield reinforcements arrive. They need to do a lot of running down and chasing the ball. But the good thing for kids playing up front on their own, is that the ball is likely to come their way more often, as they are usually the only outlet. So they can see a lot of action in this position.

Clearing Strategies

Football is a complex game, but when you peel away its outer layers, what it comes down to in its simplest form is that the team that spends more of the game at the opponent's end of the pitch rather than its own is generally going to produce the most goals and probably reap the most success in terms of wins. So, a team's ability to extricate itself from trouble by effectively clearing the ball out of the area in front of its goal is crucial to its success.

Fending off the opponent's attack doesn't require any magical moves or Houdini-like manoeuvres from your players. Simply coaching the kids in basic clearing principles involving their goalie and the touchlines should be enough to help them move the ball out of danger and begin mounting an attack of their own.

The back pass to the keeper

During the heat of competition when your team is under attack and struggling to clear the ball out of its own end of the pitch, players can easily forget that their goalie can be a huge asset in times of trouble. For example, when your defenders have possession of the ball and are under pressure but have limited passing or dribbling options because teammates are all marked and they have no space to move into, then players can turn to their goalie.

A back pass to the goalie can bring the opponent's attack to a halt. Once the goalie has the ball, she can kick it up the pitch to give his team the chance to recover, or she can deliver a long pass to a teammate moving toward the other end of the pitch.

Make sure to tell your players that they should only use a back pass when they see no threat of the ball being intercepted by an opposing player. Also, while the back pass to the goalie should be firm, it shouldn't be so hard that it actually challenges the youngster in the goal to make a save from one of her own players. In fact, your players should play the ball to the side of the goal nearest the defender if possible. By doing this, they ensure that if the ball is over-hit, it goes off for a corner and not in for an own goal.

Mastering this skill takes time and it may be while before youngsters are comfortable resorting to of the back pass during an actual game. But they eventually click, through experience, that they need to remember to use their goalie, if that turns out to be the best option for the team to keep possession.

Work with your goalies during practice games, or any type of exercises that you are running, so that they know to be vocal and let their teammates know that they are available for a back pass if they sense the team struggling to move the ball and they don't see any other options from their vantage point. During the exciting of games, players can often forget that the goalie is there to help them, if needed. A simple verbal reminder from the goalie lets teammates know that she is ready to receive a pass. Communication among your players is a vital asset for successfully stopping an attack.

Clearing toward the touchlines

Whenever your team is under pressure, one of the best escape routes to relay to them is always to play the ball toward the touchlines, as this involves the least amount of risk. Players, especially the relatively inexperienced ones, are always tempted to move the ball straight ahead, dribbling or passing, and that usually moves them directly into trouble. The centre of the pitch represents the most dangerous territory to a defensive team looking to clear the ball. One poorly timed pass or a mistake while dribbling can be costly. Always instruct your players to look to the nearest touchline for a teammate to clear the ball towards. Even if the ball happens to be intercepted in that area, there won't be nearly as many options for the opposing player as if the ball was lost in the middle of the pitch. Good attacking sides find ways to get the ball into the middle of the pitch; good defences work the ball to the flanks.

As players begin working out how to get the ball in the air, there is a gradual temptation when clearing the ball to simply kick it over the head of an oncoming opponent. Doing so can be problematic simply because it can be risky as it can produce an immediate scoring opportunity for the opposing player if the ball isn't kicked high enough in the air. Remind your players, especially your fullbacks and players positioned near the goal, that, if possible, they should try to pass the ball around opposing players to minimise the threat of losing it in the vicinity of their own goal. Sometimes, however, when the pressure is really on, a big kick up the pitch, or off of the pitch for a throw, or even off for a corner, is the best option.

Introducing New Defensive Skills

As your players begin getting comfortable with different playing styles, you can start introducing them to additional defensive tactics that they can employ, as well. Helping to upgrade this area of their game allows them to enjoy more success in their one-on-one battles for the ball, and also enhances the team's overall play in their own half.

Chasing down

One of the basic tenets of good defensive play revolves around jockeying attackers. If defenders don't chase down the player with the ball, bad things are generally going to result, specifically in the form of attacking pressure, good scoring chances for the opposition, and more than likely, opposition goals too.

Often, in youth football, a player dribbling the ball is treated as if he has the chicken pox – everyone keeps their distance from him. Over players avoiding him allows the player a free run towards the goal and leaves you wondering what happened to all the good defensive work that your team put in during training over the past week.

When your team understands that every time the opponent takes possession of the ball, the nearest player has to immediately go over to close that youngster down and cut off his passing options, your defence begins to take shape. Disrupting the opponent from the outset not only makes it that much more difficult for the opposition to begin its attack, it also forces it to control the ball under intense pressure and make an additional pass or two to get started. The more times you force the opposition attackers to pass or dribble with a defender in their face, the more chance your squad has to gain possession of the ball, and start an attack of its own.

Man marking

Man marking simply means that one or two of your defenders are assigned to follow specific attackers on the opposing team, wherever they go on the pitch. Man marking typically works well with younger kids starting out in the game because you can assign a player for them to mark and you can track relatively easily who has lost their player. This style of play also ensures that your players won't become bored or lose concentration during the game, simply because they have to stay focused on sticking to their assigned player. Man marking is also good for practice games because it allows players to get used to dealing with tight marking. It can also be pretty effective at winning possession as e one of your players is always right on top of the player dribbling the ball, and others are guarding her teammates tightly, so passing opportunities are cut down.

Moving out

Moving out is a key defensive concept that basically prevents the opposing players from goal hanging and waiting for a pass. When the opposing team has the ball, an attacking player has only a couple of ways of advancing towards the goal. He can move in when the ball is closer to the goal than the other player is, or if one of your defensive players (excluding your goalie) is closer to the goal than the attacking player. So, train your defensive players in the tactic of not backing towards the goal and bunching up near the goalie. If your players are hovering around the goal, so can the opposing players.

When it comes to working with your defenders, you want them to focus on staying up the pitch because that ensures that the forwards on the opposing team can't advance further than where they are situated on the pitch, unless they have the ball. Keep in mind though that your defensive players must begin retreating as the ball approaches, because everyone can advance at least as far as the ball. Remember that if no offside is being played, as in mini-soccer, the opposing players can stand as near to your goal as they like, and your players have to mark them.

Offside trap

The *offside trap* is a defensive strategy that can be used to gain possession of the ball (see Figure 15-4). Your defenders on the goal side of the ball have to step up together, past the players they are marking, leaving the defender who is about to receive the ball with only the goalkeeper in front of them. As soon as that person receives the pass, she is offside. The referee calls offside and awards the ball to your team for an indirect free kick.

Figure 15-4:
If the offside trap isn't successful, your opponent has an immediate advantage.

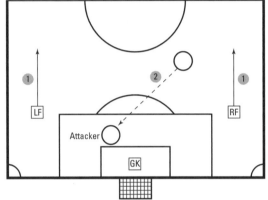

At the more advanced levels of youth football, or at least with a team that has many players who have playing the game for several years, this tactic is often used to stem an opponent's attack and win possession of the ball. In mini-soccer, however, offside is not played.

When attempting an offside trap, keep the following in mind:

✔ **All your defenders need to be aware.** If you have signalled to your team to attempt the offside trap, make sure that all your defenders are aware of the situation. Better still, get one of the central defenders to decide when to play the offside trap and to tell the others to push up. If not all of your defenders have pushed up past the opponent who receives the pass, then he is not offside and suddenly has a golden scoring opportunity landing in his lap because your entire team wasn't aware they were playing offside.

✔ **It can be dangerous.** Playing offside is all about timing. If your defender is attempting to step up past the opponent but is a step or two slow when the opponent receives the ball, then your defence has put itself in a highly compromising position because the attacking player may have already been moving forward when he received the ball and now can continue in on goal or fire off an immediate shot.

✔ **The referees factor in.** Youth football officials are out there doing the best they can for the kids and giving decisions as fairly as they possibly can. But, the offside trap is not always an easy decision to make and the referee may not make this decision or may simply not deem it to have been offside. In either case, the result is going to be an immediate advantage for the opponent.

You may want to consider working with your players to raise their hand to get the referee's attention when you are attempting to use the offside trap so that they are aware of it – without giving away your intentions to the other team. In any event, whether the decision is made or not, You have hopefully continually told your players to play to the whistle, that is keep playing as if the game is going on until the referee blows the whistle, and to respect the officials at all times – even during those instances when decisions don't work out in their favour.

Chapter 16

Coaching Set Pieces

. . . .

In This Chapter

▶ Mastering attacking opportunities

▶ Making a defensive stand

. . . .

*W*hile shooting, passing, and tackling are some basic skills youngsters must have a good command of in order to excel on the pitch, plenty of other areas of the game deserve your attention, too. (See Chapter 3 for more on these basic skills.) In this chapter, we introduce you to those aspects of the game that make playing football so truly unique and exciting – and coaching it constantly challenging and fascinating.

Direct and indirect free kicks, penalty kicks, corner kicks, and throw-ins – known as *set pieces* – provide enormous advantages for the attacking team, and helping your youngsters figure out how to capitalise on these opportunities will enhance their hopefully already growing enjoyment of the sport. Furthermore, developing their ability to make defensive stands in these situations when the opposing team is in attacking mode can be equally rewarding.

Attacking from Set Pieces

During your games this season, the majority of your team's scoring chances may come in the form of throw ins, penalty kicks, corner kicks, and free kicks. Being prepared to take advantage of these wonderful scoring opportunities when they arise can have a major impact on the game.

Fortunately, you can incorporate drills into your training sessions to coach your team in these special skills and basic tactics they can employ during games to take full advantage of these special situations whenever they occur.

Throw-ins

When the ball crosses the touchline during the course of action, play comes to a brief stop. The team that knocks the ball out of play loses possession, and the opponents get to throw the ball in to start play again.

In theory, this *throw-in* occurs as quickly as possible, which is in your team's advantage if the opposing team is not in proper position to defend it. Sometimes, though, especially when the team is under pressure, you may want to organise your team before taking the throw in.

With inexperienced football players, tell them to always throw the ball in the direction of the other team's goal.

Keep in mind that the player mustn't throw the ball into the goal. It must touch another player first. In addition, the attacking team can't be offside on a throw-in. (See Chapter 3 for the low-down on the offside law.)

The player throwing in the ball holds it behind his head with both hands, as shown in Figure 16-1, with his body facing the direction that he's throwing the ball. When the ball goes behind the head, the child's elbows should point out to the side to ensure that he has the most power behind his throw.

Figure 16-1:
Taking a throw-in.

Both feet must remain on the ground; a running start or jumping in the air is not permitted.

Here are a few additional tips to keep in mind during the throw in:

✔ Make sure that the player drags the toes on her rear foot hard enough so that she can hear it. This movement helps to ensure that she doesn't give away a foul throw during the game because she lifted her foot.

✔ The throwing motion must consist of a continuous forward thrust until the ball is released in front of the head. When the player follows through with the throw-in, they should snap their wrists.

✔ The player can throw the ball to the feet of a teammate so it can be easily controlled and the team can begin its attack. Alternatively, they can throw the ball to the teammate's head so that they can flick it on, or at chest level so that they can trap the ball with their chest and then bring it down under control.

A good throw-in drill to incorporate into your training sessions is to stage a mini tournament with your players. Here's a sample one that works quite well for any age group:

1. Place a cone several yards away from the sideline and have each youngster take five throws and record who gets the ball closest to the target, or who hits the target the most number of times.

2. Set up several cones around the pitch at the same distance from the touchline so that a number of kids can be throwing simultaneously. Doing this avoids having the kids waiting to throw. You never want your players waiting too long during drills, as it really cuts down on the amount of improvement taking place.

You can also stage a throw in competition by seeing who can throw the ball the furthest and with the most accuracy. When conducting these types of mini competitions, make sure that the team is using good technique on every throw-in Any time you notice incorrect technique being used, make it clear that that throw cannot count in the competition, even if it happens to hit the target.

Having a throw-in at the opponent's end of the pitch represents an excellent opportunity to create scoring opportunities. The following is a basic tactic that your team can use (see Figure 16-2). Here's how it works:

1. Player A is throwing the ball in. She tells Player B to be ready for the pass, which makes the defensive players (D) think the ball is going to that Player B and other defensive players may relax their marking a little bit on the other attacking players.

2. Player B moves forward as if she will be receiving the pass and while she is doing so, Player C sprints down the sideline.

3. Player B, moving forward, creates a partial block to help enable Player C to get free of their marker to receive the pass.

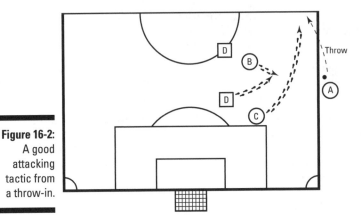

Figure 16-2:
A good attacking tactic from a throw-in.

Penalty kicks

The referee awards a penalty kick to the attacking team when a defensive player commits a foul inside the penalty area. A *penalty kick* is a free shot at the goal that is taken from a spot 12 yards in front of the goal. (The spot is a lot closer for younger players in mini-soccer leagues.) Penalty kicks are golden opportunities to score a goal because the goalie is at an overwhelming disadvantage.

You need to know your league's rules, particularly when it comes to those rules that have been adjusted to meet the age and skill level of the players you are coaching. You will be pretty embarrassed if your team has been practising penalty kicks from 12 yards away during the week, on match day, all of a sudden your team is awarded a penalty, only to find out that the league rule is that these kicks are taken from 7 yards away.

During the kick, the goalie must have his heels on the goal line, and he can only move along the goal line until the ball is kicked. All other players must stand out of the penalty area. Penalty takers have two basic choices. They can hit the ball as hard as they can. Or they can try to place it. At the younger levels of play, you may want your players to take the shot using a side-foot pass. Using the inside of the foot delivers a more accurate shot than an instep kick from this short distance (see Chapter 9). The youngster should concentrate on getting enough force behind the ball to beat the goalie. The more experienced your team is, the more you can get them to place their shot when they are awarded a penalty kick.

The most difficult penalties to stop are those that are just inside post at or near ground level, or in the top corners. At the more advanced levels of football, players are often able to use powerful instep kicks. Let penalty-takers know that they should decide what they are going to do and where they are going to place the ball and then stick to that decision, not change their minds on the run up.

A good way to help young players hone their penalty-kicking skills is to set up a cone in the goal about two feet away from each goal post. If players become comfortable at hitting the target, then when it comes time to deliver the kick in a game with a goalie standing in their way they are sure to enjoy the same amount of success. A goalie finds it virtually impossible to stop a well-placed penalty kick with even a decent amount of pace behind it, at any level of play.

As youngsters often tend to feel a little more pressure than normal when taking a penalty shot, because all eyes are on them, devise drills that incorporate that factor into the equation. For example, at the end of training have each player take a few penalty shots on the goalie with the entire team watching to get them comfortable performing the skill with an audience.

Corner kicks

When a team knocks the ball past its own goal line, the opposing team is awarded a *corner kick* from the corner arch on the side of the pitch where the ball went out of play (see Figure 16-3). Taking a corner kick is certainly one of those rare times when a youngster is going to enjoy being sent to the corner! During the kick, defensive players must be at least ten yards from the player kicking the ball, while the teammates of the youngster delivering the corner kick may position themselves anywhere they choose. Generally speaking, the more players positioned in the goal area the more difficult the goalkeeper will find it to clear the ball with all the players around her.

One of the more effective techniques for corner kicks is for the child to use his instep and to kick low on the ball to get it airborne. The instep works best because this is easier for the child to control. With older and more experienced players, you can work with them to come across the ball slightly as they are making contact with it, which generates spin on the ball. Extra spin makes it more difficult for the goalie to handle the incoming ball.

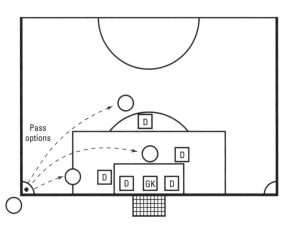

Figure 16-3:
Your team can use several tactics when attempting a corner kick.

If you happen to have a strong-footed kicker on your team who can deliver the ball to the goal post that is the furthest away, and a player who is pretty good at headers to make contact with the pass, then you have a pretty potent tandem that your team can use to its advantage to create great scoring opportunities.

The following training drill is great for honing those corner-kick skills and can be run simultaneously in all four corners of the pitch in order to eliminate any standing around time by your players.

1. Position a player about ten yards in front of the goal.

2. The player delivering the corner kick must try to get the ball to this player in the air.

3. The player receiving the ball can work on their heading skills and attempt to head the ball into the goal, or work on their trapping skills by controlling the ball and then taking a quick shot on goal.

4. By having this drill going on in all corners of the pitch, the goalie also has to react quickly and make several saves in succession. The difficulty of the drill can be increased by adding a defender to the mix, which also makes the drill more game-like in nature. One thing to keep in mind while observing your players delivering corner kicks is to make sure that they aren't sending the ball too close to the front post. Ideally, you want them to position the kicks about five yards or so out from the goal, which makes getting to the ball a little more difficult for the goalie. Inswinging corners that curl in towards the goal can be very difficult to defend. If the team has a left-footed player, she can take the kick from the right hand side, with a right-footer taking it from the left.

You can employ a number of different tactics on a corner kick:

✔ If your team has a height advantage over the other team, you can send a high corner kick in front of the goal that your taller players can attempt to head into the goal.

✔ Inexperienced players, or those that don't have the leg strength to boot the ball toward the goal, can take a short corner kick. Here, the ball is simply passed to a teammate positioned just a short distance away. Then, the attack simply begins from there. This can also be a highly effective play when the player receiving the ball is a skilled dribbler who can help work the ball into the opposition's penalty area to get off a shot or deliver a pass to a teammate to generate a scoring chance.

✔ The corner kick can also be used as a back pass, where the youngster sends the ball back towards midfield. Taking this approach allows the team to get its players positioned for the ensuing attack.

Free kicks

Free kicks, which are awarded when fouls are committed, are a great opportunity for your team to get organised, run a training ground move that it has practised during the week and take control of the action on the pitch. The opposing players must be at least ten yards away from the ball during a free kick. Free kicks come in two types:

- ✔ **Direct free kick:** A direct free kick may be kicked directly at the goal.

- ✔ **Indirect free kick:** an indirect free kick must touch another player before a goal can be scored.

Direct free kicks

Direct free kicks (see Figure 16-4) provide the opportunity for you to get a little creative with your coaching. The more experienced and talented your players are, the more room you are afforded with your set moves and the more options you have at your disposal. Working on a series of different options in training gives your team a better choice on match day.

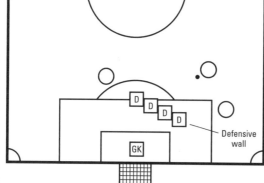

Figure 16-4: You can get creative when setting up to take a direct free kick.

Here are a few key points to consider when taking a direct free kick:

- ✔ **Go for the goal:** Anytime your team is set up for a direct free kick in the vicinity of the opposing team's goal, the less time you spend on passes and the quicker you get the shot on goal the better because this means more scoring chances. During your training sessions, you should focus on getting players to take a direct shot, or at least limit the team to one pass before shooting. Anything that involves multiple passes provides the defence with plenty of time to react to what is going on and recover in order to win the ball or disrupt the play.

✔ **Attack quickly:** When setting up to take a direct kick, regardless of whether the kick is in your opponent's half of the pitch or in the shadows of your own goal, do so quickly. These are wonderful opportunities to begin a successful attack, and your team will enjoy greater success and encounter fewer problems if they are able to act quickly before the other team has an opportunity to get organised. If the defence is already in position, don't rush as no tactical advantage exists. In this case, get the team ready first and then proceed.

✔ **Use decoys:** These are the type of free kicks that your team can, excuse the pun, get a real kick out of. They're fun to discover and practise, and when the deception translates into a goal during a game everyone gets a pretty good feeling seeing it all come together. For example, you can have a player charge up to the ball as if he is going to deliver a kick, but at the last second step over the ball and look to receive a pass from another player who actually takes the free kick.

✔ **Use your good passer:** If you have a child on your team who has emerged as an excellent passer, you can take advantage of those skills by having him take the free kick in a key situation. The ability to chip the ball over the wall is an excellent asset that can really put the defence on its heels and force them to scramble to recover.

✔ **Take it from all areas:** Free kicks are going to occur at random spots all over the pitch during games, so be sure to practise everywhere in your training sessions. Simply practising free kicks near the goal isn't going to do your team a whole lot of good when, during the game, they are forced to take one down in their half of the pitch far away from the opponent's goal. Being prepared to take free kicks from all areas of the pitch and at different angles is crucial in order to exploit all these opportunities to the full.

✔ **Take direct shots:** Just because the defensive team has set up a wall doesn't necessarily mean that your player taking the direct kick should look to pass rather than to shoot. If your team is in a prime scoring area of the pitch, tell your players to take a good look at the wall before passing up a shot. The defensive team may have a wall set up poorly – with gaps between players or room to shoot at either end – and your player can exploit it by shooting. If the player can get off a shot, they should be strongly encouraged to take advantage of the opportunity.

✔ **Use the swerve:** If the player is able to spin the ball, he can curve it around the wall, which creates all sorts of additional scoring chances. Swerve shots can be particularly difficult for goalies to contend with because they aren't able to see the full shot. Swerves are the type of skill primarily associated with players at the much more advanced levels of football.

Indirect free kicks

Indirect free kicks are taken in much the same way as direct kicks, with the minor exception that another player has to touch the ball after the kick before a goal can be scored. A good pass from the player taking the indirect free kick can create a good scoring opportunity for the team when they are near to the opposing team's goal. An option for an indirect free kick is the following (see Figure 16-5a). The player taking the kick sends the ball to a teammate positioned far enough past the wall that they can get an immediate shot on goal. Another option is for the player taking the kick to send the ball wide to a teammate, and then take off to get a return pass and catch the defenders off guard, as they often converge on the player with the ball and neglect the first player (see Figure 16-5b).

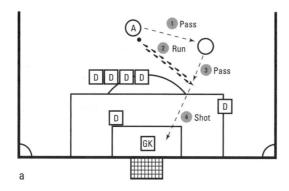

a

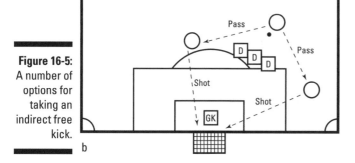

Figure 16-5: A number of options for taking an indirect free kick.

b

While it's certainly an advantage to have your player with the strongest legs take the direct kick, or your best passer take the indirect kick, make sure during your training sessions that all the kids get plenty of work in these areas of the game. There may be times during the game when your strongest player may be at the other end of the pitch and doesn't have time to run over and take the kick. Also, you should work closely with all of your kids so that each one has enough confidence to take the kick; and regardless of how proficient they are in this area of the game, each should have equal opportunities to try these kicks during the course of the game.

Defending Set Pieces

While corner kicks and direct kicks can provide fantastic scoring opportunities when your team has possession of the ball (see the preceding section), they can be equally problematic when your team finds itself on the other side and is faced with trying to stop them. Being able to take away even the slightest advantage the attack has is key to performing well when confronted with defending these situations. Denying a scoring chance on a corner kick or preventing a player from getting a quality shot off on a direct free kick can provide your team with a big boost of confidence. Furthermore, defending set pieces well can dramatically shift the momentum of the game in your favour. The following sections take a look at what it takes to defend well in these situations.

Throw-ins

When defending a throw-in, one of the main points your team must keep in mind is that the opposing team is probably going to use a standard throw-in that they have worked on in training. It may even be one that your team uses or something similar that they quickly recognise. Regardless, work with your team to keep the following points in mind on defending throw-ins:

- ✔ **Maintain the advantage:** Don't put a defensive player on the youngster that is handling the throw-in, because this gives away the slight advantage you have with more defenders on the pitch of play than attackers. The player making the throw-in can't touch the ball until someone else on the pitch does.

- ✔ **Don't get picked off:** Your best defensive bet may be to assign players to be responsible for a certain area of the pitch so that a lot of the confusion of trying to stick to an individual player is eliminated.

✔ **Keep an eye on the best player:** Once the game gets under way, you and your team are going to have a good idea who some of the best players are on the opposing squad. Throw-ins represent wonderful opportunities for teams to get the ball to these players. Consequently, you may want to consider putting your best defender on the team's most dangerous player and have her shadow this player all over the pitch to help ensure that the player doesn't break free with the ball following the throw-in.

✔ **Allow no offside:** Your team must constantly be aware during throw-ins that an attacking player cannot be given offside. That means that your players have no reason to ever allow a player from the opposing team to break free while receiving a throw-in.

✔ **Don't forget the player who threw the ball in:** After the player throws the ball in, she must be accounted for after play resumes. If not, she may race down the sideline and receive a return pass from the player she just threw the ball to. Your team needs to keep an eye on this player because she poses a risk once the ball is in play.

The wall

The *wall* is your team's best weapon to defend against free kicks that take place at your end of the pitch. The wall is exactly what it sounds like – a wall of stationary players lined up to serve as an obstacle to the opposing player taking the free kick. One of the main purposes of the wall is to cover the near post half of the goal (see Figure 16-6) while the goalie's primary responsibility is on the other half of the goal. On a direct free kick, the players comprising the wall must remain still until the ball is kicked. Here are a few other tips to keep in mind when it comes to the wall:

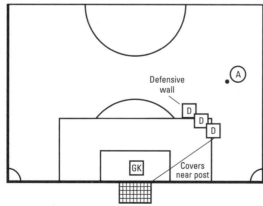

Figure 16-6: When players form the wall, they help the goalie defend against a shot.

✔ **Be quick:** The players need to get lined up quickly so that the attack isn't able to get an advantage. With younger teams, you may want to designate ahead of time a player or two to be in the wall so that you are always assured of having a couple players who rush to get set up and then, depending on the position on the pitch, other teammates can join in quickly as well.

✔ **Choose the number of players:** With more experienced teams, you can rely on the goalie to choose the number of players for the wall. With less experienced teams, you need to take a more vocal role in helping select the number of players required. The goalie is also responsible for instructing in which direction he needs the wall to move in order to be in its most effective position with the end player lined up with the post.

✔ **Don't move:** Inexperienced players not accustomed to standing still while a ball is kicked toward them have a tendency to turn their back on it. Turning is a bad habit for players to get into for a couple of reasons. First, turning sideways creates unwanted gaps for the ball to slip through and second, the players are at a disadvantage because they won't be able to see where the ball is and react as quickly.

✔ **Remember that height matters:** The tallest player in the wall should be lined up with the near post. The remaining players comprising the wall should stand shoulder to shoulder – from tallest to shortest – with no gaps between them.

Goal keeper's drop kicks

While goalkeepers are primarily thought of as defensive specialists, they can also play very important roles with your team's attack. A properly executed drop kick can accomplish a couple of very important things. First, if your team has been under an enormous amount of pressure from the opposing team's attack and much of the game has been played in your end of the pitch, the drop kick can give your team a reprieve from the assault. Second, a drop kick that connects with a teammate has quickly eliminated a portion of the pitch that the team has to negotiate, which may correlate into extra scoring chances for the squad.

Take a look at the keys to executing a successful drop kick (see Figure 16-7):

✔ Have the youngster focus on striking the centre of the ball with the top of his shoelaces.

✔ The toe of the kicking foot should be pointed and the ankle locked.

✔ The player should take a step forward with his non-kicking foot while dropping the ball on the kicking foot. Some children, when first beginning to practise this skill, have a tendency to throw the ball at their foot rather than letting it drop out of their hands.

Figure 16-7:
The goalie can help your attack by executing a successful clearing kick.

To help your goalies get a good feel for properly connecting with their kicks, here's a great drill to help them on their way. Position two goalkeepers approximately ten yards apart. The purpose of the drill is for the player to kick the ball to their partner. By starting the players off close together, their focus is on making contact with the ball in the centre. When they become proficient in kicking the ball back and forth to each other, you can start moving them farther apart. Once they are accurate, they can start kicking for distance. Another added benefit of this exercise is that, by catching their partner's kicks, they are building their hand-eye co-ordination and getting great practice catching high shots.

Goalie throws

Besides being able to kick the ball, another key skill for a goalie to have in their arsenal is the throw. While kicking is the most effective way to make the ball travel a long distance, when a ball is being booted that far, the other team is inevitably going to take possession of the ball some of the time. Whenever possible, your goalie should throw the ball to a teammate to help get an attack started. The throw is much easier to control than the kick and is much safer when it comes to maintaining possession of the ball.

The following tips help coach your youngsters in the art of throwing the ball to a teammate:

✔ Younger kids may need both hands in order to bring the ball back into the proper throwing position.

✔ As the child brings the ball over his throwing shoulder, he should spread his fingers, which provides added control of the ball. Then, he steps forward and follows through toward his intended target (see Figure 16-8).

Figure 16-8:
A goalie's
throw is
intercepted
less often
than a kick.

Defending corner kicks

Teams that are delivering corner kicks are in a great position to create good scoring opportunities. Experienced football teams score a lot of their goals with headers from corner kicks. Therefore, make sure that the front of your goal is guarded by three defenders. With this set up, the defenders have a good chance to move the ball away from the goal if it comes into the penalty area.

Position one defender directly in the goal area near or next to the goal post, while making sure that they don't obstruct the goalie's view. The second defender is positioned at the goal post at the far end. If the goalie is forced to leave the box, the defenders can collapse to the middle of the goal area to protect both halves.

Defending penalty kicks

Winning the lottery. Never getting sick a day in your life. And stopping a penalty kick. All involve enormous odds stacked heavily against you. After all, a well-struck football can travel from the penalty spot to the goal in less than a second, which means that the goalie is basically left wondering which direction the shot is headed in, and their attempt to save the ball falls into the category of guessing.

As your goalie becomes more skilled and masters the basic techniques of playing in goal, you can begin to work with them on the ultra difficult aspect of contending with a penalty shot. Here are a few tips to help them:

✔ **Take a cue from the kicker:** Have your goalie get used to checking out the direction the penalty taker's plant foot is pointing in and even the posture of his body. Try to read him as he approaches the ball. Is the player already looking at a certain part of the net and unknowingly giving away where he intends to kick the ball? Is he approaching the ball at a certain angle to get a better shot at one side of the net? While a goalie certainly won't be able to pick up all that information in the short amount of time he has to work with, he may pick up on one titbit of information that he can use to his advantage.

✔ **Use game knowledge:** If the penalty kick is taking place in the second half, your goalie may well already have a feel for the type of player taking the kick. Perhaps he has already had to save this youngster's shots, so he may know that the player has a tendency to aim all his shots to the left, or the right. Is he a finesse or power player? Have all his shots been low to the ground or in the air? These are all factors that can help the goalie make a big save for the team.

✔ **Pay close attention prior to the shot:** Make sure that your goalkeeper pays close attention to the player before the shot. Maybe he can pick up something in the way the youngster takes a warm-up swing with his leg before the shot that gives away what type of shot he is thinking of taking. Or maybe right before he lines up to run towards the ball, he glances at which side of the net he plans to aim his shot at.

The bottom line is that if the player taking the penalty shot and the goalie are both equally talented at their respective positions, the player kicking the ball has a distinct advantage in this situation. So, any little thing the goalie can do to help minimise that advantage is key in their efforts to save penalty shots.

Defending direct and indirect kicks

Free kicks can present real problems for defenders, especially at the more advanced levels of football when players have the ability to kick hard and accurate shots from long distances. These types of players pose big threats and if your team isn't prepared, they can quickly exploit your defensive weaknesses and put the ball in the back of the net. Assembling a wall (see the section 'The wall' earlier in this chapter) and positioning it properly, is vital for establishing that first line of defence against a free kick.

Whenever the attacking team is in range to get a good shot on goal, you must get a wall set up to help block the shot or disrupt the attacking team's set play. In a full-scale football game of eleven-a-side, the wall is usually comprised of three, four or five players stationed ten yards away from the ball. In smaller scale games of football involving kids at the beginner levels, such as six-a-side, the wall can be as small as one or two players. Your league's rules regarding how far away the wall must be positioned from the ball can vary greatly from the official rules of football. In smaller-scale games with younger kids the distance can be as little as five yards. (Refer to Chapter 2, for more on league rules.)

When a direct or indirect kick takes place far from your own goal, you really have no special defensive tactics to rely on. Basically, you want your defenders to move quickly and maintain their proper positioning, with themselves between the ball and the goal. On an indirect kick, for the overwhelming majority of the time, the attacking player will deliver a short pass to a teammate to the left or right of the wall. Because this is most often the case, defenders should already be focused on marking their man so they don't allow the attacking team any type of advantage.

Chapter 17

Implementing Advanced Exercises

In This Chapter

▶ Getting your players in condition

▶ Developing a challenging exercise regime

Along with those smiling faces, one of the best indicators that you're doing a pretty good coaching job is that your team members are gobbling up your instructions, putting your feedback to good use, and really developing as young players. Now, more than ever, is the ideal time to take full advantage of this momentum. Unveiling new – and even more challenging – exercises is just what your team needs at this point to propel them to even higher levels of play, and that's exactly what you find in this chapter.

Also, we address the issue of conditioning, one of those topics that make kids cringe and instantly puts horrible images in their heads of excruciating exercises and non-stop running. While conditioning is important in all youth sports, it arguably takes on an even greater importance in football, where running is at the foundation of the game. We shed some light on this topic, and show you why conditioning doesn't have to have an unpleasant label attached to it.

Conditioning Your Players

Because of the nature of football, which involves lots of continuous running mixed in with short bursts of high intensity sprints, youngsters are going to need a combination of aerobic and anaerobic fitness in order to perform at their maximum level all game long. *Aerobic* stamina refers to the level at which youngsters can take in and use oxygen. The stronger a youngster's heart and lungs are, the longer he is able to run up and down the pitch without tiring. *Anaerobic* fitness pertains to how long a youngster can perform at a high intensity, which includes sprinting after a ball.

Just how important is conditioning in a sport like football? Well, think about it this way. A highly skilled player who has not been properly conditioned and tires easily is not going to enjoy the sport as much, or be an asset to the team, if she's gasping for air midway through the game and can't chase down balls or keep up with opposing players. Clearly, less talented players with plenty of stamina who are just as effective late in the second half of games as they are at the start of games are more beneficial to the team over the long term, and derive far more satisfaction from their participation.

Because the positions in football are so varied and require such diverse skills, the conditioning needs for each position are quite different, as well. For example, a midfielder has the responsibility of covering a lot of territory. Because the position requires a large amount of continuous running, a midfielder is better prepared to handle those duties if he has strong aerobic fitness. On the other hand, your centre backs, for example, are counted on to do far less non-stop running. Because these positions entail short bursts of running to cover attacking players, their bodies are better able to fulfil their responsibilities if they possess strong anaerobic fitness.

Youngsters who are fatigued are much more likely to suffer injuries than those operating on a full tank of energy because they become sloppier in their technique. So, keep an eye out during games for players who are tiring. Giving them a breather for a few minutes is usually enough to catch that second wind and get them back on track.

The most effective conditioning takes place when you incorporate it into your training sessions and the kids don't even realise what you're doing. If you played sports as a youngster, think back to those experiences. What often happened? At the end of training, your coach announced that it was time for conditioning – you and your teammates let out a groan – and you began running endless laps around the pitch until you heard the whistle blow. As you got older, you may have realised that if you started conserving energy toward the end of training, you fared better in the running, while unknowingly compromising your development in the process.

Training sessions in which time is set aside simply for mind-numbing running aren't going to be effective – or fun – for the kids. When you use exercises that emphasise constant movement and eliminate standing-around time, the youngsters on your team emerge as well-conditioned players simply because of the nature of your training sessions. Sure, having the kids run laps around the football pitch for 20 minutes is going to get them into shape – and probably make them dread coming to training, too. Instead, using that 20 minutes for fun-filled exercises that focus on skill development, while also requiring running and continual movement, is not only better received by your players, but that much more productive in their development as football players.

Developing Challenging Exercises

Are you looking to add some flair and excitement to your attacking exercises? How about giving your players situations that really test their defensive abilities? The following exercises are designed to push players who have already become pretty proficient in the sport to the next level.

✔ **Wall pass heading combination** (see Figure 17-1) has it all – throw-ins, ball handling, dribbling, passing, and heading.

How it works: Position Player A on the touchline, who begins the drill by executing a throw-in to Player B. After Player B receives the throw-in, she dribbles to the centre of the pitch and delivers a pass between a pair of cones to Player C, who executes a wall pass back to Player B. Then, Player B sends a long pass to Player D, who is positioned at the top of the penalty area. (While all this is taking place, Player A, who delivered the throw-in, has run into the penalty area to defend against Players C and D.) Player D sends a square pass to Player C, who executes a chipped pass that Player D attempts to head into the net. You can easily increase the difficulty of the exercise by incorporating another defender into the mix to make the passing that much more complicated.

Begin by keeping a close eye on the youngster taking the throw-in. There's simply no reason why your team should ever concede possession of the ball by committing a foul throw. In order for the youngsters to really benefit from this exercise, stress the importance of performing it at full speed, just as they would in a game situation. You may even want to let them know that you are only giving them ten seconds to perform the exercise, to reinforce the emphasis on being fast with the ball and making quick decisions.

Figure 17-1: This drill gives five players the chance to work on their skills.

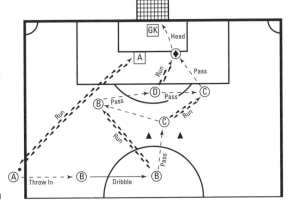

✔ **Near and far post crosses** help your players become proficient at delivering crossing passes to both the near and far posts while facing defensive pressure. *How it works:* Player A (see Figure 17-2) starts with a ball at the top of the penalty area and delivers a pass to Player B, who is moving toward the goal line. After Player A delivers the pass, she moves toward the near post and receives a cross from Player B. Player B has to focus on making an accurate pass that can't be intercepted by the defender stationed in the penalty area. After Player B delivers the cross and Player A attempts to head the ball into the goal, Player B sprints to the corner kick area and delivers a corner kick to the far post that Player A also attempts to head into the goal while dealing with the defender.

This exercise can get pretty competitive with older and more skilful kids who jostle for position in front of the goal to get in a header or defend them, so keep a close watch to make sure that is the kids are not indulging in illegal pushing or committing any fouls.

✔ **Spin and shoot** helps players, while dribbling the ball, make quick and accurate decisions on who to distribute the ball to when a goal-scoring opportunity presents itself. *How it works:* The exercise begins (see Figure 17-3) with you throwing a high pass to Player A, who must trap it with his chest and gain control of it. The players flanked on both his left and right near the top of the penalty box execute spin away and head towards the goal. Player A immediately passes the ball so that one of the two players can run onto it. The player who receives the pass dribbles forward and either takes a shot on goal or passes to the other attacking player to let them shoot. At the start of the exercise, a defender is also positioned in the penalty area, which puts extra pressure on the attacking players to make an accurate pass.

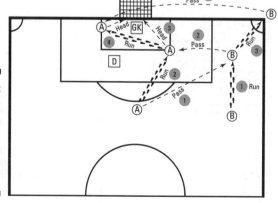

Figure 17-2:
Practising
passing
while facing
defensive
pressure is
important.

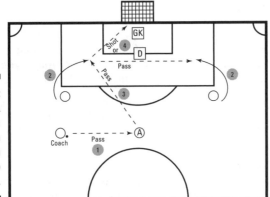

Figure 17-3:
Player A
makes a
decision
about which
player to
pass to.

Work with the attacking players to make sure that they don't spend too much time dribbling the ball. Players sometimes have a tendency to want to run with the ball for too long when, in a situation like a three-on-one, they need to find out how to take advantage of having the extra numbers in attack and pass to a teammate to produce a better scoring chance.

✔ **Move and react** gives players chances to work on their one-on-one moves while being closely marked, as well as their shooting and passing skills. *How it works:* Player A begins with the ball outside the penalty area (see Figure 17-4). Player B, who is attacking with her, is at an angle outside the penalty box as well, facing Player A. A defender starts a couple of yards behind Player B. The exercise begins with Player A passing to Player B, who spins away to either her left or right and, depending on whether she gets away from the marker, takes a shot on goal, or looks to pass to Player A, who is following up. If Player B shoots and there's a rebound, Player A is there to knock it in.

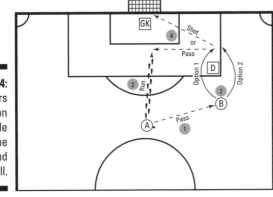

Figure 17-4:
Players
work on
multiple
skills in the
move and
react drill.

Kids naturally love taking shots on goal, so watch Player B closely and make sure that she is distributing the ball to Player A if spinning away from the marker hasn't produced an opening to get a good shot in. If she should have passed the ball instead of shooting, don't hesitate to interrupt the exercise. Show her that there was a better chance to score by demonstrating that Player A was without a defender near her.

✔ **Under attack** is a good conditioning exercise because it's fast-paced and allows little time for recovery. Besides working on skills like throw-ins and corner kicks, it also generates a game-type atmosphere with two-on-two and three-on-two play.

How it works: Position two attacking players and two defenders in the penalty area (see Figure 17-5). Also, place an additional attacking player starting on the touchline. The additional player begins the exercise by sending a corner kick that the attacking players attempt to score a goal with while the defenders try to clear the ball out of danger. While this is going on, the player who delivered the corner kick rushes up the touchline, picks up a ball and delivers a throw-in, which produces a game of two-on-two. To keep the game moving, only allow for 15 seconds of play. You can award a point to the attacking team if they get a shot on goal (two points if they score a goal) and a point for the defending team if they prevent a shot on goal. The exercise concludes with the player who began the exercise rushing up the touchline again, delivering another throw-in and joining the action for a three-on-two opportunity. Again, allow just 15 seconds to keep the exercise moving. Keeping score also helps keep the kids' interest and ensures that they are competing as hard as they would if they were in a game situation.

Particularly with the three-on-two portion of this exercise, make sure that the attacking trio is properly spaced out. Whenever the team has a tactical advantage with an extra player, they shouldn't minimise that advantage by bunching up close together, which makes it much easier for the defenders.

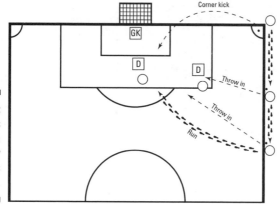

Figure 17-5:
Players work on specialty skills in this drill.

✔ **Crisscrossing** puts a premium on good ball control and passing, and also gives both forwards and defenders work on one-on-one situations, which occur all game long all over the pitch and play a big part in how success-ful the team is.

✔ *How it works:* Player A starts in midfield (see Figure 17-6) and dribbles the ball against a defender to a pre-determined spot, where he makes a square pass to Player B, and then runs at an angle toward the penalty area. Player B gains control of the ball and sends a pass forward to Player A, and then moves diagonally to the outer edge of the penalty box. Player A sends a pass to Player B in the penalty box area, who must now beat the defender there and get a shot on goal.

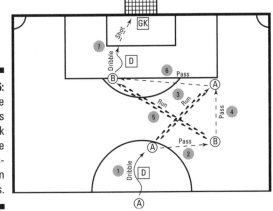

Figure 17-6:
The
defenders
try to break
up the
crisscross-
ing pattern
of passes.

No matter what the age level or ability of your players, always stress the fundamentals when it comes to passing and receiving. You never want your players to get into the habit of straying from the fundamentals, which only prove more difficult to correct later on.

✔ **Goalie tester** gives your goalie, regardless of her age or ability, the chance to hone her skills and receive a lot of good practice in a short period of time.

How it works: The goalie takes her normal position in front of goal. You take a spot approximately 10 yards away from the goalie and kneel down with a large supply of balls at your disposal. You begin the exercise by throwing balls at the goal one at a time, so the youngster is forced to make the save and then quickly return to her starting position to stop the next ball. By squatting down, you are able to send a wide variety of balls at the goalie. You can roll them, bounce them or throw them in the air. A lot of times in exercises, goalies aren't really tested and forced to extend far to their left and right to make saves. By delivering the balls with your hands, you ensure that the goalie has to make all the types of saves that they have to make in actual games. You can even increase the difficulty level of this exercise in a couple of ways. One, you can place a defender a few yards in front of the goalie to obstruct the her vision and make sure that she only sees the ball late, which often happens during a game, with players battling for position around the goal. And two, you can position players to the left and right of you and, periodically, instead of throwing a ball at the goal, you can roll one to your left or right for a player to take a shot on goal. Again, this forces the goalie to really be alert and react quickly to all sorts of different situations, which is exactly what she will confront during an actual game.

Footwork and technique are the key elements to successful goalkeeping. Watch that the youngster uses the proper technique when she reaches up high for a ball or is forced to get down low to scoop up a rolling ball.

Part V
The Finer Details

'We've had such an amazing response for
new team members that some of you are
going to be a little disappointed.'

In this part . . .

What your team does before it takes the field can have a major impact on how well it performs. In this part, we serve up some pre- and post-match routines, including warm-ups and nutritional tips that will fuel your players, and examine how you can best protect your team from annoying injuries. And, in the event you have to deal with a problem parent or child, we provide some useful solutions. For those of you interested in tackling the more challenging role of coaching a team in an organised league, you find all sorts of useful information here, too.

Chapter 18

Keeping Kids Injury Free and Healthy

*B*eing a well-rounded football player requires a lot of skills in many different areas. The same goes for being a well-rounded football coach. Besides coaching kids in the basic skills, techniques and strategies of the game, you've also got to have a handle on those aspects of the game that often slip under the radar of most volunteer coaches: injury prevention, recognition, and treatment, as well as the do's and don'ts of pre- and post-game nutrition.

While you certainly don't need a medical background or have to be an expert in the sports nutrition pitch, at least being familiar with these aspects and how they influence kids' performances on the football pitch makes a big difference to how much your players enjoy the game – as well as how successful you are in helping them have fun fulfilling their potential. In fact, many leagues recommend that team coaches have a certified knowledge of first aid. This chapter shows you how you can help your kids to remain injury free and fuel their young bodies to perform at their maximum capability.

Warming Up to Injury Prevention

You simply can't get around the fact that any youngster who steps onto the football pitch – regardless of their age, level of ability or experience playing the sport – is vulnerable to suffering an injury. While you can't eliminate the threat of injuries occurring during both training sessions and games, you can take several steps to help reduce the chances of a child suffering an injury.

In addition, having your team follow a sound stretching regimen – both before and after games and training sessions – goes a long way in not only promoting better flexibility but providing added protection against those unwanted aches and pains.

For children up to the age of eight, only a light warm up is required. This should involve pulse raising physical activity such as jogging, skipping, jumping, plus some mobilisation of joints such as hip swivelling and arm swinging.

Once children get to eight the warm up should include some light slow moving stretches, which help to ensure that a youngster's muscles, joints, and limbs have been carefully taken through a full range of motion and are ready for intense physical activity. When these moves are consistently performed correctly throughout the course of the season, child's normal range of motion is significantly increased. This is an enormous benefit to youngsters, as the greater their range of motion the greater the amount of force that can be applied to kicking a ball or chasing down an attacking player, for example.

Players who are also able to increase their flexibility enjoy the benefits of seeing dramatic improvements in their techniques, which translates into more effective football. For example, a youngster with especially tight hamstrings is going to be limited in how strongly and accurately he is able to kick a football at the goal or deliver a pass to a teammate. If you can help that child stretch out those hamstrings and gain increased flexibility, he should enjoy a fuller range of motion, which leads to more forceful kicks, probably more goals scored, and, with this added success, more fun as well.

Passive stretching is the most beneficial type of stretching for children. Rather than bouncing and straining to reach a desired position, which can result in injury, passive stretching stresses the individual slowly moving to the desired position, just slightly beyond discomfort, holding that position for a short period of time, and then relaxing. Remind kids that mild tension – not pain – is what they need to be striving to achieve on any type of stretch, for example, slowly bending down and touching their toes, counting to five, then relaxing and returning to an upright position.

During any stretching exercises, make sure that you have one-on-one contact with all kids, especially those new to football or stretching. For example, when a child is stretching out their hamstrings, place the child's hand on the back of their leg so that they can feel the exact area of their body being stretched and prepared for competition. This also helps to ensure that they are applying the correct technique.

Stretching to improve flexibility

Maintaining and improving a child's flexibility is essential for not only preventing injuries, but also for giving them the solid foundation of strength, balance and co-ordination that they need to reach their full potential. Incorporating a variety of stretches and strength-building exercises for the legs into your pre-training routine is a key component for preparing youngsters for the rigorous demands of football.

You can use several different stretches during warm-ups to help prepare a youngster's legs for training sessions and games.

- **Standing squats:** The child holds the football in the centre of her body with her elbows flexed. The feet should be about shoulder width apart. In a slow and controlled manner the child squats down into a deep bend at the knees, with her body weight centered over the heels. After a one-second pause, she lifts up, keeping the upper body steady.

- **Backward lunges:** The child begins by holding the ball out in front of her with flexed elbows. Next, she steps backward, landing on the ball of her foot while her stationary knee is in line with her ankle. She lowers her body by bending the knees. Using the rear leg, she lifts the stationary leg back so that her feet are together. Then, she repeats using the other leg.

- **Alternating leg raise:** The child lays face down and places her elbows under her shoulders with her forearms on the ground. She places her legs hip-distance apart and curls her toes under while lifting her body up onto her elbows and toes. While maintaining a neutral posture, she alternates leg raises from the hip with a straight knee.

- **Calf stretch:** The child stands in a lunge position with her front knee bent, though that front knee should not extend past the ankle. The child places her hands on the front of her thigh and presses forward, keeping her back leg straight while pressing the rear heel down.

- **Knee bends:** While the child is seated, she bends her left knee and places her left foot flat on the floor. She follows this by placing her right foot and ankle on her left thigh just above the knee. She places her hands on the floor behind her hips and presses her chest toward her knee and foot. Her upper torso, neck, and shoulders should remain open and straight; do not let her round her upper back.

- **Hip flexor:** The child stands with her feet in a lunge position and her front knee is slightly bent. She pushes up using the toes on her back foot. She also presses her hips forward while tightening her buttocks and then slowly lowers her body until a stretch is felt in the front of the hip. While performing this, her upper body remains upright and centred directly over the hips.

✔ **Hamstrings:** While sitting, the child extends her right leg fully and bends her left leg, placing the inside of the foot along her right calf. While keeping her back straight, she brings her chest towards her knee and reaches with both her hands towards her toes. Depending on how much flexibility the child has, she places her hands on the floor alongside her legs or holds her toes.

✔ **Quadriceps:** The child stands and grabs her right foot or ankle and lifts it behind her body. She presses her foot into her hand while pressing her hips slightly forward. Her lower leg and foot should be directly behind her upper leg and there shouldn't be any twisting in or out. Make sure that the child does not rest her foot against her buttocks. If any of the kids have trouble balancing on one leg, have them perform the stretch with a partner so that they can use their free hand to put on their partner's shoulder to balance themselves.

✔ **Groin:** The child sits on the ground and places the soles of her feet together with her knees off to the sides. Leaning forward, the child slowly presses forward until a mild tension is felt in the groin.

Just as your team has vastly different characteristics and levels of ability, the same holds true when it comes to how flexible they are going to be. Some kids are going to be extremely flexible while others won't even come close to being able to touch their toes. After the warm-up, make sure that the team knows that, if anyone doesn't feel that they are sufficiently loosened up, they can spend a few extra moments doing additional stretching until they are comfortable and feel that they are ready to proceed with the game.

Breaking a sweat

Because football requires large amounts of running with players moving almost continuously throughout the game, you don't want to send your team out on the pitch without first getting their bodies warmed up and their hearts pumping for this type of strenuous activity. During your warm-up period, you want the kids to get loosened up with jumping jacks or light jogging while dribbling a football.

For example, you can have the kids dribble a football down the pitch to help get their hearts beating a little faster to get them ready for when they are required to run at full speed during the game. Or, you can have the players jog down the pitch in pairs dribbling the ball and passing it back and forth to one another.

Incorporating skills used in the game into the warm-up is doubly effective. You want to avoid doing a lot of one-on-one drills that put kids in a competitive situation where they tend to exert more energy than you would like. You want them working at about 50 per cent of their normal speed during this phase so that they have a full tank of energy to start the game with.

Here are a few other tips to keep in mind:

- **Keep moving:** After the players are warmed up, make sure that their bodies don't have a chance to cool down before they step onto the pitch. Sometimes, a game preceding theirs may run into extra time, and a team's warm-up can lose a lot of its effectiveness if kids wind up just standing on the sidelines waiting to take the pitch. The same goes for those youngsters who are starting the game. You don't want them planting themselves on the bench once the game begins. So, encourage players to keep moving around, lightly jogging in place, and doing light stretches to keep their legs loose and their bodies warm.

- **Pay attention to conditions:** If the weather is extremely hot, you may want to shorten the warm-up; or if your team is involved in a tournament and is playing several games that day or over the course of a weekend, you should reduce the amount of time they spend warming up because they are already expending more energy than they are accustomed to.

Cooling off

While the warm-up gets all the attention because the focus is on preparing kids for games, the post-training and post-game warm-downs are equally important for the long-term health of your team. The warm-down helps reduce muscle soreness in your players, while aiding circulation and helping to clear waste products from the muscles. Doing some of the light stretches that you use in the pre-game warm-up help to prevent the tightening of muscles that accompanies vigorous exercise. See the section 'Stretching to improve flexibility', earlier in this chapter.

You can make this post-game stretching period fun for the kids by talking to them about the game while they are going through the exercises. Joke with them about anything unusual or funny that may have happened in the game. Point out how well they may have executed a three-on-two or how well they defended an attack. Ask them what they enjoyed most about playing.

Handling Injuries

While you can't eliminate the threat of injuries occurring during both training sessions and games, how you handle them when they do pop up can have a pretty significant impact on how the child views his future football participation.

The overwhelming majority of injuries you are likely to encounter during your football coaching career involve minor bumps, bruises, cuts, and twisted ankles. Of course, while these injuries may seem minor to you, they may, in fact, be pretty major in the eyes of a child who suddenly sees blood on his leg or feels the kind of pain he has never felt before in his young life when he tries to put any pressure on his ankle. Acting quickly, administering the proper treatment, and comforting the youngster can help him bounce back and return to action fairly quickly.

Kids are obviously going to be curious about what is happening to an injured teammate, but they should be kept back from the event. You don't want the entire team crowding around the injured child, which may make him panic more than he already is, seeing everyone hovering over him and staring at him with concerned looks on their faces. During a serious injury to a player on the opposing team during a game, your team should return to its touch-line. Immediately check on the injured child with the other coaches and provide any assistance that is needed. You don't want your players to be a distraction or unnecessarily get in the way while treatment is being provided.

Dealing with blood

Any time one of your players suffers a cut or has an open wound, the first thing you should do is grab a pair of latex gloves, or use some other type of blood barrier to keep yourself from coming into contact with blood.

You are right to be fearful of AIDS, but that should never be a factor in providing help to an injured player on your team. You are only at risk if you allow the blood of an HIV-positive person to come in contact with an open wound. Should one of your players have AIDS, or is HIV-positive, this is something that the parents certainly should have made you aware of during your pre-season parents meeting (refer to Chapter 4). Regardless, the fact that you are wearing latex gloves provides the protection you need in order to treat the injured child.

Once you have the gloves on, follow these steps:

1. **Apply direct pressure.** You can stop any bleeding that may be occurring by applying direct pressure to the wound with a clean dressing. If you're having trouble stopping the bleeding, then elevate the child's injured area above their heart while maintaining the pressure.

2. **Clean the wound.** After you have stopped the bleeding, you need to clean the wound. Pre-moistened towelettes can be used for cleaning minor cuts and scrapes, or you can use alcohol swabs or antibiotic creams that are readily available over the counter.

3. **Cover the wound.** Use a bandage or piece of sterile gauze to cover the cut and be sure to secure it tightly in place, particularly if the child is able and wants to continuing playing.

4. **Discard rubbish.** Place your gloves and any other used materials that may have blood on them in a sealed bag and place it in the rubbish bin so that no one else is at risk of coming into contact with the materials.

Soothing strains and sprains

Football is a physically demanding sport that requires players to run, make sudden stops and starts, and execute sharp turns, while often coming into contact with other players in the process. These movements – and some of the collisions that accompany them – can result in muscle strains and sprains. Because much of football is played below the waist, the majority of these types of injuries involve the ankle and knee.

When a player has strained a muscle or twisted their ankle, keep in mind the RICE method for treatment:

- ✔ **Rest:** Immediately get the child to the sideline so that they can rest the injury. If the child has twisted her ankle, for example, have an assistant coach or a parent from the stands help you carry the child off the pitch so that she doesn't put any additional pressure on the injured area.

- ✔ **Ice:** Apply ice to the injured area. Ice helps to reduce the swelling and pain. Don't apply the ice directly to the skin. Wrap the bag in a towel and then place it on the injured area.

- ✔ **Compress:** Compress the injured area by using athletic tape or any other type of material to hold the ice in place.

- ✔ **Elevate:** Have the child elevate the injury above their heart level to prevent blood from pooling in the injured area.

Only after any swelling, discoloration, or pain has subsided, should the youngster be allowed to play again. If any of these symptoms are present for more than a couple days, the player should be examined by a doctor before you allow them back on the pitch. You never want a child to return to the pitch when their injury hasn't completely healed because this puts them at greater risk of re-injuring the area and spending even longer out of the game.

Coping with more serious injuries

At the more competitive levels of football, as the players become bigger and stronger and are capable of kicking the ball with tremendous force, this force opens up the door for the possibility of other types of injuries to occur. The following list takes a quick look at a few of these and how you should respond.

- ✔ **Concussion:** A jarring injury to the head, face, or jaw resulting in a disturbance of the brain. Concussions are classified as mild or severe. Symptoms are a brief loss of consciousness, headache, grogginess, confusion, a glassy-eyed look, amnesia, disturbed balance, and slight dizziness. Immediate care should include rest on the sidelines with an adult in attendance to provide careful observation. If you see any evidence of something more serious, such as unconsciousness, change in the size of eye pupils or convulsions, get them immediately by ambulance to a hospital for further observation. Mild concussions may require up to a week for recovery and the decision to return must be made by a physician. Severe concussions require at least four weeks of recovery and permission to return should be given only by a head injuries specialist.

- ✔ **Eye injuries:** Any foreign body, such as a fleck of dirt, lodged in the eye needs attention. Usually this is a nuisance condition but if the irritation doesn't go away it needs to be evaluated by an eye specialist. Symptoms are tearing, pain, and redness. Most foreign objects can be easily removed with a cotton swab and saline wash. If the surface of the eye has not been seriously injured and vision is not impaired, the youngster can return to competition as soon as the foreign object has been removed.

  However, when a child suffers a direct injury to the eyeball, you have an immediate medical emergency. Symptoms are extreme pain, loss of vision, hazy vision, double vision, change in vision colours or obvious lacerations or abrasions of the eye. If the vision loss is the result of a direct eye injury rather than a head injury, a dry, sterile eye patch or piece of gauze should be applied to the eye along with a bag of soft, crushed ice. The youngster should immediately be taken to an emergency facility.

  When a youngster has been poked in the eye, examine the eye and if you see minimal redness, no discharge or bleeding, and the child is not in significant pain, simply clean the area out with cool water and allow the athlete to rest for a while before allowing them to return to play. Anything more serious requires immediate medical attention.

- ✔ **Orbital fracture:** This is a fracture of the bony frame around the eye. All orbital fractures are serious and require expert medical treatment. Symptoms are severe pain, with possible double vision or other vision problems. The fracture may be accompanied by cuts, abrasions, bleeding, and black and blue marks. Any youngster who has suffered significant injury to the area around the eye should be transported to a facility where he can be x-rayed to determine whether a fracture has occurred.

✔ **Shin splints**: This injury is common in a sport like football where lots of repetitive running is involved. The primary cause of the injury is related to the weight pounding down on the shin. Other factors that can also contribute are muscle weakness, poor flexibility, improper warm-up and warm-down exercises, and improper footwear. Symptoms are typically easy to identify because the athlete will have pain on the shin. The four stages associated with shin splints are pain after activity; pain before and after activity without affecting performance; pain before, during and after activity, adversely affecting performance; and constant pain that prohibits activity. The early stages of shin splints are relatively mild but later stages can become much more severe. If the injury is not properly managed, it can result in a stress fracture. If a player develops shin splints, ice can be used to reduce pain and swelling and any weight-bearing activities should be eliminated to allow the affected area time to heal.

✔ **Winded**: A youngster who has had the wind knocked out of him for the first time is likely to begin panicking when he has trouble breathing. Comfort the youngster and have him take short, quick breaths and pant like a dog until he is able to resume breathing normally again.

✔ **Tooth knocked out**: If a child has a tooth knocked out, retrieve the tooth and place it in a sterile gauze pad with saline and take the child to a dentist as soon as possible.

✔ **Nosebleeds**: These can be fairly common in youth football. As long as you are sure that the child has not sustained a nasal fracture, then simply squeezing the nostrils together and holding the nose in this position for a couple of minutes should be all that is needed to stop the bleeding.

Any time a child suffers an injury that you have provided any type of treatment for, be sure to write down exactly what you did. In a separate logbook, write down the nature of the injury, how it happened, and what treatment you provided. Do so the same day while the event is still fresh in your mind.

Heading off lawsuits

Unfortunately, we live in a litigious society these days, so having an accurate account of everything that transpired the day of an injury – should you need to recount what happened – will help protect you in a court of law. Don't discard these records after the season is over. Keep these accounts, along with your dated training plans and notes, for several years.

It may be unlikely but a former player, years from now, may come forward and sue you for an injury suffered while playing for you. If you have detailed notes of everything that happened, you can go some way to protect yourself from unwarranted accusations. These detailed training plans, with dates, will come in handy if you need evidence that you safely and properly taught your players specific skills, and to protect yourself against ridiculous and totally unfounded lawsuits.

Handling emergency situations

You always want to proceed cautiously when dealing with any type of injury, and that is particularly the case any time you are dealing with an injury that involves the head, neck, or spine. Never attempt to move a player who is lying on the ground with such an injury because doing so is likely to cause further damage. Medical assistance should always be called immediately whenever you are dealing with a serious injury.

Being able to assess sports injuries is an integral part of coaching football. You must be prepared for any type of injury, including when a child gets knocked down and may have lost consciousness. The acronym COACH is a handy reminder of how to respond.

- ✔ **Conscious:** The first step is to determine whether the child is conscious.

- ✔ **Oxygen:** Are they breathing and getting oxygen? (If the answer is yes to these two questions, move on.)

- ✔ **Ask:** Ask the youngster where they are hurt.

- ✔ **Control:** Control the area that is painful.

- ✔ **Help:** What type of help is required? Make the decision of whether you need to call for immediate medical assistance and take the child to hospital.

When you're approaching an injured child, look at their lip colour, feel the chest or put your cheek next to their nose to see whether they are breathing. If they are not breathing and you can feel no palpable pulse in their neck or wrist, you must immediately initiate CPR and have someone call for immediate medical assistance. If the injury sustained is to the head or neck, the athlete must be calmed and restrained in the position found while emergency medical assistance is responding.

All youth football coaches should receive CPR and first-aid training from the Red Cross or other nationally recognised organisation. Remember, every training session and game you are responsible for the safety and well being of every single player. So, do your club, your team, and yourself a huge favour and take the time to go through the training. You, and your team, may be glad you did.

Be prepared for emergencies

If a serious injury occurs, are you prepared to handle it? Much like you spend time practising corner kicks, you need to practise how you are going to respond in an emergency situation. How you respond – and how quickly – can make the difference in saving a youngster's life. The following are steps to keep in mind:

✔ **Know where you are playing:** Be aware of the name of the facility that you are playing at, as well as its address. In the event that you have to call 999, being able to provide as much accurate information as possible quickly helps to ensure that emergency medical personnel arrive as quickly as possible at the proper location.

✔ **Have each child's emergency information on hand:** These important forms (see Chapter 4) are crucial in the event that medical personnel need to know whether the child is allergic to any type of medication, for example. Always carry these forms in your first-aid kit and have them easily accessible in the event of an emergency.

✔ **Provide first aid:** While awaiting the arrival of medical personnel, provide only the first-aid care that you have been trained to perform.

✔ **Comfort:** If the child is conscious, comfort them by talking in a calm and relaxed voice. Let them know that they are going to be OK and that medical help is on the way.

✔ **Phone calls:** If the child's parents are not in attendance, one of your assistant coaches should have the responsibility to call them to let them know what is going on. Your foremost responsibility at a time like this is to the child, so if you have already designated someone else to make that initial call to the parents, you won't have to waste unnecessary time when all your attention needs to be focused on the youngster.

Watching the Weather

Mother Nature and her tremendous power should never be taken lightly. Severe weather poses a great risk to youngsters and you must meet your responsibility to get them off of the pitch before trouble arrives. During a game, don't rely on the referee or the opposing team's coach to stop the game when bad weather is approaching. Never try to squeeze in another minute, or try to get the game finished so that you don't have to deal with the hassle of rescheduling. Think about it. Endangering the safety of your players is never worth the risk simply to finish a game.

Lightning is a big concern simply because it can show up so quickly. If a storm moves in on you unexpectedly and lightning is in the area, safe places to retreat to with the kids are enclosed buildings, fully enclosed vehicles with the windows up, and low ground. Be sure to stay away from trees, water, wide open areas, metal stands, light poles, fences or any other metallic objects.

Lightning isn't the only issue Mother Nature can cause. Children do not acclimatise to heat as well as adults, so several points need to be considered. You should be aware that certain temperatures present an extreme stress to kids.

As a general rule, when the humidity rises above 70 per cent and the temperature is above 80 degrees you need to exercise extra caution with your team. Kids should be encouraged to drink extra water and to wear lighter clothing. When the temperature rises above 90 degrees with the humidity between 70 and 80 per cent, this presents a pretty dangerous area for heat illnesses to occur. When these types of conditions are present, training sessions or games should be suspended, or at the very least significantly curtailed. Only cool, porous clothing should be worn and water should never be withheld as a form of discipline, no matter how serious the infraction or broken team rule. (See the section 'Getting enough water', later in this chapter.)

Exposure to the sun is an often overlooked health risk when it comes to youth football. Our skin is an excellent record keeper of our time outdoors and every moment we spend in the sun adds up, accumulating like money in the bank. Unfortunately, the payoff is often skin damage and skin cancer. The best defence to protect your athletes when outdoors is to encourage them to use a sunscreen with an SPF of 30. Make sun safety a priority with your team.

Following a Healthy Diet

You can coach kids in the proper way to head a ball, deliver a corner kick or make a tackle, but if they aren't eating the right foods before arriving at the pitch, their performance is going to be compromised. While you can't control what your team eats before training sessions and games, you can spend time discussing the importance of following good nutritional habits in order to maximise performance. Discussing nutrition with your team (and even their parents) and how fuelling the body can improve performance by giving them energy and added strength can make a difference.

Fluids and glucose are the two primary ingredients for fuelling a child's muscles during training sessions and games – and they get used up the longer the activity goes on. Kids lose fluids through perspiration, which is why water is such a vital ingredient to keep a child's body temperature from rising during exercise. The longer a child exercises without replacing lost fluids, and the more extreme the temperatures and conditions they are competing in, the less effective their performance and the worse they are going to feel.

In addition, *glucose,* a sugar derived from carbohydrates, is an important muscle fuel. Glucose is carried to the working muscles through the bloodstream and gets stored in the child's muscles in long chains called glycogen. With all the running, stopping, and starting required in a game, a child's glycogen stores are steadily depleted. The more carbohydrate fuel a child loses during competition, the less energy they are going to have to perform at their peak.

What the kids eat and drink before, during and after games impacts on their performance, as well as how quickly they recover before the next outing.

What to eat – pre-game

When your players show up at games without eating, or after having devoured a burger, fries, and a fizzy drink, their energy levels are going to be down and they're going to have trouble both performing and concentrating. A nutritious pre-game meal – while often overlooked – clears the way for the child to perform at their optimum level. Youngsters who eat a healthy meal – or at least healthy snacks – comprised of plenty of carbohydrates are going to have the muscle energy to play and play well. The pre-game meal needs to be comprised of foods that have most of their calories coming from carbohydrates because they convert into energy quicker and more efficiently than other nutrients. The following are pre-game meal tips to share with your squad and their parents:

- The pre-game meal should be consumed between two to three hours prior to the game. Players should avoid eating within an hour of game time because their bodies spend the first half digesting their food, which detracts from their performance.

- For the most nutritional punch, youngsters should opt for pastas, breads, cereals, and whole grains, along with fruits and vegetables.

- Good pre-game snacks are bagels, yogurt, dried fruit, fresh fruit, crackers and energy bars, fruit granola bars, and whole grain crackers with peanut butter or cheese. Stay away from sweets, biscuits, doughnuts, and regular and diet fizzy drinks.

- TV commercials sing the praises of chocolate bars packed with caramel centres, but nutrition is found in the four basic food groups, not in sweets. Children bring home ideas from many sources and they can bring home healthier eating habits from you if you take the time to explain these habits to them.

 If your players feel sluggish in the second half of games, or really seem to tire and not perform as well as they do in the first half of games, their diet may be the culprit. Advise them to experiment by changing their eating habits on training days. Encourage them to consume healthy snacks prior to training and see whether they notice any difference in their energy levels. If so, they can use that knowledge and feed their body those types of food prior to their games, too.

 If your team has a morning game and the kids simply aren't going to be able to get up early enough to have a proper pre-game meal, make sure that they focus on eating a nutritionally sound meal the night before, which helps to prepare their bodies when they step on the pitch the following morning. The meal should be a big serving of pasta with vegetables, chicken or fish. Even the night before a game, kids should steer clear of sweets, ice cream and fizzy drinks, for example, which have the ability to rob them of much-needed energy on game day.

What to eat post-game

What you say – and how you say it – following your team's game impacts each child's confidence and self-esteem. Similarly, what the team eats following a contest impacts on their bodies and how they feel. While it's certainly fun to reward kids for a game well played with a tasty snack, giving them junk food sends the wrong message about the importance of following proper nutritional habits. The following are a few post-game tips to keep in mind:

- ✔ **Think carbohydrates:** Foods rich in carbohydrates that also have protein value are the most beneficial for youngsters. Ideally, the post-game meal or snack should look a lot like the pre-game meal (see preceding section), with the only difference being that the portions should be a little bit smaller. Turkey sandwiches, fresh fruit, and crackers and cheese are great post-game foods to let your team eat.

- ✔ **The sooner the better:** The sooner your team digs into its post-game food the better. Plenty of research out there indicates that foods packed with carbohydrates, consumed within 30 minutes of a game or training session, are going to provide the most benefits for youngsters.

If you talk to kids about how what they are eating today can affect their health years from now, they're unlikely to listen. But if you frame your discussion in terms of how their meal this morning will affect their performance in the game this afternoon, your chances of grabbing their attention are much more likely and they may be much more interested in what you have to say on the topic.

Getting enough water

The importance of children consuming lots of fluids – and the right kinds – simply can't be stated enough. When kids are running up and down the pitch chasing the football and exerting all of this energy their body temperature rises. The younger the child, the less they are going to typically sweat because their sweat glands are not completely developed at this stage in their life. This is one of the reasons why their bodies soak up more heat when games are played in high temperatures and humidity. Children who don't consume adequate amounts of water during games, especially those contested in hot and humid conditions, are at increased risk of becoming dehydrated and suffering muscle cramps, heat exhaustion or, even worse, heat stroke.

So how much water should kids be consuming? Well, the amount varies, because the game conditions dictate whether they need to increase their water consumption to remain sufficiently hydrated. Also, with so many different body types, kids are going to sweat at different rates and need different levels of fluids. Generally speaking, you want kids consuming water whenever possible: drinking a glass of water with their pre-game meal; consuming water during the pre-game warm-ups; and taking sips of water whenever they come out of the game.

When it comes to fluids, here are a few additional tips to quench that knowledge:

- ✔ **Be specific:** With younger children, even though they hear you telling them to drink water, they probably aren't consuming enough. During a break in training, or during time out during a game, encourage the players to take ten sips of water, for example. Ten sips help to ensure that the kids are getting enough fluids into their bodies.

- ✔ **Help the internal organs:** After exerting themselves, kids need to consume lots of fluids to help replenish the fluids they lose throughout the game. Giving the body water after a game helps the liver and kidneys clear out all the waste, which is a key element in recovery.

- ✔ **Don't worry about too much water:** You don't need to worry about kids drinking too much water. Most kids are going to drink based on need, as drinking is a voluntary habit and thirst is the mechanism that tells them to drink. With plenty of water breaks, you don't have to worry about them sitting on the touchlines swigging too much water and not being able to perform on the pitch.

- ✔ **Encourage drinking even if they are not thirsty:** Often, kids are so immersed in the game that they don't even think about drinking any water. You've got to encourage them to drink. During breaks in play and at half-time when you are providing encouragement and discussing game strategy, make sure that you stress drinking water, too. Kids should be sipping water from their water bottles while you are talking to them.

- ✔ **Encourage parents:** A great way to help ensure that kids are properly hydrated is to work with parents so that on the car ride over to the game they can have their child drink some water. Spreading the water intake out helps to ensure that the body remains hydrated, and kids won't become bloated by trying to drink too much in one sitting.

- ✔ **Bring extra water:** Always have extra water on hand to refill children's water bottles if they happen to run out. Designate a couple of different parents each week to be responsible for bringing extra water. Water is simply something you should never have a shortage of at any training session or game.

- ✔ **Say no to caffeine:** Beverages with caffeine in them act as a diuretic, which is exactly the opposite of what you are trying to accomplish in keeping the kids hydrated. Also, keep kids away from carbonated drinks.

Chapter 19

Challenges Every Coach Faces

. . . .

. . . .

*P*articipating in organised football provides children with a lifetime of memorable moments – though unfortunately a few of those memories may not turn out to be such happy ones. While every child that laces up a pair of football boots and straps on a pair of shinguards should be able to look back on their participation with fondness and a big smile years from now, inappropriate behaviour by parents and opposing coaches on the touchline can quickly squash the fun and ruin the entire experience for everyone involved.

You must never allow any type of bad behaviour from parents, coaches or spectators to infringe on a child's football experience and cast an unpleasant shadow over your team and the entire season. The same goes for disruptive players on your own squad who affect their teammates' enjoyment. Hopefully, you will have few, if any, times when you need to discipline a youngster on your team or – even worse – deal with inappropriate comments from an opposing coach, parent, or spectator. In the event that you are forced into a position at some point this season of addressing an uncomfortable issue with another adult – or a challenging matter with one of your players – this chapter is here to lend a hand in helping you negotiate your way through the unpleasantness.

Dealing with Problem Parents

Face it – a lot of the childish behaviour seen at youth football games around the country doesn't take place among the kids on the pitch, but rather among the adult spectators and the coaches pacing the touchlines. Sure, minor conflicts arising throughout the course of a football season are going to be inevitable. Anytime you bring together a group of parents with different backgrounds, motivations and sports experiences – all of whom happen to be looking for something different out of their child's football experience – you have a formula for occasional problems to pop up.

If you held a pre-season parents meeting (see Chapter 4), then you have already laid some of the key groundwork in preventing parental problems from escalating into something that is no longer manageable. During the meeting, you should have detailed your expectations regarding parent behaviour during games and clearly explained what constitutes appropriate and inappropriate behaviour from both them and their children during the season.

While laying out your expectations for parental behaviour before the first football is ever kicked is an important step, it cannot guarantee that every parent is going to be a model of good behaviour all season long. So, you've got to be prepared to step forward at the first indication of trouble. Now, many football coaches aren't willing to do that, or simply fail to understand the importance of doing something about it right away. Some coaches, well aware that a problem exists, simply cross their fingers and hope that it resolves itself on its own without any intervention on their behalf. Clearly, this type of approach is not conducive to maintaining a smooth-running season. Anytime a problem is allowed to linger and go untouched for too long, the potential for it to blossom into something much worse greatly increases.

The upcoming sections take a look at some of the more common problems involving parents that you may be dealing with at some point this season, and what approaches you can implement, to help ensure that they are taken care of quickly and effectively and don't negatively impact on any child's experience.

Parents who want to win at all costs

Parents invest a lot of time, money, and energy into their child's football experience, and it is only natural that they are going to want to see them excel in the sport and reap the benefits of participating. Often that means they are going to place unrealistic expectations on their child to perform at exceedingly high levels. They are also probably going to pile unrealistic expectations on you to help their child become a star player. They also look to you to guide the team to a large number of wins and nothing less than a league championship is satisfactory in their eyes.

Such unhealthy behaviour can place an enormous burden on you and your ability to work with all the youngsters. The additional pressure also certainly infringes on some of the other kids' enjoyment of the game and – most importantly – it puts the youngster whose parents have the skyrocketing expectations in a really uncomfortable and pressure-filled position.

Win-at-all-cost parents typically resort to any means possible to ensure that their child's team wins – and that their child looks good in the process. Blinded by their visions of league championships, shiny first-place trophies, and post-season accolades, these parents do whatever it takes. They shout disparaging remarks at referees. They even go so far as to try to intimidate referees into giving favourable decisions for the team, and some of these referees may be teenagers out there on the pitch simply doing their best to do a good job. These parents may even verbally criticise the opposing coach and the techniques his team is using, especially if the opposition happens to be winning the game or doing a really good job of marking the parent's child and not allowing him to show off any of his skills.

You are also going to be on their radar screen and a big target for criticism and questions about your coaching style whenever the outcome of a game doesn't turn out in your team's favour. These are the parents, regardless of the age level of the youngsters, that are likely to confront you about the importance of playing the more athletic kids for longer stretches in the game and to substitute the less skilful players, all to help ensure that the team wins more games and their child receives more playing time on the pitch. They may also criticise your game strategy following losses, question your line-up, analyse your substitutions and offer their unsolicited advice regarding your tactics in both attack and defence.

Of course, following losses they are most definitely going to confront you about why all the play doesn't revolve around their talented child. These win-at-all-cost parents equate wins with winning the lottery and view losses as catastrophes of truly epic proportions. This unhealthy outlook, and what they're drumming into the child at home about how important winning is, goes against everything you're trying to impart to the kids regarding doing their best and having fun doing so.

So how do you deal with a win-at-all costs parent? Again, make sure, from the outset of the season, that you share with the parents your coaching philosophy and what role winning plays at the level of football that you are coaching. Hopefully, any parents looking for something more competitive for their child have understood that this may not be the right fit and signed their child up for something else. Some parents, however, may not have realised that there wasn't going to be quite as much emphasis on winning as there was on skill development and acquiring some of the basics of the game.

While you don't have a say in what the parents say to their child at home about winning and how important it may be to them, you do have a say in what is said while you are coaching a game. Look at the football pitch as a classroom, where you are coaching the kids not only in football skills, but other important values such as teamwork, good sportsmanship, and doing the best they can at all times. You can't allow outside influences to disrupt the messages that you are trying to get across to the kids.

Chances are that during the course of the season some parents may begin adopting a rather intense interest in the outcome of games. You may start noticing that their comments and reactions during the game, or what they say to their kids afterward, are becoming problematic and counterproductive to what you are trying to get across to the youngsters. Groans when your goalie fumbles a shot that results in a goal, or feet stomping in disgust when one of your players fails to convert a golden scoring opportunity are clear signals that their behaviour is taking on the tone of a professional rather than a youth game.

To help stem the competitive tide and prevent it from enveloping the other parents of your players, give a brief and friendly talk to the parents before your next game. Spending a couple of minutes talking to the entire group and reminding them that this is for fun and that winning the game is not the most important factor may help to put them in the proper frame of mind.

If the group chat doesn't prove to be beneficial and the win-at-all-costs attitude continues to be prevalent, arrange to speak with the parent privately and share your concerns that their comments affecting their child's development, and the rest of the team. Be sure to reiterate that you are trying to help all the kids develop skills and that, while winning a game is one of the objectives, it is not the only one by any means. Let the parent know that if they are not happy with your philosophy on coaching kids that perhaps they should look into signing their child up for a more competitive team. In the meantime, you've got to have their co-operation. Tell them that the last thing you want is for them not to be a part of this exciting time in their child's life, but if the improper behaviour continues to detract from the values you are coaching the kids in, then the only other recourse you have is not to pick their child for the team. Don't be confrontational in your discussion, but be firm in your stance because you've got the welfare of a group of kids to look out for.

Parents who think you're a baby-sitter

Most parents these days juggle chaotic schedules in which they attempt to maintain their sanity while herding their kids to all their assorted activities. Sometimes, parents view your training sessions – and even games – as a convenient baby-sitting service where they can drop their youngster off and return an hour or so later. Yes, in today's era where single parenting plays an ever increasing role in family life, mum or dad may simply not have the luxury of being able to hang out at the football pitch and watch their child participate, with all the other responsibilities they have to fulfil in their lives.

Ideally, you want parents to be – at least to some extent – a part of the training regimen whenever possible and to be there on the day of a game providing positive support and encouragement for not just their own child, but for the entire team. After a couple weeks of training sessions and games, you start to get a pretty good sense of which parents simply can't be there all the time and which are simply taking advantage of you and are basically using you as an unpaid baby-sitting service. During your interactions with the kids, you also start to be able to gauge what type of family life they have at home, and your conversations with parents before training sessions and games should also give you a pretty good feel for what type of people they are in general.

One of the best ways to get parents to stick around during training is to include them in some of your drills. Practice games between the kids and their parents are a fun-filled way to get everyone involved (refer to Chapter 6). Or, you can incorporate some drills in which the parents serve as the goalies and the kids are shooting at them, which are also great ways to strengthen the parent-child bond. When those parents who typically didn't hang around after dropping their child off see all the fun that's taking place, and how involved the other parents are with their children, they're going to start hanging around and wanting to be a part of the action. Furthermore, if you hold these parent-child practice games or drills at the end of training, those parents who are just showing up to pick up their child start to see what they have missed, which may help spur their interest in sticking around for the entire training session next time the team gets together.

Remember, a lot of the parents that you come in contact with may be unfamiliar with their roles and responsibilities when it comes to a team sport like football, and perhaps what you outlined for them at your preseason parents meeting didn't really sink in at the time. A quick, casual conversation with parents when they arrive to pick their child up may be all that is needed to make a difference. Let those parents know that you think their child may really benefit from having them take a more active interest in their football and being a part of training sessions and games. A child who scores a goal or makes a great tackle is going to derive a lot more satisfaction if they are able to glance over to the touchline and see a thumbs up or a nod of approval and a smile from their mum or dad.

Let the parents know that their presence, even during a routine training session during the middle of the week, can do a lot for a child's confidence while also maintaining their interest in the sport. You can even mention a drill you've completed in practice that their child has really taken a liking to that that they can work on with their youngster at home. Not only does it help the child improve that particular area of their game, but it also gets the parent more involved in their child's development, which is good news for everyone.

Parents who want their child to play all the time

A lot of parents track their child's playing time more closely than their investment portfolio. When it comes to youth football, playing time is like gold, and parents can't get enough of it for their child. After all, many parents view their child's status on the team as a true reflection of their parenting skills. The more skilful their child is – and the more playing time she receives because of those skills – then the better job of parenting they assume they must be doing. In their eyes, their child's playing time becomes a status symbol among the rest of the team as well as the parents they are standing next to on the touchline all season long.

You can't avoid the simple fact these days that a lot of parents have ridiculously unrealistic expectations when it comes to their kid's football ability. Every time they see their child sitting on the bench they think their future is being compromised and their chances of playing football for their country is being put in jeopardy. Despite the league rule that is most likely in place (especially at the beginner's level) regarding equal playing time for all kids – regardless of their ability – all of a sudden, once the season gets under way, some parents are not in agreement with this policy. Now, when they see their child taking their turn sitting on the subs bench they think that you are hindering their development.

Dealing with a parent that is disappointed with the amount of playing time their child has been receiving is all too common in football, and fairly easy to handle. Here are a couple points to keep in mind:

- **League policy:** If your league has a policy on equal playing time for all the kids, and you explained that policy at the start of the season to all the parents, then you have made a pretty convincing case for why you are rotating the kids in and out of the line-up. Sometimes, you may have a large number of kids in the squad, which means that a group of them are always on the bench. Let the parent know that you enjoy coaching their child and that you wish you were able to provide more playing time, but that you have to be fair to all your players.

- **Reminder:** Another important reason why you should hold a pre-season parents meeting (refer to Chapter 4), is that if at the time you stated your policy that every child would receive an equal amount of playing time – based on regularly attending training sessions and not ability – now is a good time to remind the parent of that discussion you outlined.

- **Charting playing time:** If the parent questions whether the playing time is being distributed equally among all the players, hopefully you can refer to your line-up to show them that you (or an assistant coach if you have delegated this responsibility) carefully monitor the playing time of each child to ensure that everyone gets an equal amount. Written documentation of the great lengths you go to make it fair for everyone is usually enough to make your point.

Disruptive parents

Over-involved parents who regularly wander across the line of good behaviour have become increasingly commonplace in youth football programs. Why some parents act irresponsibly and behave poorly while watching a youth football game is difficult to figure out and probably involves a lot of factors that are completely out of your control. But what is in your control is your ability to not allow the type of negative behaviour that embarrasses their child and disrupts the game to continue.

If a parent displays inappropriate behaviour, you should address it as soon as possible. Ignoring the actions of these parents or being afraid to step forward and address the situation sends a terrible message that this type of behaviour is acceptable and everything that you hopefully talked about during that pre-season parents meeting was really just hollow words. Parents need to be made aware that you do not tolerate inappropriate words and actions in any form whatsoever. Dealing with it swiftly also lets the other team's parents know that if they step or act out of line, they can expect to be dealt with accordingly. The entire team of parents should then appreciate your commitment to ensuring that each child on the team has a safe and fun-filled experience that doesn't include loud-mouth insults, swearing, ranting, raving, or frightening violence that has found its way into an increasing number of junior football leagues, and youth sports programs in general.

How do you handle a parent who has just shouted an embarrassing comment? What do you do when they yell across the pitch at the coach who appears to be getting the better of your team? What do you do when tensions seem to be rising among parents who are suddenly not happy with how the game is unfolding? You can use the following approaches to help keep everyone's tempers in check and the game continuing on without any unnecessary disruptions for the kids.

- **Try a friendly reminder.** Often, parents may not even realise that they are behaving inappropriately and a firm – but friendly – reminder to keep their emotions in check and their comments about the play on the pitch or the referee's decisions to themselves may be all that is required.

- **Don't embarrass the parent.** Being the parent of a youth football player isn't easy. Parents want the best for their young players, and if they see their child knocked down or tripped by an opposing player and the referee doesn't blow the whistle, it can be extremely difficult to refrain from voicing their displeasure. If you hear a comment shouted from the touchline, sometimes all that is necessary is a look over your shoulder at the offending parent. That brief eye contact exchange to let them know that what they just said is unacceptable and to tone it down may just be enough to remedy the situation. You also need to take the time to follow up and meet with the parent after the game – if you get an opportunity to speak with them alone – and remind them that negative comments detract from everyone's enjoyment of the game. For example, something along the lines of, 'I know that foul the referee gave against your son in the second half was debatable, but you know all the decisions aren't going to go our way this season. I am going to need you and all the other parents to set an example of good sportsmanship and any negative comments that are made detract from all the kids' enjoyment. I know it's difficult, but please don't let it happen again.'

✔ **Don't get physical.** You should never attempt to physically confront a parent or spectator who refuses to abide by your request to behave. Obviously a last resort is to call the police. Hopefully, however, matters will never get that out of hand. For persistent offenders, issue a polite warning that the child can expect to have to play for another team if the behaviour continues. A warning is usually sufficient.

✔ **Never punish the child.** No matter how poorly behaved mum or dad is, never take out your frustration on the child. Remember, the youngster on your team has no control over how their parents behave on match day, so don't trim down their playing time, switch their position on the pitch, or take any other drastic measures in an effort to rein in the emotional outbursts of their parents. Continue coaching the child, working with them and applauding their efforts, and hopefully your chats with the parents can start to have the desired effect, and they get themselves under control.

✔ **Don't tolerate surprise attacks in the car park following the game.** These situations where the parent is visibly upset and tensions are running high are not conducive to a mature discussion and nothing good can come of it. Explain to the parent that you are happy to meet with them and discuss any concerns they may have at a time that is convenient for both of you, not in front of their child or the rest of the team.

✔ **Make sure that civility rules.** You can quickly defuse an often-tense situation between you and an upset parent when it comes to any issue following a game by maintaining a calm and friendly demeanour at all times. Setting a civil tone right from the start is a critical building block for a productive discussion. Granted, this may be difficult at times, particularly if the parent is unleashing a verbal assault, accusing you of being an inept football coach with no sense of what is right for the kids.

✔ **Acknowledge the child.** Parents want the best for their child, so the fact that they are requesting a meeting with you and are willing to take the time to speak with you on their child's behalf shows that they are a caring and concerned parent. Let them know that you understand that they want the best for their child, as do you. Acknowledge their child's attributes, and let them know how proud you are of how they have developed so far this season, what a pleasure they are to coach, and what a valuable member of the team they are.

✔ **Be prepared to listen.** If you're not willing to listen to what the parent has to say, how can you realistically expect them to listen to you? Focus as much on listening as you are on trying to get your point across and the parent may be a lot more likely to work with you and not against you.

✔ **The right tone.** Just as your tone and body language influence your interactions with the kids, they have the same impact on your dealings with parents. For example, if a parent poses a question to you about why their child only got to play in half the game and before responding you put your hands on your hips, they are going to perceive you as being upset before you have even had a chance to respond to the question. Mixed body language signals or a negative tone are quick routes to an unproductive and unhealthy conversation.

✔ **Don't fire back.** Parents often use these meetings as an opportunity to bombard coaches with accusations, complaints, and other negative comments. No matter how frustrated or upset you are, you have to resist the urge to fire back at the parent in defence of your coaching abilities because doing so accomplishes absolutely nothing.

✔ **Parent policies.** An increasing number of football leagues around the country are instituting parental codes of conduct – both voluntary and mandatory – to help give parents a clear understanding of their roles and responsibilities. If your local league doesn't do this, then you may want to recommend to the appropriate league official that the league adopts a program so that all the parents work together to ensure that the best interests of all the kids are met. The FA also runs the Soccer Parent programme. Check out Chapter 23 for resources you can use.

Coping with Problem Coaches

Unfortunately, you can't get around the sad fact that at some point during your football coaching career you are going to come across other coaches who just don't get it when it comes to kids and football. While rude and out-of control behaviour is more likely to be seen if you are coaching the older age groups and in the more advanced levels of football when the competition becomes more intense, it also can be found with the younger kids.

The best way to combat this type of offensive behaviour by opposing coaches is to maintain a level head and a calm demeanour while everyone else is losing theirs. These are the situations when you are tested on how well you can adhere to that coaching philosophy of yours that we discussed in Chapter 2. Remember, your top priority at all times is to protect the best interests of your squad. The players on your team take their cues from you and how you act when the tension rises and blood pressures escalate. What are you going to do when the opposing coach's tactics endanger your play-ers? How are you going to deal with a coach on the other side of the pitch whose behaviour is embarrassingly out of control? And what about assistant coaches on your own team who suddenly show you a side of themselves that you never knew existed when you enlisted their help on the touchlines?

Coaches who encourage unsafe play

Ensuring the safety of your players should always be your top priority. Of course, in a contact sport like football, injuries are going to occur and you simply can't avoid some of the normal bumps and bruises that occur during the course of a season. But if you find your team playing against a squad that is being encouraged to use unsafe methods that are putting your team's safety and well-being in jeopardy, you've got to take immediate action. What steps should you take?

- **Talk to the referee.** Address your concerns in a respectable manner to the referee and express that your players are being put at unnecessary risk. Make sure that you are clear that you are concerned about the welfare of all the kids, and not the referee's decision making. Never hesitate to address a safety issue when it comes to your players. One of the referee's most important responsibilities is to ensure the safety of all the players, so by working with referees – not against them – you can help make that happen.

- **Don't confront the opposing coach.** Use the referee as your intermediary to resolve the situation. Heading over to the other coach typically just creates the potential for more conflict. It can also antagonise the coach, who may feel threatened that you've come over and are questioning his coaching techniques in front of all the spectators. The coach may react negatively and view it as a ploy to affect his team's play, particularly if they are winning the game.

- **Stop the game.** If, after speaking with the referee, in the next few minutes of the game you don't feel that the tone and nature of the game has changed enough and that physical and unsafe play continues to prevail, then your only recourse is to remove your team from the pitch. Certainly, you hope that the nature of the play never escalates to such a degree that you have to resort to this, but completing a football game simply to get it in the records – at the risk of injury to a child – is never worth it.

- **Speak with the league.** You can often file a report, or a complaint, to the league in the case of bad behaviour by another team's coach. The league should have its own disciplinary procedures. Anyone manhandling the referee, for example, can expect to get a lengthy ban.

Coaches who model poor sportsmanship

You're in for quite a surprise if you head into the season thinking that every opposing team's coach is going to be a mild-mannered individual who is going to be a model of good behaviour and human decency. Unfortunately, that's not going to be the case. Football coaches do exist – hopefully not in your league – who prowl the touchlines like hungry tigers. These coaches are the ones wearing out their lungs by screaming at their players to run faster and kick harder. They fire negative comments at referees, contest every decision that goes against their team, and give their team the perception that every one is against them. These are the coaches who behave like every game is a World Cup final, every decision carries with it life or death consequences, and every victory is an affirmation of what a wonderful job they are doing as a coach. They view the shiny first-place trophies on their mantelpiece as indications of what wonderful coaches they are.

What's the best way to combat opposing coaches who are sabotaging the experience for everyone involved? Here are a few tips to keep in mind when the game heats up:

- ✔ **Keep a level head.** Opposing coaches who operate with unsportsmanlike behaviour challenge your patience, test your poise, and cause havoc with your blood pressure. You want to avoid retaliating and remain a model of good behaviour for your team.

- ✔ **Make an example.** Point out to your team the type of boorish behaviour that is taking place and explain that they have to rise above it. Demonstrate that they can be much better behaved than that.

- ✔ **Meet with the league officials.** Make officials aware that they have a coach who is really setting a poor example for the kids on her team and that she's not the type of individual who should be coaching in your league.

- ✔ **Tune out distractions.** Tell players to ignore her shouting and to play their own game. Keep talking to them in a positive manner and keep their attention focused on the game and on utilising their skills. Don't allow them to be distracted by her loud-mouthed behaviour.

Disagreeable assistants

Assistants play a vital role in the success of your team (see Chapter 4). They are extra sets of eyes and ears during games, and they can help provide instruction and keep drills moving during training sessions. However you need to exercise great caution before selecting individuals to hold these key positions. The following are a few of the problems that you can run into with your assistant coaches?

- ✔ **They want their child to play more.** Perhaps an assistant had ulterior motives from the start, thinking that to grab an assistant's role would help ensure that their child got extra playing time, or was guaranteed playing a certain position.

✔ **They are a distraction during games.** Even the most laid back, mild-mannered parents can turn into raving, screaming lunatics once the game begins. As soon as the whistle blows for kick-off, you may think a switch has flipped in their head and they go into a mode of screaming and running up and down the touchlines.

✔ **They are poor coaches.** The last thing you ever want to do is coach a youngster in the wrong way to perform a skill or, worst of all, an unsafe technique that can not only put them at unnecessary risk, but poses an injury risk for the kids they are playing against. Even though you may have some great, well-meaning parents that have raised their hands and volunteered to help you out, if their knowledge of football skills is limited, or non-existent, it opens the door for all sorts of problems to occur.

✔ **They don't interact with the kids well.** Especially during your first few training sessions of the season, you must monitor closely how your assistants interact with the kids.

✔ **You have different philosophies.** During your pre-season meeting with the parents, you (hopefully) stressed that winning was going to take a backseat to skill development and fun. While all the parents may have nodded their heads in agreement with those statements back then, you may discover that when the games begin and results are being recorded that they don't exactly share those same views anymore. Basically, they've bailed out on you and are preaching to the kids everything that you are preaching against.

Remember, your assistant coaches are an extension of you – which makes everything they say and do on your behalf extremely important to the overall success of the season. If they're not getting the job done or are not adhering to the philosophies you are looking to instil in your team, you've got to have a one-to-one talk with them right away and reinforce what you are looking to accomplish this season. Usually this chat is enough to get them back on the right track. If problems continue, let them know that you think it's in the best interest of the team that they step down from their assistant duties. Be sure to thank them for their time and effort. But the position is simply too important to let any problems linger any longer than necessary.

Handling Discipline Problems

Coaching kids in the finer points of heading and how to deliver accurate corner kicks are just some of the areas of the game that challenge your coaching skills. Making sure that youngsters listen to your instructions, respect your authority and abide by the team rules you have set out can pose a whole new set of challenges that you may not have been completely aware of – or prepared for – when you raised your hand to volunteer this season.

The chances are pretty good that at some point during the season you may have to discipline a child who has stepped over the line. Children often act in a disruptive manner because they are frustrated at their lack of progress in football, they feel like their contributions aren't valued by the coach, or they get a sense that their teammates don't value them or even like them being a part of the team.

Operate a 'three-strikes and you're out' technique approach to discipline that can be used to resolve other player problems, as well. Implementing some type of three-strike technique that allows the child a little room for error and time to restructure their behaviour should do the trick for you in most scenarios that you encounter. Here's how it works:

✔ **Strike one:** The first time a child displays a form of behaviour that you deem unacceptable, give them a verbal warning. The warning lets them know that you are not pleased with what they have said or done, and that if it happens again they will be punished. Typically, the types of behaviours that merit a 'strike one' warning may be a child swearing during a game or displaying some type of unsportsmanlike conduct, such as refusing to shake the hand of an opposing player following a game. In most cases, when a child knows that a stricter measure will be enforced if they repeat the same behaviour, they are not likely to do it again. Of course, kids are kids, and there are those who can't break their bad behaviour habits or simply may have to test your authority and see whether you were serious about punishing them if they misbehaved again. Think of it as being like telling a child not to touch something because it can burn them, and they still proceed to touch it, much to your disapproval. So be prepared and don't allow a child to trample your authority. Be willing to go to the next discipline level.

✔ **Strike two:** If the youngster continues to disobey your instructions and they are still swearing during games, for example, you've got to bump up the severity of the punishment in order to derail this negative behaviour before it becomes even more bothersome and a total distraction to the team. Taking away a portion of their playing time in the next game sends a pretty clear message that you are not negotiating and that if they don't stop this behaviour immediately, they are not going to get back on the pitch. Let the player know in clear and specific terms that if they misbehave any more they have jeopardised their future with the team. After a strike two warning, you probably want to meet with the parents and let them know what has taken place with their child. Let the parents know that you want their child to be a part of your team and that there you will take no repercussions the rest of the season if the child behaves in an appropriate manner. Relay to the parent exactly what you spoke to the child about, so that they can reinforce what you've said at home and make the child aware of the seriousness of their behaviour. Let the parents know that their child will be sitting out for an extended period of time as punishment for their behaviour. If you are coaching in a league and the offending child is a starter, not allowing them to start is usually all that is needed to warrant a turnaround in their behaviour.

✔ **Strike three:** Rarely do youngsters venture into strike three territory. With this three-tiered approach to passing out punishment, and with coveted playing time at stake, most youngsters behave accordingly after the verbal warning is issued at the first hint of a problem. In the rare event where the child simply refuses to adhere to your instructions and their behaviour continues to be unacceptable, you may have no recourse but to remove the child from the team. You have a responsibility to all the kids on your team and you simply can't allow the behaviour of one child to disrupt the experience of everyone else. Ideally, you never want to be in a position to force a child away from a sport. In order to give the child every opportunity to make amends, you can even go so far as to allow the child to return to the team if they are willing to apologise to you and the team and promise to be a model of good behaviour. Kids can turn over a new leaf, and maybe a few days away from the team will make them realise how much they miss playing football.

When dealing with behaviour problems among your players, the following are a few other tips to keep in mind:

✔ **Stay away from laps.** It can be really easy when a child has just mouthed off to you to send them on a lap or two around the pitch as punishment. Keep in mind that conditioning drills should never be used as a form of punishment with players. If children begin relating conditioning and running with punishment, they are more likely to develop a more negative outlook on conditioning, which can be disruptive to their development.

✔ **Be true to your word.** When you have outlined to a particular player the discipline that results if they don't behave appropriately, you've got to follow through with the punishment to maintain your authority and respect with the team. You don't want to lose credibility, and the rest of your team's trust or respect, by failing to follow through if another team violation occurs.

✔ **Apply team rules evenly.** One of the most disastrous moves you can make when it comes to disciplining children is to have favourites and allow some kids to get away with certain behaviours while punishing others for the same infraction. A youngster's ability to kick a football harder or more accurately than their teammate should not generate a separate set of team rules for them. Doing so divides the team and cause resentment among players, which quickly sabotages team chemistry.

✔ **Make sure that the punishment is fair.** Don't go overboard ruling and enforcing team policies. If a child forgets their water bottle at training, that certainly shouldn't be viewed as the same type of infraction as swearing during a training session or game.

✔ **Avoid the doghouse syndrome.** As soon as the discipline with the child is completed, put that incident behind you and move on. Don't hold a grudge for the remainder of the season or treat the child differently than you had before the problem occurred. Don't be unfair and keep the child in the doghouse when they have already been punished for their transgression. Forgive, forget, and focus on making sure that the youngster feels like a valued member of the team again.

✔ **Maintain a level head.** Shouting at athletes or losing your temper distorts the discipline you are trying to enforce and sets a really poor example for the team regarding acceptable behaviour.

✔ **Don't discipline for playing mistakes.** Never resort to disciplining a child who lets in a goal or makes a bad pass that results in the game-winning goal for the opposing team. On the other hand, if a player intentionally tries to injure a player by tripping them, for example, this type of behaviour requires immediate removal from the game and may warrant further disciplinary action on your part, depending on the severity of the action, the intent and other factors that led up to the tripping incident.

The non-listener

Some kids arrive at the pitch with a know-it-all attitude and they won't believe that they need to listen to your instructions. Instead, they just do their own thing. Such children can be especially troublesome if they employ techniques that, despite your continued instruction on how to perform them the right way, pose injury risks for other players. For example, they may be tackling in such a way that the other players' feet are continually taken out from under them. The following are ideas on what to do if this occurs:

✔ Ask the child why they aren't performing the skill like the rest of the team? Maybe they didn't understand your instructions and out of frustration have tried doing it how they think it should be done.

✔ Sit them down in training and have them watch how the rest of the team is following instructions. After a few minutes, ask them whether they are ready to return to play and listen to what you have to say. Your non-listener is likely to be much more receptive to your instruction after they have spent any length of time by your side while their teammates are on the pitch.

✔ When it comes to dealing with problems with your players, you always hold the trump card – playing time. It can be a great equaliser, attitude adjuster, personality changer, and attention getter all rolled up into one. Let's face it. No one enjoys having their backside stuck on the bench while their friends and teammates are out on the pitch on the day of the game. Taking away playing time from a child who misbehaves is no different than a parent taking away TV time, computer games or treats from their child at home when they have misbehaved.

The talker

You may encounter some kids on your team who are more talkative than a used car salesman and throw out one-liners like a stand-up comedian. That can create a lot of problems at times. Kids more interested in talking, rather than listening to what you have to say, can cause all sorts of unwanted distractions. If only bits and pieces of your instructions to the team on a particular skill or drill are being heard because of a chatterbox, your effectiveness as a coach is compromised, as well as the development of the rest of your squad. How do you curb the vocal cords of those kids whose mouths seem to be on the perpetual move? The following are a few tips:

- ✔ At the first indication of a problem, remind the team that when you are speaking that all the team members must remain quiet and listen to your instructions.

- ✔ If that fails, the second time call the player out. For example, 'Jimmy, please don't talk while I'm addressing the team. It's important that everyone hears what I'm going over. If you have a comment or question, please hold it until I'm finished.'

- ✔ If the player's talking continues to cause problems, pull the player aside and be firm in your stance that the child must abide by your rules or face the consequences – and then spell those out clearly for the child so he knows the penalties for his future actions. If you have to reprimand him again to be quiet, let him know that he's going to lose significant amounts of playing time. Usually the reprimand is enough to get his attention – and close his mouth.

The perpetually late child

Coaching youth football has many positive aspects, but one of the least positive is the child who is consistently late for training. They miss the warm-up, your pre-training instructions and show up at your side halfway through a drill. Or, equally worse, they make an appearance midway through the first half of your game, throwing your line-up all out of whack and creating chaos with your substitutions. These late-arriving players are a nuisance, an inconvenience, and they totally disrupt the flow of your training session while distracting other team members in the process.

Yes, the perpetually late child can have you reaching for the aspirin. Besides posing a big headache for yourself, if the problem isn't rectified immediately and is allowed to drag on for weeks, the consequences can be even more severe. There may come a point in the season where the child's late arrival at a game forces you to forfeit the game because you didn't have enough players available. One of the last things you ever want to have happen is one child's lateness affect the playing experience of the entire team.

The following are a few tips that you can incorporate to help get the kids to your training sessions and games on time

- **Team talk:** As soon as you get a sense that late arrivals are beginning to create problems, talk to the entire team to reinforce your expectations on attendance. Stress that being part of a team is a commitment – one that needs to be kept regardless of whether your holding a mid-week training session or a championship game. Make it clear that you are on time for all training sessions and games, and that you expect and deserve the same consideration from every one of your players. If the problem isn't addressed at the first hint of trouble, you are slowly going to lose control of the season, and the respect of your players who do show up on time. These are the kids who are committed to you, but can become frustrated by the lack of care and concern of other players who cut into the quality of the training session with their late-arriving habits.

- **Big deal:** Make a really big thing of attendance by taking a roll call during the team's warm-up at training. Turn it into an entertaining exercise by calling out a funny nickname for a player, or using an amusing voice that gets a chuckle from the kids. Even if you only have seven kids on your team and a roll call isn't necessary from the standpoint of knowing who is there and who hasn't arrived yet, it can still be a fun moment that the kids enjoy being part of, and not want to miss in the future.

- **Fun games:** While you can't force a player to arrive on time for training, there certainly are a few things you can do to help entice them to begin showing up on time more often than not. Throw in a fun little game before training begins. You may be pleasantly surprised by the number of kids who are suddenly showing up at training well ahead of time. Hopefully, they start to pester their parents to get them to training so they don't miss out on the fun game with their friends.

- **Individual drills:** When a player arrives late, don't immediately send her to the drill being run – especially an older player who hasn't gone through the proper stretching and warm-ups that the rest of the team has completed. Instead, have her work on individual drills, such as dribbling, before integrating her into the training session. If you are coaching a team of older players who are more susceptible to muscle strains and pulls, make sure that they go through proper stretching before you allow them to start training drills. Just because a player is late doesn't mean that they can overlook this important aspect of the game. You don't want to put them at unnecessary risk of suffering an injury that is easily avoided.

- **Reduced playing time:** A youngster constantly late for training should have their playing time in games reduced because you are simply not being fair to the rest of the team that shows up on time week after week, if you do not take action about this.

Granted, you're going to find it difficult to punish a youngster who doesn't drive for the irresponsible behaviour of their parents. As we discussed in Chapter 4, during your pre-season parents meeting you, hopefully, addressed the importance of everyone showing up on time for training sessions and games and explained how crucial it was for both the season to run smoothly and for you to keep your sanity.

Anytime you address being late for training with the child, be sure to follow up with the parent. Many parents simply may not have realised what a big disruption their being late to training with their child has been causing for the rest of the team. Hopefully, a brief conversation reminding them of the importance of having everyone arrive on time is all that is needed to prevent the problem from occurring during the remainder of the season.

How do you go about discussing the issue of late arrivals with parents? The following are a few tips to keep in mind to ensure that the discussion goes smoothly and all parties are happy at the conclusion:

- **Stress team inconvenience.** Let them know that the late arrival is a disruption that inconveniences you and detracts from the time you have to coach the entire team. Stress that you really need the child to be on time at each and every training session, for both their and their team's development. The more training time they miss, the fewer number of touches they get, which, during the course of the season, will impact on their development.

- **Offer possible solutions.** You can perhaps help the parent find a solution that works for everyone. It may be as simple as having another parent with a child on your team and who lives nearby pick up the youngster and bring him to training.

- **Give the playing time reminder.** Remind the parent that playing time in games is distributed based on training attendance and you'd hate to see their child penalised, but that the punishment the fairest way for the kids who are on time.

- **Emphasise building on skills.** As e you're trying to build up the players' skills, it puts you and their child in a tough spot. Many of the skills you are working on gradually build on skills covered earlier. When a child is late and misses valuable instruction time, their development is compromised and their practice with that particular skill is limited.

Chapter 20

Getting More Competitive

· ·

· ·

*A*s youngsters acquire and develop their skills, some become deeply passionate about football and look to take their game to higher levels and compete against stronger competition. And some coaches, when they have been around the sport for a few seasons, seek opportunities to work with kids in a more competitive setting. Competitive football usually involves older children and may involve a competitive league with away games throughout a particular county, plus football trips, tours, football festivals, and tournaments.

These teams provide all sorts of new coaching challenges: The players are more skilled, the teams are more talented, and the competition is more intense; training sessions are highly structured, games are more frequent, and there may be trials to organise, players to evaluate, and team sheets to put together. If you think you're ready, this chapter provides useful information to help make your transition to a more competitive situation a smooth one.

Enjoying Top-Level Competition: Competitive Football

Serious competitive football is vastly different from what you have been used to in a local fun situation. After all, games tend to be highly competitive, as well as the fact that now your team is facing opponents from different communities and towns and, in the case of tours, different counties, and even different countries. As long as you maintain your focus on providing for the best interests of all the kids, the experience can be a richly rewarding one for everyone involved.

Most football is competitive to some degree. But some football leagues are much more competitive than others. A team that competes in a competitive county league represents an opportunity for youngsters who are interested in focusing on football as their main sport and want to play against top-level competition on a regular basis. These teams provide youngsters with the chance to play in highly competitive tournaments against other talented teams from a neighbouring community, nearby town, and in cup cases, some tournaments, and on tour, from all over the country. They require a much greater time commitment on the child's part, as well as the parents' part, than local fun football with a few teams from the same town. A typical week in a more competitive team usually involves a couple of training sessions, and when playing away, one day on the weekend travelling to the away game, or tournament.

Generally speaking, this type of competitive football is better suited to kids age 12 and older who have a deep interest and passion for the sport and want to test their skills against other talented players. The competitive game is especially suited to those about to make the transition to adult football. Because of the increased level of play, the added pressure and a fuller schedule of training sessions and games, this is not ideal for kids below the age of 12. That is a general guideline because, clearly, kids mature at vastly different rates both emotionally and physically, and certainly some 11-year-olds may be better equipped to handle a more competitive experience than some other 13-year-olds, for example.

Because of the time commitment associated with football at a more competitive level, experts suggest that kids under the age of 12 should be introduced to a variety of sports and activities that allow them to develop a wide range of skills – including such things as balance, co-ordination, and agility – before specialising in one sport.

Each decision must be made on an individual basis. The best sports experiences are the ones that are suited to the motivation and skill level of the individual player. It doesn't matter if the parents to want their child to play at a more competitive level; the child must want it too. The youngster must have the true desire and motivation to play more frequently. If his interest and motivation is suspect, then he is probably better off sticking with recreational football. The situation can be revisited again next season to see whether he is emotionally and physically ready to take that step.

Families must also analyse whether the competitive game is not only the right move for their child, but for the family also, because travelling to away games inevitably requires more commitment and expense for them.

I Want You and You: The Selection Process

Choosing players to play in a competitive team is a challenging process. Besides analysing the skills and abilities of the players, the task is made that much more unpleasant by the fact that you have to break the bad news to some players and their parents that they didn't make the team.

Orchestrating a well-run trial speaks volumes about your coaching ability, as well as making it that much easier to choose the players best suited to play on the team. Trials come into play at the beginning of a season when new players to the club, as well as existing players, have an opportunity to show you what they can do on the pitch. And as coach you get an opportunity to select the players you think suit the positions and style of play you plan to use.

Take a look at the following trial tips:

- ✔ **Introduce yourself.** Spend a couple of minutes at the start of the trial introducing yourself and outlining how the session is going to be structured. Giving kids an outline of how things are going to proceed helps ease stress, allows them to focus on performing to the best of their ability, and eliminates any unnecessary surprises.

- ✔ **Be positive.** Kids are naturally going to be nervous and probably a little uptight before trials begin. Be friendly to them when they arrive at the pitch, greet them with a warm smile and exude a positive attitude at all times. Football is fun and even though the kids feel pressure because coveted spots on the team are at stake, the last thing you want to do is turn the trial into a negative experience that is even more stressful than necessary and lacking in fun.

- ✔ **Warm up.** Even though this is a trial and you may never see some of these kids again, you've got to keep their best interests in mind at all times. That means approaching the session the same way you would an ordinary training session, which you would start off by having the kids stretch. If you leave the kids to stretch on their own, you're probably going to have some who don't do an adequate job and put themselves at an increased risk of suffering an injury. So, run them through a series of stretches so that you are comfortable knowing that their bodies are adequately prepared to participate in the trial.

    Avoid choosing players to lead the stretches. Even if you are quite familiar with some of the kids and know they would do a great job leading the stretches, that sends the message that you are already playing favourites and have these kids earmarked for a place on the team before they have even begun the trial.

- ✔ **Don't overdo it.** Limit the trial sessions to one hour for kids ages 12 and under. For older kids you can bump it up to one and a half to two hours. If you need to hold a couple of sessions in order to effectively evaluate all the kids, that's fine. You're much better off holding a pair of one-hour sessions than one lengthy two-hour session.

- ✔ **Avoid offering coaching pointers.** You don't want to get too caught up in coaching, simply because that takes away from the purpose of the trial, which is to evaluate the kids' skills. But sprinkling your trial with some coaching pointers isn't a bad idea. After all, it gives you a chance to observe how the kids react to instruction, feedback, and even constructive criticism. You are going to be coaching some of these kids for several months, so you need to gain some insight into how receptive they're going to be to your feedback.

✔ **Simulate game situations.** Timed sprints or determining how quickly a youngster can dribble the ball through a series of cones are useful but you have better evaluation tools at your disposal. For example, if one player dribbles the ball through the cones in 18 seconds and another youngster takes 19 or 20 seconds to manoeuvre through them, what have you really found out about the talent level of these two individuals? Not a whole lot, especially if the player had her head down the entire time she was dribbling, which doesn't bode well once she's on the pitch in a game setting and needs to be aware of where her teammates are as well as any defenders converging on her.

The best approach to assessing talent and determining whether players are ready for competition at this level is to put them in situations that closely mirror game conditions, and see how they respond to pressure, and what types of decisions they make while playing both attack and defence.

✔ **Arrange for lots of touches.** Observing players in small-sided games of six-a-side, for example, provides a wealth of information on their abilities. The more situations you put them in that allow plenty of touches of the ball helps you to determine how they move from attack to defence, how they recognise various situations, and how their thought processes work in determining when they should best attack and when they are best to regroup with the ball. Does the player cover a lot of territory or is he content to stick to one area of the pitch? Does he look to pass the ball or is he inclined to dribble down the pitch himself? Is he good at spotting unmarked teammates and delivering the ball to them, or is he more passive and fearful of losing the ball? Is he a fierce tackler? Is he good at reading and anticipating moves? Taking in all of this information and noticing these types of tendencies is vital for getting a true evaluation of a youngster's abilities. Also, this information can prove to be extremely valuable for any of the players that you do end up choosing because you can use it to help determine which positions they are best suited for.

✔ **Don't go station crazy.** If you do elect to use some stations, such as a shooting station to evaluate a goalie, as well as other players' shooting skills, limit how many you have going at one time. Having too many stations running simultaneously won't allow you to effectively monitor all the players. Plus, if the kids see that you are not at their station watching them, they may, understandably, not be quite as focused on giving it their best effort, which detracts from the effectiveness of the entire trial process.

Selecting players

A well-structured trial is the first step to putting together your team. Now, as the kids are running, kicking, and competing, you've got to keep close tabs on all of them to determine which ones deserve the chance to play for you this season. Let's take a look at some areas of the selection process that sometimes are easily overlooked.

- **Teamwork:** Assessing how players work with their teammates is crucial. A player that is great on the ball is an asset to the team if she looks for unmarked teammates; and she's a liability if she is reluctant to give up possession of the ball. A highly skilled player must be a team player in order to fit into the framework of your squad.

- **Attitude:** Does the player get noticeably upset when a teammate fails to deliver an accurate pass to him that may have resulted in a good scoring opportunity? Does he get visibly frustrated when his pass isn't controlled well and results in the opposing team gaining possession of the ball? You want players on your team who are supportive, rather than negative toward their teammates.

- **Mental muscle:** Don't neglect the mental aspect. Keep a close watch to see what type of competitors the kids are. For example, when they lose the ball to a defender, are they focused on regaining possession of it or do they tend to become frustrated and lack the competitive fire to go after it? Do they behave in a sporting like way and play within the rules, or do they resort to unfavourable tactics at times? Keep in mind that these aren't automatic disqualifiers, as each child has to be evaluated on a case-by-case basis. Certainly, if you elect to choose a child that has exhibited the occasional tendency to behave inappropriately, you, as the coach, have the responsibility to work with that youngster and coach him in the importance of behaving in a respectful manner, otherwise he is at risk of being dismissed from the team.

- **Get assistance:** Particularly if you have a large turnout, you can do with a few more sets of eyes watching the kids. If you're taking the place of a coach who looked after the team the previous season, ask his advice or see whether he can come out and give you his input because he has valuable experience of what type of kids it takes to play and compete at this level.

- **Be comprehensive:** If you have several adults helping you out, make sure that they get a chance to see all the kids, otherwise their evaluations won't be as accurate and comprehensive as they should be.

- **Skills list:** Make a list of the skills you want your evaluators to monitor, such as speed, shooting, passing, receiving, trapping, shielding, aggressiveness, and one-on-one abilities, both attacking and defensive.

Breaking the good and bad news to players

Letting a child know that she has made the team and seeing that smile on her face is one of the great things about coaching a football team. Unfortunately, at the other end of the spectrum is the unpleasant task of breaking the news to a youngster who hasn't made it. You, and the players who gave it their best during the trial, will experience a wide range of emotions when it comes to this part of the process. There will be happiness and heartbreak, smiles and sadness, and delirium and disappointment.

Here are some do's and don'ts when it comes to informing kids whether they are to be in the squad this season.

- ✔ **Do notify everyone.** Of course, it would be so much easier on you if all you had to do was deliver the good news to the kids who made it, but in fairness to every youngster who sweated and performed to the best of their ability, you've got to personally let every child know whether they made it or not.

- ✔ **Do be timely.** Make your decisions in a timely manner. Think about when you've gone to job interviews for a position you really want and how nerve-wracked you felt waiting to hear whether you got the job or not. The same goes for kids wanting to be in your team. They are naturally going to be anxious to hear whether they made it or not, so be as prompt as possible in your decision-making process.

- ✔ **Do be careful of your phrasing when delivering bad news.** You simply can't get around the fact that breaking the news to a child that he didn't make the team is going to be like telling him that there won't be any Christmas presents for him to open this year. Such news can be crushing to a child's confidence and self-esteem and you've got to do everything you can to soften the blow of this setback. You don't want your news to squash his enthusiasm for the sport, or derail his interest in playing. Be clear in how you phrase your words that this is not a judgement on the child as a person. Let the youngster and his parents know what areas of his game you were impressed with, and let him know which areas he should devote a little more focus to. Also, offer recommendations on how he can go about improving those areas of his game, and make sure that you encourage him to attend any trials next season. It may simply be a case that he just needs one more season of playing at a less competitive level to hone his skills before he makes the jump to this level of play.

A letter telling a child he didn't make the team is the easy way out for you – but not the right way. The youngster gave her best for you, and she deserves to hear in person your evaluation of her play. In most instances, her parents will appreciate your willingness to talk one-to-one, and, after the initial hurt wears off, should appreciate your encouraging words and helpful feedback on areas to work on to prepare themselves better for the next time trials arrive. If a large number of players attended the trials and you simply can't have one-on-one conversations in person, then at the very least deliver the news over the phone.

You don't want the child regretting that he came to the trial. Yes, there will be disappointment when he doesn't make it, but what you say – and how you say it – can determine whether that disappointment lingers for a couple of days or months, and whether or not your words are used as motivation to work on skills.

✔ **Do say thank you.** At the conclusion of the trial, always be sure to thank the players for following instructions and giving it their best effort. Also, thank the parents for their willingness to get the kids to the trial or trials on time and adjusting their busy schedules to accommodate the dates and times when you conducted the trials. With this nice touch, you demonstrate how much you are concerned for them and their child.

✔ **Do remind parents that playing time varies.** When informing kids that they made the team, be sure to clearly explain to them and their parents that playing time is determined by ability. Some parents may be under the impression that once their child makes the squad that the kid will be starting every game. Make sure that they understand that competitive football is vastly different to recreational football, and while players receive plenty of work in training sessions, playing time in games is for players who, in your opinion, can help the team win the most games.

Keeping the Energy Up All Season

Often, it takes youngsters a little while to adjust to the competitive team schedule. After all, they have more training sessions and games to play in during the week than they are normally accustomed to; and new places to play in for out-of-town games; and they are conscious of increased competition for playing time to adjust to, because their teammates are quicker, faster, and stronger than a lot of the kids that they may have played with in the past. The following sections discuss how you can help your players avoid being overwhelmed by the experience.

Avoiding burnout

Competitive seasons can stretch on for several months, which increases the chances of players suffering burnout. *Burnout* occurs when players grow tired of playing and it typically involves a combination of physical and emotional exhaustion. Even though kids love playing football, if they are subjected to a heavy training schedule that they normally aren't accustomed to, as well as an increased number of games, then they are susceptible to suffering burnout. Here are some steps to consider to keep your team energised.

✔ **Keep it fresh.** With the extra training load, you need to, more than ever, provide kids with a wide range of exercises throughout the week. The more variety you are able to spice your training sessions up with, the less likely the kids are to become drained from participating. (For more on structuring training sessions, refer back to Chapters 6 and 13.)

✔ **Downplay winning.** The pressure to win can be a heavy burden on a team and eventually it can sap your kids' energy and cripple their enthusiasm, some of the first signs of burnout.

✔ **Ease back.** If you've got a heavy fixture schedule on the horizon, or know you're going to be playing a lot of games within a short time span, ease back on the training schedule leading up to those games. Easing back helps keep the kids' energy and enthusiasm at optimum levels. Taking these types of measures can help to prevent potential problems, because once burnout settles in, the only real solution is plenty of rest and time away from the sport.

Keeping everyone in the game

Even though this is competitive football and the bulk of the playing time is handed out to the most talented players at this level, you can't lose your focus on the fact that every child – whether they are the team's leading scorer or the least talented of the group – has an important role. You have the responsibility to make sure that they are fully aware of that, too.

When players are on the bench during games, you want them actively involved in cheering their teammates on and supporting them. Also encourage them to monitor the action closely. Besides keeping the kids' busy, they may also spot a defensive tendency displayed by the opposing team that can be exploited. Encouraging players to take an active role in all areas of the game, regardless of whether they are on the pitch or not, enhances their experience and further instils the sense that they are valuable members of the team.

Competing in weekend tournaments

If you are coaching at a weekend tournament, it will be dramatically different from working the touchlines in the usual league game for a number of reasons. One of the biggest differences you have to deal with is that tournaments typically involve several games played in a short period of time. Consequently, you need to do plenty of juggling and employing different strategies to help ensure that you don't wear your players out. You may find that you also have to adjust your pre-game warm-ups accordingly, the deeper into the tournament you go, so as not to exhaust your players.

Because of the heavy playing schedule, which often doesn't leave much recovery time in-between games, making sure that kids are consuming adequate amounts of fluids takes on greater importance. Your non-starters also play more prominent roles during a weekend tournament. In games that you are comfortably well ahead in, they can be inserted to spare the regulars and give them valuable rest for the upcoming games.

Also, depending on the fixture schedule and the condition of your players, you may need to alter your playing strategy at times. For example, if you typically employ an aggressive attacking strategy that requires a large amount of running from all of your players and you are several goals ahead in a game, scaling back and taking a more defensive posture to help ensure that your players have enough fuel in their tank to compete in the next game may be worth considering.

Hitting the Road

Coaching a team that travels to away fixtures involves so much more than figuring out what type of attacking system best fits your team or who should start in goal in the upcoming game. A number of issues arise – away from the pitch – that must be dealt with that directly impact on everyone's experience.

Just being in charge of a large group of youngsters for an out-of-town game is big responsibility. You've got to ensure the safety of every child, not just on the football pitch, but on the road to and from events, as well as at the game. You're accountable for all the kids at all times. Besides being the coach, you are also the chaperone and need to closely monitor and know the whereabouts of every player.

Occasionally there may be opportunities for your team to play further afield, in another part of the country, or even abroad. In these cases, where you are probably staying overnight and no doubt enlisting the help of a number of parents, coaching the team is not all about creating good scoring chances from corner kicks, or successfully defending three-on-twos. While what happens on the pitch is certainly a major responsibility of yours, what takes place away from the pitch should also have your full attention. When you take a team of kids – and their parents – to a weekend tournament, for example, a number of issues are likely to pop up at some point:

✔ **Curfews:** Children are naturally going to enjoy staying away, but in order for them to perform at their best, curfews must be enforced. Certainly the ages of the kids dictate the curfew, as well as the starting time of their game the following day. Again, let the kids and their parents know in advance at what time you are setting the curfew.

✔ **Extra-curricular activities:** Competing in tournaments in different locations provides opportunities for sightseeing and participating in extra-curricular activities away from the football pitch. Several factors must be taken into account when determining what activities, if any, are going to be included. As the coach, the last thing you want to happen is for your players to be so exhausted from sightseeing that they are unable to give you their best effort.

Before departing for the event, go over the tournament schedule with the players and their parents, and let them know well in advance whether there is any time for extra-curricular activities. Clearly, if you happen to be playing four games over a two-day period, that's not going to allow time for the parents to arrange any type of activities for their kids. If there happens to be a break in the tournament schedule, you are going to have to decide whether you want to organise a team activity or allow the parents and their kids to do their own thing.

Obviously the group probably has varied interests, so organising a team activity can prove to be somewhat tricky. Also, keep in mind the added expense of these sorts of activities as you don't want to put a financial strain on some parents or force them to participate in an activity that they may not be able to afford. For example, going to a nearby amusement park may seem like a great way for the team to spend an off day, but not if tickets are out of range of some parents' pockets. Always discuss these plans with the entire team before leaving.

✔ **Problems with partying parents:** For many busy families these days, weekend tournaments are a welcome break for parents who come along to help. So, the parents may want to enjoy themselves. Of course, that's perfectly fine, as long as the good times don't escalate into problems, such as excessive drinking or loud noise in the hotel. Before departing for any tournaments that require an overnight stay, let the parents know that you want them to have a good time and enjoy themselves, but to keep in mind that this is a youth football event and to be a model of good behaviour and set a good example at all times.

Part VI

The Part of Tens

'This new coach <u>is</u> keen.'

In this part . . .

The Part of Tens introduces you to some unique ways you can go about making sure that all children on your team look back on their season with you and smile. If you use some of the ideas we present here, or if you use them to generate creative options of your own, your kids will carry fond memories of their season with you for the rest of their lives.

We also give you a rundown of useful football organisations who can help you get to grips with the rules and regulations of the game.

Chapter 21

Ten Ways to Make the Season Memorable

A child's experience in organised football can be a defining moment in their young lives. Years from now, they aren't going to remember what their team's record was, or how many goals they scored during the season. But they will easily recall whether the time they spent with you was a positive or negative experience. This chapter covers methods you can use to ensure that your players are treated to a memorable season that will bring a smile to their face for years to come, as well as have them begging to play for you again next season.

Challenge the Coach Day

What do youngsters like most about playing football? Well, besides scoring goals and wearing the cool shinguards, they love opportunities to play – and beat – you, the coach, in any type of skill challenge. Reflect back for a moment on your own sports experiences growing up and that first time you were able to beat your mum, dad, or perhaps even your coach, in a game. That feeling becomes entrenched in our memory banks forever. Kids genuinely love these types of challenges, so set aside one training session at some point during the season in which each player on the team gets the chance to challenge you in some aspect of football.

With younger kids, give them choices to consider. It can be a simple race against you for the length of the pitch, dribbling a football. Other options are dribbling through a series of cones to see who can do it the fastest; seeing who can control the ball the longest in a designated area with the other person serving as the defender; playing a game of one-on-one in a scaled down area with a cone serving as the goal that players must hit with the ball; among others.

Bring Your Parent to Training Day

In many schools around the country, kids have the chance to bring their parents with them for the day; and it works great in organised football, too. By doing this early in the season, you send the message that you really want the parents to be actively involved in their child's football experience. You don't just want parents showing up and reading a book on the touchlines or talking on their mobile. Have them shadow their child during the entire training session and participate right alongside them. They should go through the warm-ups with their youngsters and take part in all the exercises. A good idea in this training session is to run a lot of exercises that involve two-on-two or four-on-four so that the youngster and their parent are competing against another child and his parent. Conducting this type of training session serves as a great bonding experience for both the parent and child, and gives parents a better appreciation of what their child goes through during the course of a regular training session, particularly if they never played football while growing up themselves.

New Exercises

Nothing sabotages fun and discovery quicker than subjecting youngsters to the same boring training sessions week after week. Taking the time to introduce a new exercise during every training session infuses your sessions with lots of excitement and help to ensure that the kids never get in a rut performing the same mind-numbing exercises all season long. To give them something to look forward to at each training session, introduce the new exercise at the same point in your sessions. You may find it works best to unveil the new exercise at the start of training, when youngsters are often the most focused and attentive. Or, you may discover that building the anticipation and saving the new exercise for the last few minutes of training is a great way to conclude the session. Once you establish a routine, you should find that the kids eagerly anticipate the chance to participate in a fun new exercise every time they step on the pitch.

Contest Day

One of the most effective ways to promote team camaraderie is to devote a training session to a series of special contests. But rather than having the players compete among themselves, which only gives your more skilled youngsters the chance to further showcase their talents while alienating the lesser skilled kids, pair up the players ahead of time. By putting a talented child with a youngster who may not be quite as skilled, you force the two of them to work together, which not only improves their skills but allows them the chance to get to know one another better and build teamwork.

As you know, the more familiar kids are with each other, the deeper they are going to care about each other, and that translates into more inspired play on the pitch. It also leads to more supportive teammates who want one another to succeed and who step forward to offer encouraging words when things don't work out as planned. It also plants the seeds for long-term friendships, which are one of the special benefits that come from participating in organised football. If you played football, or any sport growing up for that matter, you can probably easily recall some of the friendships that you forged with teammates.

Samples of mini contests you can hold include having the pairs pass the ball back and forth between them a set number of times while running the length of the pitch and timing them; or completing headers where the player tosses the ball to their partner, who must head it back to them. (The last exercise forces the players to work together because the better they throw, the easier it is for their partners to head the ball.) Encourage the kids to support their partners, and you can even let them know before the contests begin that you will be awarding bonus points to those pairs that demonstrate the most support for one another.

Midseason Report Cards

Remember your days in school when you'd bring home those progress reports with the smiley face from your teacher that said what a great student you were and how well you were doing? Reports gave you a sense of accomplishment and served as a springboard for continuing to work hard and improve for the rest of the term. Well, issuing midseason cards to your squad can accomplish much of the same and give players a real boost of confidence. A handwritten note extolling their talents and recognising what areas of the game they have really excelled in so far this season is a nice touch and really lets players know that you appreciate the effort they are putting in this season.

Everyone loves to be recognised for their skills and hard work, and a written note that players can look back at and read all season long often carries more weight than a verbal accolade and serves as the impetus for them to continue striving to give you their best each time they step onto the pitch. Even with older players, these hand-written notes can be just as effective. You can even go so far as to touch on an area of the game where you challenge them to make improvements during the remainder of the season. Besides applauding those areas that they are excelling in, giving them a target to strive for gives them something extra to concentrate on during training. The target serves to help maintain their focus through the second half of the season.

Bringing in New Faces

Even if you're doing a great job of coaching, every once in a while kids may enjoy a break from you, particularly if the season is long and they are with you for several months. Bringing in a new face to talk to the kids about a particular aspect of football provides a new perspective that can be refreshing and re-energising for them. You should find lots of possibilities within your community. A school football coach, a well-known local football player, or coaches or players from nearby teams are all excellent resources.

Just giving the players on your team the chance to see a new face that can offer different tips on performing a specific skill, or words of encouragement on what it takes to reach the next level, can be enormously beneficial in a youngster's growth and development in the sport. Other options include bringing in a sports nutritionist, which would be especially good for older kids who are at an age where they are exploring all sorts of ways to improve their skills. Hearing about the importance of eating correctly and drinking the proper fluids is going to be much more effective coming from an expert in the field than from you, however much they admire you.

Team Votes

One of the basic facts of growing up is that kids have to endure being told what to do much of the time. Between school, home, and other assorted activities, they are constantly being instructed, ordered around and told how things are going to be. Once in a while, let your kids decide what they want to do. Giving them chances to voice their opinions shows that you respect them as both football players and people, and that you value their thoughts and opinions.

If the league allows, letting the players vote on the team name or the colour of the strips, not only builds camaraderie among the players, but sends the message before the season even gets under way that what they think matters to you. You can also let the youngsters work together to come up with a team chant to repeat before they take to the pitch for their games. These types of exercises promote team unity and create a bond that isn't likely to be broken during the course of the season.

Team Captain for the Day

Rotating team captains every training session is a great way to give each child a little extra attention. At the start of each training session, let the team know who you have designated as the team captain for the day. Or, you may find the kids are more receptive to being told at the end of training who is to be captain at the following training session so that they have something to look forward to.

Make this honour something that really carries weight. Besides the basic stuff of letting the designated captain lead the team warm-ups, allow them the authority to choose the first team exercise of the day, or how they would like to have training conclude. You can even go so far as to have a captain's armband or a specially coloured jersey made that says 'Team Captain' on the back, that you give to the child at the start of training . Listening to kids' ideas, and then following through with them, truly gives each child the sense that they are an important and contributing member of the team.

Carnival Day

Kids love carnivals, games, and the chance to win prizes – and you can easily recreate that type of atmosphere by devising off-the-wall activities at one of your training sessions during the season. For example, set up a football bowling station where a youngster has to kick a ball and knock over a couple of plastic bowling pins or cones. Or lay a hula hoop on the ground and challenge kids to kick the ball from a specified distance and have the ball end up inside the hoop. At each of the stations, you can have a bucket of sweets, or a little toy so that when the kids are successful, they earn a small prize.

Holiday or Birthday Themes

With younger children, a training session based around a holiday can be a fun way to mix up the routine. If your football season runs during autumn, then

Halloween is a natural time to encourage kids to come to training in their costumes. Of course, you should adjust the exercises accordingly so that you don't have youngsters running all over the pitch risking injury or damaging their costumes. Simply having the kids practise their shooting, for example, can be a fun-filled activity for them. You can even show up in a costume yourself, play goalie, and let the kids take shots at you.

You don't have to limit your creativity to Halloween. If a child is having a birthday during the season, give the kids birthday hats to wear during training. Other holidays provide plenty of opportunities for you to get creative, too. For example, around Easter, set up an exercise where, when a youngster completes the skill successfully, he gets the chance to look for chocolate eggs that you've hidden around the pitch.

Chapter 22

Ten Fun Ways to End on a High Note

In This Chapter

▶ Coming up with creative team awards

▶ Thinking about clever mementos

*A*s your youth football season winds to a close, you need to start thinking about what your plans are for concluding the season in a memorable way for the youngsters. While pizza parties and participation medals are some common routes many coaches take, you can go a step further and use your creativity to wrap up the season on a high note that has the kids craving to return to the football pitch again next season. This chapter covers ten clever season-ending ideas that send the kids home with a smile on their faces.

Jazzing Up Team Awards

Innovative team awards are a great way to recognise the contributions of the youngsters on your squad. When you give out any type of awards to your team, you need to recognise each player in some way. Singling out only a select few players can leave the others feeling isolated, hurt and not a valued and contributing part of the team. Handing out awards you have created yourself is a great opportunity to recognise the children for any special skills or attributes that meant the most to you during the course of the season.

With a little imagination, you can come up with ways to highlight each child's efforts during the season. You don't have to hand out the old standby, Best Player Award. First, everyone knows who the best player on the team is already and second, presenting this type of award gives the impression that this individual was more important than any of the other team members, and that's the last type of message you want to send the team home with at the end of the season.

There are a number of creative awards that you can come up with. For example, you can hand out a Most Likely to Block a Shot During a Game Award. Creative awards are a great way to show your appreciation for the child that was always willing to do all the little things that must be done during the game in order for the team to be successful. Plus, this type of award is an ideal way to recognise a youngster whose contributions otherwise may have been overlooked. Even this slightest bit of recognition is often enough to give that child a boost of confidence and the encouragement to return to the sport the following season.

You can design the certificates and print them on a computer at home or recruit an interested parent with artistic ability to do it for you. Or, you can even collect a few pounds from each parent and do miniature trophies with the player's name and the name of the award engraved on it.

The following are just some ideas of different types of awards you can present to your team. Use your imagination and you can come up with plenty of others that your players can treasure.

- Most Dedicated
- Best Sportsmanship
- Most Improved
- Hardest Worker
- Most Enthusiastic
- Model Teammate
- Best Defender
- Best Passer
- Corner Kick Specialist
- Penalty Kick Specialist
- Best Dribbler
- Best Tackler

Record Your Team

Recordings are a great way to capture the excitement of the season for the youngsters and their parents, who can then enjoy viewing it for years to come. Kids, excuse the pun, get a real kick out of watching footage of themselves, and their teammates. If you have a parent with experience of using a camcorder, recruit him to record the kids at different training sessions and games throughout the season and put together a montage of the season.

If you have a parent or two who are interested and willing to undertake this project, just make sure that you have adequate footage of each child on the team. The last thing you want to do is have a child's feelings hurt because she doesn't appear anywhere in the piece, or has limited appearances compared to the rest of her teammates.

You can also check with the parents to see whether they are willing to chip in to hire a professional cameraman. Bring this up at your pre-season parents meeting (see Chapter 4). At the same time, make sure that all parents are willing to allow their kids to be recorded. The Football Association (`www.thefa.com`) has a number of forms related to parental permission for photographing and filming kids, as well as guidance on the issues involved. A professionally filmed piece makes a great keepsake that the kids and their parents can treasure for years. You can cut down on the cost by having the professional come out for just a game or two during the season, and remember to ensure that he gets footage of each child.

Create Individual Recordings of Each Child

If you have the financial resources to hire a professional, or a parent with spare time on his hands, you can put together individual recordings for each child that highlights their play throughout the season. Even a two- to three-minute recording makes a great keepsake for the kids. If you decide to go down this route, before handing out the tapes, gather the team together so that they can watch them all as a team. It makes for a fun night and everyone can have a great time looking back at the team's play from the season.

Distribute Team Stickers

Kids love stickers of their favourite sports heroes to look at and swap with their friends, so working with a local photographer to design football cards with the kids' photos on the front and some interesting facts about them on the back should be a big success. You can include basic information, such as date of birth, height and weight, as well as fun information, such as the nickname you call them by during training, or a quote from you on what you admire most about their game. Give each kid a dozen or so that they can swap with their teammates, give to friends, or send to grandparents. Again, you can discuss this with the parents prior to the season to see whether they are willing to contribute extra money to fund this.

Hold One-on-One Meetings

A season-ending meeting with each player individually, especially the older kids, is a great way to end the season on a high note, motivate them to work hard, and have them look forward to returning next season. During the one-on-one, talk to them about the area of the game where they made the most improvement this season and how proud you are of their efforts. Kids will respond in a positive manner to the compliment and recognition, and it may just be the spark that ignites their enthusiasm to return to the pitch next season.

Keep in mind that the recognition doesn't even have to come in the form of praise for a specific football skill. For example, maybe the child wasn't much of a team player at the start of the season for whatever reason, but as the season progressed, he came around and started shouting encouragement to his teammates or congratulating them more enthusiastically for a goal or other excellent play. Or maybe he emerged as a better sport and no longer displayed any unsportsmanlike tendencies. There are a variety of areas you can highlight that all go into the youth football experience. Football is so much more than passing, shooting, and scoring, and it's important that you are fully aware of that when evaluating each player's all-round game.

With older children, particularly those that you know will be on your team next season, or that are simply interested in improving their play, you can talk with them in a positive way about areas of their game that they can concentrate on working on and improving during the break. Talk to them about how impressed you are with whatever the strongest aspect of their game is, and then follow it up by mentioning that if they devote a little extra attention to this other area, they are really going to be tough to stop next season. Remember, positive and encouraging words can fuel their desire to improve and take their game to the next level.

When holding these meetings with your players, make sure that you are in an area where there aren't any distractions. You don't want your complimentary words and feedback to go unheard or unrecognised by a youngster whose attention is diverted by kids playing nearby, or by her teammates lingering around listening in to what you are saying.

Create a Team Newsletter

A newsletter captures the excitement of the season and is a wonderful keepsake for any child's scrapbook, as well as a fond remembrance of their time with you. Some of the things that can be featured in the newsletter are different action photos from various training sessions and games during the season; capsule summaries of each game (make sure that each child is mentioned at some point if you are recapping the season); brief bios of each player, listing their favourite TV show, school subject, or how many brothers and sisters they have. You can also include a comment from you about each player, such as how they are the team's hardest worker, they displayed the best sportsmanship during the season, or they displayed the best attitude. You may be able to recruit parents to help in this endeavour by putting together some of the text for the pages, or laying out the pages with the photos and headlines.

Design your newsletter in a newspaper format and have a column written by yourself, talking about how much fun you had coaching the kids this season and how enjoyable it was to watch them develop and progress in the sport. Be sure to thank the parents for all their hard work and positive support, too.

Create a Team Photo Album

A team photo album makes a great end-of-season gift that the children can enjoy looking at and is something that they can hold on to and cherish for a lifetime. Before the season starts, designate another parent to take photos during games. Or choose a different parent each game to take pictures of all the kids. By doing this, you ensure that you have a wide variety of shots to choose from when putting together the albums. Once you pick out the photo files you want, simply get copies made to make each album identical for all of the players. If you or another parent has time, you can get really creative and make individual albums for each player that feature a team photo, and then a variety of shots of that particular child participating in training sessions or games. Make sure that you get the parents' permission to take the pictures first.

Schedule a Crazy Training Session

All season long, your training sessions have been well organized, efficient, and focused on helping the kids develop and improve a variety of skills. A great reward for the players who have shown up on time all season long and given you their complete attention is to stage a crazy training session during one of your last sessions with the team, one that is sure to be embraced by all the players.

There are a number of different approaches you can take. For example, you can have the kids wear mismatched kit to training, or have them wear their shirts and shorts backwards. The younger the players are, the more excited they get to have the chance to be silly together and laugh with one another. Don't forget to join in the fun too. The kids probably get the most laughs seeing you and your assistant coaches dressed in strange outfits or wearing your clothes the wrong way.

Take a Football Photo

All kids love receiving gifts, especially a cool sports gift related to the sport of football that they love. A football emblazoned with the team photo makes a great present and can make great collectables that the youngsters can proudly display on their bedroom shelves at home. It's also more eye-catching than the traditional team photo stuck in a frame. Firms can be found on the Internet that provide services like this.

Have a Team Memento

If you want to hand out some type of participation memento, you can go with a medal shaped like a football, or even a miniature football trophy because all kids love receiving trophies to display in their room. Or you can give them miniature footballs that can be purchased at various sports shops. You can jazz up the balls by having the team name written on them, or the team's record if you coached in a competitive league and the team won the title or finished in a good position.

Chapter 23

Ten Recommended Resources and Organisations

In This Chapter

▶ Taking advantage of invaluable resources

▶ Contacting important organisations

M ost of the time, coaching is great fun, the time passes by, the children improve their football skills, the team gets better, and the parents are happy. But like anything else in life, coaching has its challenges. You have drills to sort out, matches to prepare for, tricky kids and parents to deal with. What with the training, matches, inevitable paperwork, and all the other planning, organisation, and admin to do, it can sometimes seem like an uphill battle. Hopefully, you are always able to rely on your assistants, parents, and even friends with some sporting background or knowledge for help and advice when you need it. But that's not all the help that's available. As a football coach, you are not alone. You have a whole football infrastructure out there to help you, from the Football Association and other governing bodies to a variety of Internet resources. You just have to find them.

The FA

In the UK, the game of football is run by the individual national football associations: The English FA, the Scottish FA, The FA of Wales, and the Irish Football Association. The Web sites of these organisations are essential destinations for anyone who is coaching football or interested in coaching in that particular part of the country. Each provides a range of resources for coaches from details of education courses to information about grassroots football. They should be your first port of call on your online travels:

www.scottishfa.co.uk – Scotland

www.thefa.com – England

www.irishfa.com – Northern Ireland

www.faw.org.uk - Wales

Getting a Handle on Small-Sided Games

Small-sided games are football, but not quite as we know it. In 1999, the Football Association, the governing body for football in England, introduced mini-soccer as its preferred game for under-10s (even some older children now play mini-soccer).

Mini-soccer is essentially football scaled down for children. The pitch is smaller and the teams are smaller, originally ranging from 4-a-side, to 7-a-side and now 9-a-side for the under-11 to under-14 age group. The emphasis is on fun and participation with features like equal playing time, and roll on, roll off substitutions at the younger levels. For the under-7s, results are not collected, league standings don't exist and neither do winner's prizes. The rules and regulations are modified as well. (They do not have offside, for example, which players and officials often find confusing at an adult level, let alone in youth football.)

The aim of mini-soccer is partly to allow children to get more touches on the ball than in 11-a-side. The FA says that to become comfortable on the ball, a youngster should have had 10,000 touches on the ball by the time they are 16. Mini-soccer improves the chances of that happening.

The other football associations in Scotland, Wales and Northern Ireland all operate their own versions of small-sided games for young children. Scotland even has mini-kickers for 3 to 5-year-olds.

To get to know about mini-soccer in its various guises, you can visit the football association Web sites, and in some cases, download the mini-soccer handbook:

www.thefa.com/Grassroots/ClubDevelopment/MiniSoccer

www.scottishfa.co.uk/scottish_football.cfm?curpageid=448

Helping Football Parents Be Model Parents

You may find it hard, if not impossible, to be a successful coach without the help and support of the kids' parents. Why? Because being a football coach is about so much more than knowing a 101 football drills, or being able to recite the rules of the game in your sleep. You have to work with your players, and in order to organise training and matches effectively and work the kids, you need the co-operation of the parents.

Being a good football parent' is about getting involved and stepping back as and when necessary. They need to provide support and encouragement in a positive way, acting as role model and understanding and supporting what the coach is trying to achieve. The model football parent gets their kid to training on time with all the required kit, joins in if required, supports little Johnny on match day, providing positive encouragement no matter how well or badly little Johnny plays, and communicates with the coach in a polite way, being entirely sympathetic to the equal playing time rule.

The not-so-model football parent gets their child to practise at random times, often after training is underway, without all the kit needed, won't join in, rarely turns up at games, and worse, when he does turn up, hurls abuse from the touchline, threatens to thump the ref/the opposing coach/you, and insists on little Johnny playing up front all of the time. Most football parents, of course, fall somewhere in-between these two extremes. Fortunately, when it comes to encouraging parents toward the model parent end of the scale, help is at hand.

Soccer Parent is the English FA's free online course for coaches and parents, which is there to provide some pointers on the key issues involved when a child joins a football team. A book published by the FA also covers similar ground. By pointing out the benefits of such a course to the parents of your players, you are doing yourself a favour. The more helpful and supportive the parents are, remember, the easier your job seems.

`www.thefa.com/TheFA/FALearning/Soccer+Parent/`

Being Up to Speed on First Aid

Football is a contact sport, and while it would be wonderful if the season passed by without having to open the first-aid kit at all, the likelihood is that the kids are going to get some bumps and scrapes along the way. Even the youngest kids can fall over and graze their knees, while at a more competitive level the tackles are going in thick and fast – twisted ankles, tweaked ligaments, pulled muscles and even the occasional broken bone are possible. With parents entrusting the care of their children to you on the football pitch and training ground, you must ensure that someone associated with the team has a good knowledge of first aid. There needs to be someone competent at first aid always in attendance. That someone can be an assistant, but it really should be you.

You have a number of options for finding out about becoming a certified first-aider. The Red Cross is one popular option. It runs one day courses on sports first aid. The FA also runs a specialised first aid for sport course.

`www.redcross.org.uk`

Exploring the Treatment Room

Yes, you need to get first-aid training (see preceding section), and you also need to know a little more about the various sports injuries that your players may suffer. What is that mysterious metatarsal that Wayne Rooney fractured in the run up to the World Cup in 2006? What is an Anterior Cruciate Ligament and why is it so important? What is bursitis when it's at home? For the coach curious to get the lowdown on these sporting injuries and more, what better way to find out than to check out who is suffering from what in the English Premier Division?

The Physio Room Web site has all the details of which Premier division players are on the treatment table, what injury they have, and how long they can expect to take to recover. The site has excellent details and diagrams on a huge range of footballing injuries. Plus you are then in a good position to tell your young football fans when their favourite professional player is going to be back in action again.

www.physioroom.com/news/english_premier_league/
epl_injury_table.php

Being Part of the Beautiful Game

Football is the beautiful game, the stuff of legends. Pele, Johan Cruyff, Diego Maradona, Bobby Moore, Ronaldinho, are some of the greatest players of the world's most popular sport. As a football coach, you are part of a great sporting tradition, and who knows, one of those kids you are coaching may turn out to be the next world football star. Football is more than just skills and drills, it also has a rich history of fun and competition. Your kids are going to ask you all sorts of questions, from what team you support, to who won the World Cup. If you are already a football history buff, a season ticket holder, and a walking sport encyclopedia, no problem. If not, it may be a good idea to get up to speed on what has happened, is happening and is about to happen in the world of football.

Some good places to start are the Fédération Internationale de Football Association (FIFA) Web site, where you can discover all kinds of unusual and interesting facts about the game from the world's governing body (including the fact that during the 100 years' war between England and France, from 1338 to 1453, a succession of kings made football illegal as the soldier's love of playing the game meant they weren't getting enough archery practice in!).

www.fifa.com

Explaining Rules and Regulations

Ever tried to explain the offside rule to someone who knows very little about football? You won't find it easy, even with a pen and paper. Even the experienced football players still struggle with the idea of active and non-active players. Every week in the professional game, you can read about a number of well-publicised contested decisions. And that is just the start of it. Did you know the ball in the adult game must not weigh more than 16oz or less than 14oz at the start of the game? Or that if thermal cycling shorts are worn under the shorts, as many players wear, they have to be the same colour as the shorts (under Law 4)?

As coach you need to know the rules. Not immediately, it takes a while to absorb all the details. Rules are not great bedtime reading but it has to be done. By the end of your first season, you should be reasonably familiar with the full rules of the game and very familiar with the rules of mini-soccer and the league that you play in.

The rules of the game can be downloaded from the Football Association website:

www.thefa.com/TheFA/RulesAndRegulations/FIFALawsOfTheGame

Developing Skills and Drills

As coach, you have a selection of drills that you know well. But after a while, they become stale. So what then? Yes, you can rack your brain between training sessions trying to come up with some new ideas. But why reinvent the wheel? Thousands of other coaches have their own ideas about the game. Some are extremely experienced. Some have put their thoughts, drills, and philosophies online.

Football is not a static sport, the game changes over time as some ideas become fashionable, and some less so. Many decades ago, the four-two-four was a standard formation, yet this is fairly rare today. Not long ago, the sweeper system was popular particularly in Italy. But now the sweeper is less fashionable, whereas the five-man midfield with a lone striker and the four-three-three are becoming more popular. The Internet is a wonderful resource for discovering new drills, and keeping up with the latest skills and tactics.

The free Better Soccer More Fun Web site provides insight into the Dutch youth football coaching pages of useful information, diagrams, and animated diagrams:

www.bettersoccermorefun.com

At the soccer clinics site, which claims to be the world's largest soccer Web site, you can find more coaching information (although this site requires a subscription).

www.soccerclinics.com

Going Official: A Licence to Drill

After a season of coaching kids, you should have a pretty good idea if you want to continue to do so. You may have already decided that you want to take it further, acquire more and better coaching skills, take your coaching ability to the next level. If that's the case and you are really hooked on the game, then the next step is to take your official coaching badges. Even by taking the first few levels, you improve your ability to coach. Who knows though, you may end up doing your EUFA A Pro coaching license. Details of the different coaching schemes run by the FAs can be found on their individual Web sites (see the next section).

Finding Answers on a Coaching Forum

The coach doesn't always have the answers. Sometimes you will have a question about coaching but can't find anyone to answer it. Well now you can try posting up your question on a football forum where other coaches in a similar position to you ask and respond to questions. Hopefully, someone out there knows the answer:

http://forum.football.co.uk/forum-148.html

www.websitetoolbox.com/tool/mb/stevethefootycoach

Index

• *E* •

• *G* •

Notes

FOR DUMMIES®

Do Anything. Just Add Dummies

ROPERTY

UK editions

0-7645-7027-7

0-470-02921-8

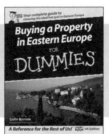
0-7645-7047-1

ERSONAL FINANCE

0-7645-7023-4

0-470-05815-3

0-7645-7039-0

USINESS

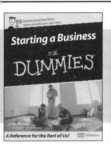
0-7645-7018-8

0-7645-7056-0

0-7645-7026-9

Answering Tough Interview
Questions For Dummies
(0-470-01903-4)

Arthritis For Dummies
(0-470-02582-4)

Being the Best Man
For Dummies
(0-470-02657-X)

British History
For Dummies
(0-470-03536-6)

Building Confidence
For Dummies
(0-470-01669-8)

Buying a Home on a Budget
For Dummies
(0-7645-7035-8)

Children's Health
For Dummies
(0-470-02735-5)

Cognitive Behavioural Therapy
For Dummies
(0-470-01838-0)

Cricket For Dummies
(0-470-03454-8)

CVs For Dummies
(0-7645-7017-X)

Detox For Dummies
(0-470-01908-5)

Diabetes For Dummies
(0-7645-7019-6)

Divorce For Dummies
(0-7645-7030-7)

DJing For Dummies
(0-470-03275-8)

eBay.co.uk For Dummies
(0-7645-7059-5)

European History
For Dummies
(0-7645-7060-9)

Gardening For Dummies
(0-470-01843-7)

Genealogy Online
For Dummies
(0-7645-7061-7)

Golf For Dummies
(0-470-01811-9)

Hypnotherapy For Dummies
(0-470-01930-1)

Irish History For Dummies
(0-7645-7040-4)

Neuro-linguistic Programming
For Dummies
(0-7645-7028-5)

Nutrition For Dummies
(0-7645-7058-7)

Parenting For Dummies
(0-470-02714-2)

Pregnancy For Dummies
(0-7645-7042-0)

Retiring Wealthy For Dummies
(0-470-02632-4)

Rugby Union For Dummies
(0-470-03537-4)

Small Business Employment
Law For Dummies
(0-7645-7052-8)

Starting a Business on
eBay.co.uk For Dummies
(0-470-02666-9)

Su Doku For Dummies
(0-470-01892-5)

The GL Diet For Dummies
(0-470-02753-3)

The Romans For Dummies
(0-470-03077-1)

Thyroid For Dummies
(0-470-03172-7)

UK Law and Your Rights
For Dummies
(0-470-02796-7)

Winning on Betfair
For Dummies
(0-470-02856-4)

FOR DUMMIES®

Do Anything. Just Add Dummies

HOBBIES

0-7645-5232-5

0-7645-6847-7

0-7645-5476-X

Also available:

Art For Dummies
(0-7645-5104-3)

Aromatherapy For Dummies
(0-7645-5171-X)

Bridge For Dummies
(0-471-92426-1)

Card Games For Dummies
(0-7645-9910-0)

Chess For Dummies
(0-7645-8404-9)

Improving Your Memory
For Dummies
(0-7645-5435-2)

Massage For Dummies
(0-7645-5172-8)

Meditation For Dummies
(0-471-77774-9)

Photography For Dummies
(0-7645-4116-1)

Quilting For Dummies
(0-7645-9799-X)

EDUCATION

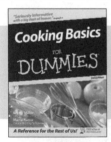

0-7645-7206-7

0-7645-5581-2

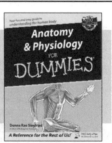

0-7645-5422-0

Also available:

Algebra For Dummies
(0-7645-5325-9)

Algebra II For Dummies
(0-471-77581-9)

Astronomy For Dummies
(0-7645-8465-0)

Buddhism For Dummies
(0-7645-5359-3)

Calculus For Dummies
(0-7645-2498-4)

Forensics For Dummies
(0-7645-5580-4)

Islam For Dummies
(0-7645-5503-0)

Philosophy For Dummies
(0-7645-5153-1)

Religion For Dummies
(0-7645-5264-3)

Trigonometry For Dummies
(0-7645-6903-1)

PETS

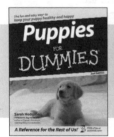

0-470-03717-2

0-7645-8418-9

0-7645-5275-9

Also available:

Labrador Retrievers
For Dummies
(0-7645-5281-3)

Aquariums For Dummies
(0-7645-5156-6)

Birds For Dummies
(0-7645-5139-6)

Dogs For Dummies
(0-7645-5274-0)

Ferrets For Dummies
(0-7645-5259-7)

Golden Retrievers
For Dummies
(0-7645-5267-8)

Horses For Dummies
(0-7645-9797-3)

Jack Russell Terriers
For Dummies
(0-7645-5268-6)

Puppies Raising & Training
Diary For Dummies
(0-7645-0876-8)

FOR DUMMIES®

The easy way to get more done and have more fun

LANGUAGES

0-7645-5194-9

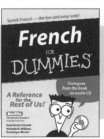

0-7645-5193-0

0-7645-5196-5

Also available:

Chinese For Dummies
(0-471-78897-X)

Chinese Phrases
For Dummies
(0-7645-8477-4)

French Phrases For Dummies
(0-7645-7202-4)

German For Dummies
(0-7645-5195-7)

Italian Phrases For Dummies
(0-7645-7203-2)

Japanese For Dummies
(0-7645-5429-8)

Latin For Dummies
(0-7645-5431-X)

Spanish Phrases
For Dummies
(0-7645-7204-0)

Spanish Verbs For Dummies
(0-471-76872-3)

Hebrew For Dummies
(0-7645-5489-1)

MUSIC AND FILM

0-7645-9904-6

0-7645-2476-3

0-7645-5105-1

Also available:

Bass Guitar For Dummies
(0-7645-2487-9)

Blues For Dummies
(0-7645-5080-2)

Classical Music For Dummies
(0-7645-5009-8)

Drums For Dummies
(0-471-79411-2)

Jazz For Dummies
(0-471-76844-8)

Opera For Dummies
(0-7645-5010-1)

Rock Guitar For Dummies
(0-7645-5356-9)

Screenwriting For Dummies
(0-7645-5486-7)

Songwriting For Dummies
(0-7645-5404-2)

Singing For Dummies
(0-7645-2475-5)

HEALTH, SPORTS & FITNESS

0-7645-7851-0

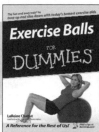

0-7645-5623-1

0-7645-4233-8

Also available:

Controlling Cholesterol
For Dummies
(0-7645-5440-9)

Dieting For Dummies
(0-7645-4149-8)

High Blood Pressure
For Dummies
(0-7645-5424-7)

Martial Arts For Dummies
(0-7645-5358-5)

Menopause For Dummies
(0-7645-5458-1)

Power Yoga For Dummies
(0-7645-5342-9)

Weight Training
For Dummies
(0-471-76845-6)

Yoga For Dummies
(0-7645-5117-5)

Available wherever books are sold. For more information or to order direct go to www.wiley.com or call 0800 243407 (Non UK call +44 1243 843296)

FOR DUMMIES®

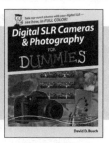